A
SCANDALOUS
JESUS

I dedicate this book
to my teachers

How Three Historic Quests
Changed Theology for the Better

Joseph A. Bessler

POLEBRIDGE PRESS

Salem, Oregon

Cover and interior design by Robaire Ream

ISBN 978-1-59815-122-0

we cautiously release notes
too carefully held too long
—Murray Bodo

Contents

Acknowledgments

Upon finishing this book I began to ask myself where it came from. Why did I ever become interested in the historical Jesus, and what nurtured that interest? I found myself going back quite a ways, to many of my previous teachers, such as Murray Bodo, Lawrence Keller, and John Krump. I owe an additional debt of gratitude to graduate school teachers and mentors over the years including Dieter Georgi, Langdon Gilkey, and David Tracy, and to colleagues such as the members of the Westar Institute. In 2005, I was asked to speak at the 20th anniversary of Westar. That same year I accepted an invitation to help keynote the Common Dreams conference in Sydney, Australia in 2007. The many people I met in these contexts have also been influential and supportive of my work.

My thanks to Kay Northcutt for improving many drafts of various chapters along the way. Brandon Scott, a wonderful senior colleague, conversation partner, and friend, has supported me throughout my career at Phillips and also in my theological musings on the historical Jesus. In addition to other faculty colleagues over the years, including Dennis Smith, Rick Lowery, and Roy Herndon Smith, I want to thank deans Elizabeth Box Price and Don Pittman, and presidents Bill Tabbernee and Gary Peluso-Verdend, for their support. My walking partners Gary Peluso-Verdend and pastor and friend Gary Blaine helped keep this project in front of me, as have my neighbors and friends Margaret McShane and Lee Anne Ziegler. Terry Warnick encouraged my progress, as did friends Pat and Bob Lucy, and Sheri and Bob Curry; Joe and Ivy Dempsey wanted updates, and the patient laughter and real knowing of Laura Dempsey kept me both sane and settled. Without these friends and their support, I would not have conceived or finished this book.

Finally, had it not been for the persistence and patience of my editor Larry Alexander, who kept me tethered to the work, and for my copy-editor Cassandra Farrin, whose careful reading kept me on track near and till the almost-end, for Mary Ann Morris' thoughtful work on the index, and for Char Matejovsky and Robaire Ream, who helped carry the project the rest of the way, I would not be writing these words acknowledging with affection the gifts and graces of so many who helped me to see something and who strengthened me to say it.

Introduction

Sometimes an answer to a problem appears so complete and compelling that it brooks no further questions. A good example of that phenomenon in the study of Christian theology can be found in Martin Kähler's rejection of, as he put it, the "so-called historical Jesus." Writing in 1895, Kähler argued ingeniously that the word *history* had two distinct meanings in German. The first, *Historie,* referred to the science of assembling evidence to explain an event or set of events that occurred in the past. The second term, *Geschichte,* sought to name and explore those persons and events that helped shape history, that were "historic." To use an American example, while *Historie* might seek to research and report objectively on the facts of George Washington's life, *Geschichte* would articulate the historic impact of Washington in shaping subsequent American history and political life.

To be sure, these two senses of history could overlap; discovering new facts about Washington's life in researching his correspondence, for example, might conceivably alter judgments about Washington's mythic status as Father of the country. In the case of the historical Jesus, however, Kähler argued that the work of *Historie*—assembling facts about Jesus of Nazareth—was effectively closed to historians. The gospel narratives were not historical records, as David Friedrich Strauss had established in 1835, and there was very little in the way of other historical evidence about Jesus to warrant any confidence that one could understand Jesus by the historical methods of *Historie.* Thankfully, argued Kähler, *Geschichte*—the study of the historic impact of Jesus, namely, *faith*—is all that the Christian community needs to know about Jesus of Nazareth.

Kähler's argument effectively divided not just history but historical *knowledge* into two camps, one kind of knowledge (*Historie*)

1

that sought to use historical methodologies to grasp what one could know about Jesus by the discipline of human reason, and another kind of knowledge (*Geschichte*) that was the knowledge of *faith*. This distinction, which affected not only historical investigation but also knowledge and reasoning, actually involved far more than the particular question of the historical Jesus. Kähler effectively used the question of the historical Jesus to create what he called a *sturmfreis Gebiet*, an "invulnerable space" secured by faith, which could exist and operate freely without the threat of secular reason. Kähler's argument dramatically influenced the shape of the twentieth-century theological movement known as neo-orthodoxy and its major representatives, Karl Barth, Rudolf Bultmann, Paul Tillich, H. Richard Niebuhr and others.

It is precisely on this point—Kähler's use of the historical Jesus question to create a space of intellectual safety for faith and Christian theology—that his argument becomes very interesting to me. Why? Because Kähler's distinction between the "so-called historical Jesus" and the "biblical Christ of faith" was not simply interested in *that* particular distinction but in a wider, larger issue, namely, the anxiety of Christian churches and their theologians as they began to face a range of new knowledge, such as the sciences, and a new civil society over which the church had dwindling control. Is it possible that that broader anxiety shaped the way Kähler himself set up his categories? Did he, in order to create his *sturmfreis Gebiet*, argue too quickly that the search for the historical Jesus was mere *Historie*, mere fact-finding, yielding only a "so-called historical Jesus"?

My proposal in this book is that Kähler, and the neo-orthodox tradition of theology that followed him, missed something—something crucial. What they missed was the possibility that the question of the historical Jesus was, in fact, not only a historical question but also a *historic question*—a question that created a series of profound social, political, and theological impacts that have continued to shape and reshape our world. It is a question that cannot be reduced to this or that particular proposal about the historical Jesus, but a question whose disturbing power has not only *not* gone away, but continues to open up new spaces of historical and theological construction and new spaces of lived faith.

In short, the "quest" for the historical Jesus is not (and was never) simply about the historical Jesus; it was always already about larger issues involving churches' theological self-understanding and their relation to broader society. And, thus, the theological rejection of historical Jesus research was almost always a refusal to deal with those larger issues. Moreover, there was not simply one quest, as in *the* quest for the historical Jesus, but differing quests that emerged within distinct periods and places, and which carried historic questions for their own time. The continuing dismissal by some theologians that the question of the historical Jesus was resolved long ago by Kähler, Albert Schweitzer, or others—and that its resurgence was simply the "same old" issue—is both defensive and incorrect.

In this book, I have sought to capture the *historic questions* that surround and shape both the question of the historical Jesus and the impact of these differing quests on theological and cultural life. In re-claiming the historic dimension of these quests, however, I do not want to avoid their various and serious attempts to get at the actual figure, or the actual teachings and acts, of Jesus of Nazareth by means of historical research. What interests me, however, is not the process of arguing whose reconstruction of Jesus or Jesus' teaching is better or best, on historical grounds. What really interests me is what Kähler seems to have either overlooked or ignored: under what circumstances does the use of historical methods to illuminate the person and work of Jesus of Nazareth become a *historic* question and not simply a historical one?

If, for example, as happens in the eighteenth and nineteenth centuries, one becomes concerned that the transcendent truth claims of Christian faith are being used, especially by the established churches in Germany or England or France or the Netherlands, to restrict the discussion of new ideas and the formation of an open civil society, then one might well be interested in using the newly available tools of historical research to ask what Jesus of Nazareth was *really* like. This, in fact, is what I argue in Part One of the book, in which I move with and against Albert Schweitzer's *The Quest of the Historical Jesus* (1906) in order to illuminate what remains largely hidden in his work: the historic quest for an open civil society, free from the imposed constraints of church dogma.

Or, if one suspects that after the success of Kähler's arguments and Karl Barth's neo-orthodoxy, Christian discourse in the mid-twentieth century had become too separated from human experience and modern culture, then one might again ask whether one could know more about the core of Jesus' teaching and practice, if not his biographical details or personality, in order to situate Jesus' own passion and concern for the depths of human experience. Part

Two discusses this "New Quest" for the historical Jesus—a quest that contributes to opening up new approaches to theology, including various liberation and feminist theologies.

Or, if one suspects that a newly politicized form of Christian fundamentalism in the United States in the late twentieth century exposes a level of biblical illiteracy that threatens civil discourse both within and well beyond the life of Christian churches, then one might well ask whether it was at all probable that Jesus, in fact, said all of the words attributed to him in the New Testament. Part Three discusses the Jesus Seminar's "Renewed Quest" for the historical Jesus in the face of a politicized Christian fundamentalism in the public sphere, on the one hand, and, on the other, the development of postliberal theology in mainline Christianity.

Each of these three major quests opens up historic questions that are at once wider than the particular figure of Jesus, but also informed and shaped by the attempt to fathom his authentic teaching. There is theological continuity across these quests in that they press the Christian institutions of their period to alter long-held theological assumptions in order to make room for a new depth and range of discourse. The first quest challenged established churches to move beyond the use of ecclesiastical power to control civil society, and to embrace greater religious freedom and an open civil society. The New Quest challenged the church to embrace the full historical humanity of Jesus and open itself more deeply to the full range of human experience in modern life, including the experiences of women, people of color, and those oppressed politically and economically. The Renewed Quest has challenged Christians and theologians of all stripes to reject the politicized power of Christian fundamentalism and open up models of faith that move beyond the too-narrow confines of right belief. Furthermore, it engages spiritual seekers of no faith tradition as well as persons of other faiths and traditions in the pursuit of wisdom. To be sure, one could come to these wider concerns quite apart from any knowledge of or interest in historical Jesus research, but historical Jesus research helped to carry the weight of these questions into arenas of public and theological debate.

To the extent that these questions have caused and continue to cause profound consternation in the circles of established religious authorities, the publication of historical Jesus scholarship has often created a climate of scandal. Blaming scholars for confusing and disturbing the faith of the simple believer, outraged officials have sought to mock and suppress such inquiry as a kind of treason against the church. Historic questions are often the most scandalous precisely because they raise basic, fundamental challenges about the assumptions governing their societies. Galileo questioned the earth-centered universe; Jefferson and company questioned governance by kingship; the research into the historical Jesus questioned the divine foundations of established churches. Such questions reverberate far beyond academic circles of science, philosophy, and biblical scholarship. Questions like these challenge institutional power. Pushing against the "certainties" of tradition, scandalous questions of a historic nature transgress the limits of authority, the limits of belonging, and the limits of institutional legitimacy, urging institutions and societies to risk openness to new knowledge, to less control, and to broader participation. Due in part to the changing world of recent centuries, and the accelerated change of more recent decades, what has often appeared scandalous in one era has appeared as grace to another. That is, finally, why I believe the quests for the historical Jesus matter deeply to theology. They have, in their differing ways, sought to argue that the central figure of Christian faith continues to hold open the horizons of religious and cultural life.

Part One

The First Quest

CHAPTER 1

Why the First Quest
for the Historical Jesus?

I was watching the first episode of Bill Moyers' 2006 PBS Series *Faith and Reason*.[1] He was talking with Salmon Rushdie, author of numerous novels including *The Satanic Verses*, which was banned by the Indian government when it was published in 1988. It was also banned in Pakistan, in Saudia Arabia, Egypt, and South Africa. In 1989 Iran's Ayattollah Ruhollah Khomeini issued a *fatwa*, or death sentence to be carried out by any Muslim not only against Rushdie but also his publishers for blaspheming Islam. For ten years Rushdie lived underground in England, moving from safe-house to safe-house until the ban was lifted in 1999. In this portion of the interview Rushdie protests the way Islamic societies—governed legally by theological law derived from the Qur'anic notion of *sharia*—have used theological claims to silence *public* discourse and to stifle the development of a genuine civil society:

> Unfortunately the degree of censorship in the Muslim world is so rigorous at the moment that very few scholars are able to go back to first principles and reexamine the bases of the faith.

He then makes a remarkable suggestion:

> Islam is unusual in that it is the only one of the great world religions which was born inside recorded history, and there's an enormous amount of factual, historical record about the life of the Prophet and about social conditions in Arabia at that time. So, it's possible to look at the origins of Islam in a scholarly way, based on historical fact.

I had been barely listening, but this last comment caught me; "Did he just . . . ?" Already, Moyers had begun to follow up:

> Do you expect Muslims to look at their faith in a historical context as opposed to supernaturally?

Rushdie: Yeah, of course; many people do. Actually, knowing a large number of Muslims around the world, many people do this. *It's just that it's the public discourse that's forbidden.* (emphasis added)

"Yes," I thought, still somewhat amazed, "he's calling for a study of the historical Mohammed." Lamenting the silencing of public discourse, Rushdie highlights the importance of historical studies as a way of moving Islam toward a more tolerant and open civil society. Such scholarship, implicitly challenging the notion that the Qur'an is a divinely revealed text, would undercut the theological argument by which Islamic states and radical clerics censor and silence public dissent. Rushdie continues:

> It's very interesting about Mohammed, the Prophet, that he has a character; that we know what he was like as a person. It's very interesting to see how Islam grew out of the social and economic conditions of his time. It's very interesting to see exactly how he learned from, and in many ways borrowed, stories and ideas from Judeo-Christian culture. That's to say, it's, to me, fascinating to see how this book came out of history. It's not an event outside history but inside history.

When pressed by Moyers to explain what prevents Islamic intellectuals and scholars from articulating a kind of historically informed skeptical faith: "What do you mean? Someone has to say, 'It's okay'?" Rushdie replies with some exasperation.

> *I mean you have to stop oppressing them.* Let's say at the moment there has been a very widespread campaign of oppression again Muslim writers and intellectuals. It's very hard to publish this kind of work; it's very hard for anyone to read it. Such scholarship has been banned outside and is banned inside the Muslim world. So, I think, if we're going to push toward the future you can't go on being hidebound by ideas which come from hundreds and hundreds of years ago. You have to enter the modern world. (emphasis added)

Why would Rushdie call for a study of the historical Mohammed in 2006? Was it perhaps merely a private interest of his, something that he found "interesting," as he says in the interview? Or does the question of a historical Mohammed raise, in effect, other questions—questions about the religious control of public discourse, about academic freedom, about the tension between religious authority and human freedom? Moyers' interview with Rushdie gives an American audience the opportunity to see the importance of the West's own history of conflict between traditional assumptions of religious authority and the creation of an open civil society. My own reading of the interview is that Rushdie sees the question of the historical Mohammed not simply as a point of inquiry but as a needed point of leverage for opening up the sphere of public discourse in Islamic societies. And Rushdie knows that leverage for such an opening of a religiously conservative culture must come not from the outside, but from the inside; not from those hostile to Islam, but from those faithful to it. And Rushdie knows as well that Islamic theologians will argue in varying ways against this or that portrait of the historical Mohammed, and often for good reasons. But the key issue at such an early phase of inquiry isn't whether a historian "gets it right." Instead, the central issue is: "You've got to stop oppressing" those who would pursue and publish such research.

◆ ◆ ◆

Rushdie's call for Islamic states to allow studies of the historical Mohammed helps contemporary readers better understand what was really at stake in the development of historical Jesus studies in the Christian West. The real historic question—at once cultural, political, and theological—that informs the eighteenth- and nineteenth-century modern quest for the historical Jesus is this: Do established churches have the authority to control and limit public discourse?

Put that directly, the question is provocative. One might well ask: How could an inquiry about the historical figure of Jesus of Nazareth really be about something else as distant as the control of public discourse? Isn't it more likely that interest in the historical Jesus developed somewhat innocently as an almost natural response to the development of historical methodology in the eighteenth century? Or, isn't it more likely that the *historical* Jesus is just one among the many changing faces of Jesus over the centuries? And, besides, isn't the history of the "quest" for the historical Jesus a fairly marginal question in the field of New Testament research? In summary: How can it be that the question of the historical Jesus is itself part of a "historic" question that asks about the ecclesiastical control of public discourse?

Prominent historical Jesus scholars from Albert Schweitzer to Martin Kähler and Hans Conzelmann have all acknowledged that the quest for the historical Jesus has always been about more than knowing the facts, as it were, about Jesus.[2] Each of these three notable scholars has said that the classic era of historical Jesus research, from the mid-eighteenth to the close of the nineteenth century, was a critique aimed at "dogmatism," or the "dogmatic Christ" of faith. But why would scholars talk about the historical Jesus in order to criticize the dogmatic Christ? What would be the point of that criticism? Schweitzer really doesn't explain his assertion; nor does Kähler; nor does Conzelmann, and perhaps they fail to do so because answering that question takes one afield from New Testament scholarship and theology, narrowly understood, and into the broader cultural and political issues of the time. To answer the question of *why* there have been quests for the historical Jesus, one must step back to view the broader cultural context, in which Jesus emerged as a figure critical of the church and its relationship to a newly emerging worldview and newly emerging nation states. When one does this, one can see the truly historic dimensions of the Quest itself.

Medieval Background and the Emergence of New Tensions

Although the actual biblical scholarship about the historical Jesus began in the eighteenth century, we need to go much farther back in European history to trace the larger social and political developments in which the Quest was rooted. Medieval legal, and educational, structures were founded on Augustine's argument that the role of the civil law in the "city of man," was to make life secure for the citizens of the "city of God." The civil law and its functionaries, including princes, were to be of service to the church. The major authority on the art of statecraft in the twelfth century, John of Salisbury, writes in his classic *Policraticus: The Statesman's Book*:

> This sword [of justice], then, the prince receives from the hand of the church, although she herself has no sword of blood at all. Nevertheless, she has this sword, but she uses it by the hand of the prince, upon whom she confers the powers of bodily coercion, retaining to herself authority over spiritual things in the person of the pontiffs. The prince is, then, as it were, a minister of the priestly power, and one who exercises that side of the sacred offices which seems unworthy of the hands of the priesthood. (Bk. 4, chap. 3)

And again,

A commonwealth, according to Plutarch, is a certain body which is endowed with life by the benefit of divine favor. . . . Those things which establish and implant in us the practice of religion and transmit to us the worship of God . . . fill the place of the soul in the body of the commonwealth. And therefore those who preside over the practice of religion should be looked up to and venerated as the soul of the body. For who doubts that the ministers of God are his representatives? Furthermore, since the soul is, as it were, the prince of the body, and has rulership over the whole thereof, so those whom our author calls the prefects of religion preside over the entire body. (Bk. 5, chap. 3)

John's analogy of the body's subordination to the soul was grounded in the Platonic Christianity of the Middle Ages in several ways. For centuries, Christian theologians had taken the Genesis image of humanity created "in the image of God" (Gen 1:26b) to mean that humans were created with a rational soul, capable of governing the passions and senses of the body. In addition, the Christology of the church began with the affirmation of the divine, eternal Word (*Logos*) of God that took on the condition of humanity in Jesus of Nazareth. Thus, even though the Council of Chalcedon (451 CE) had proclaimed that Jesus was both "fully God" and "fully human," the Christian Platonism of the Middle Ages argued that the divine nature of the Christ subsumed his human nature. While there is far more that one could add to bring home this point, John's arguments that the worldly prince is to be subordinated to the spiritual priest and that the civil law is to be subordinated to the divine law is clearly embedded in Christianity's teachings on human nature and on the nature of the Christ, Christology. Writes John: "Every censure imposed by law is vain if it does not bear the stamp of the divine law; and a statute or ordinance of the prince is nothing if it is not in conformity with the teaching of the church" (bk. 4, chap. 6).

John's logic contains yet another assumption, namely, that the "divine law" as promulgated by the teachings of the church, is based in divine revelation, that is to say in "truths" known only to faith, and which, by definition, exceed the grasp of human reason. Precisely because Europe was not only Christianized, but Christianized within a Platonic framework, this theological assumption of the priority of revealed truth was never really challenged. The assumption that civil law must be informed by divine law meant that *religious authorities were the effective censors of public discourse*, not only with respect to religious discourse per se, but also with respect to any public claim that threatened the established church and its interests, the trial of Galileo (1564–1642) being among the most famous cases.

The Middle Ages bequeathed to the early modern period an ideologically unified West, publicly informed by the logic of Christian theology. While there were ongoing tensions between ecclesiastical and civil authorities, the ideology of a unified worldview remained largely intact. Indeed, in many respects the Renaissance strengthened such legal and institutional connections rather than weakened them as one might suppose. The church held its authority not only officially, in law, but also by well-worn tradition, by education, by access to wealth, and by the power of the pulpit.

Reformation as Fragmentation

Under the aegis of "purification" and "reform," waves of Christian Reformation brought religious and political fragmentation to Europe. The ensuing religious wars between Catholics and Protestants, followed by bitter disputes between newly emerging Protestant sects — with one church anathematizing another — turned what had been the unifying discourse of Christendom into an increasingly polarized and divisive discourse. Thus, the Reformation created the terms of political and religious anxiety that would help birth a longing for certainty in the modern world. In the wake of profound religious conflict, one finds religious and political leaders grappling with a key question: How could religion, which had been essential to the public and political identity of Europe for a thousand years, continue to shape public and political identities? It seemed, on the one hand, that the power of religious communities needed to be affirmed; after all, the Reformation in its various manifestations had sought to strengthen Christianity. On the other hand, the new situation of violence and vitriol with which Christians denounced one another, to the point of extended armed conflict and persecution, raised profound new anxieties about whether religion was helpful in securing the public welfare. Thus, one of the key questions that emerged in the seventeenth century from the spiritual and political devastation resulting from the Reformation was how Christians, with now radically diverse theologies and commitments, would deal with one another.

There was another major question as well. In the face of profound new political, economic, and technological changes, what kind of public discourse would emerge to fill the vacuum left by the embittered splintering of the Christian ethos? The seventeenth century witnessed surges in economic growth and cultural complexity: the rise of nation-states as cultural bodies with distinct identities; a corresponding expansion of economic activity not only within these nations but globally with vast new trading possibilities opened to distant peoples, made possible by improved technology in shipbuilding and the competitive funding of rival states; a vast increase in publishing in vernacular languages; and the rise of intellectual and scientific bodies like England's Royal Society of London for the Improvement of Natural Knowledge, established in 1660.

The Peace of Westphalia, in 1648, provides a benchmark for observing a number of these historic trends across Europe. The Peace of Westphalia, which refers to the series of treaties which brought an end to the Thirty Years War, is often credited with establishing the basic international infrastructure of modernity, namely, the following principles: of sovereignty and political self-determination of nation states; of legal equality between nation states; of legally binding treaties between states; and of non-intervention in the internal affairs of other states. In the process, the treaty also gave rise to several new states in Europe by granting independence to the Netherlands from Spain (ending the Eighty Years War), and recognizing the independence of Switzerland. In addition, the treaty ended the legal and political influence of the Holy Roman Empire and its Emperor, Ferdinand III, putting to rest the claim that the Holy Roman Empire should have secular dominion over the whole of Christendom. Most important for our purposes is the fact that the Westphalia pact ratified the 1555 Treaty of Augsburg which had established the principle *cuius regio, eius religio,* ("whose realm, his religion"). According to this principle, the religion of a state, or region, would be dictated by the religion of the prince (a formulation which also tacitly acknowledged the facts on the ground in the English Reformation, as of 1534). The Peace of Westphalia also officially recognized Calvinism in addition to Lutheranism and Catholicism.

From even this very brief and partial summary of the treaty, one can see the increasing complexity of political, economic, and social life at work in the seventeenth century. At the heart of that complexity and stress lay religion itself. As the treaty both recognized the profound importance of religion and sought to separate religious communities in the interests of peace, national sovereignty, and commerce, the resulting fragmentation and demonization of one faith by another deepened the felt divide amidst an increasingly diverse Europe. The treaty's pragmatic solution created a new problem, namely, that of "official" or "established" churches, guided effectively not simply by the head of the church but by the political monarch in charge of the state. The more closely linked the church and state—the "altar and throne"—became throughout this period, the more one sees not only the continued emphasis on divine revelation as the source of the church's authority over public discourse but also the emergence of new theological defenses of the "Divine Right of Kings," which claimed to provide a scriptural defense for the king's absolute authority over public life.

In the newly created state churches, it was not clear how the official teachings would deal with the problem of the individual conscience. What if someone could not affirm the teachings of the state church? Would there be room for religious dissenters? Or would these dissenters be viewed not only as a threat to the "official" church but as a threat to the monarch? Didn't the Reformation itself provide a warrant for the free exercise of conscience and for the right of public discourse? How would one balance the felt need for national and religious "identity" with the arguments for the liberty of one's individual conscience?

For those whose religious views did not concur with the prince or monarch of their region and who became dissenters, several options presented themselves. The Peace of Westphalia itself allowed people three months to pick up their lives and move to a land with a more favorable religious option. Some endured this form of hardship for their faith. Others could affirm the new established religion publicly but privately maintain their former beliefs. Such persons might hold out for the time and place where their faith might become the religious establishment (as was the case, for example, with the Puritans and the Massachusetts Bay colony in the new world). Another option would be found in the newly emerging plurality of religious positions, an option that would look very different from Augsburg and Westphalia. For these voices, both within the established churches and among dissenters as well, the very plurality of religious positions, augmented by an affirmation of the inviolability of the individual conscience, would argue against any one church being elevated to the status of an official, established church.

Roger Williams was an early voice against the idea of established churches. Having been ousted from the Massachusetts Bay Colony for heresy, he wrote to Parliament in 1644 his landmark text, "The Bloudy Tenent of Persecution." In the text, Williams presents a dialogue between the figures "Truth" and "Peace" in which he argues passionately that the union of religious and civil power actually creates public discord.

> All civil states with their officers of justice, in their respective constitutions and administrations, are . . . essentially civil, and therefore not judges, governors, or defenders of the Spiritual, or Christian, State and worship. . . . It is the will and command of God that, since the coming of His Son, the Lord Jesus, a permission of the most Paganish, Jewish, Turkish or anti-Christian consciences and worship be granted to all men, in all nations and countries; and they are only to be fought against with that sword which is only, in Soul matters able to conquer, to wit; the sword of the Spirit—the Word of God. . . . God requireth not an uniformity of religion to be enacted and enforced in any civil state; which enforced uniformity, sooner or later, is the greatest occasion of civil war, ravishing consciences, persecution of Christ Jesus in His servants, and of the hypocrisy and destruction of millions of souls. . . . An enforced uniformity of religion throughout a nation or civil state confounds the civil and religious, denies the principles of Christianity and civility, and that Jesus Christ is come in the flesh.[3]

By pointing to the diversity of religious positions, and arguing for the priority of the public peace of the whole community, Williams claims that magistrates, who themselves might belong to one sect or another, are not competent in matters of religion. Magistrates should not, therefore, be in a position to rule on true religion v. false religion, or to impose penalties that would imprison, or confiscate property, or banish, or condemn those who in conscience believe differently from the majority, or ruling, faith. In a very interesting argument, Williams claims that religious communities, as diverse social groups themselves, are more like other self-governing corporations within the society, than they are analogous to the society, and its interests, as a whole.

> The *Church* or company of *worshippers* (whether true or false) is like unto a . . . *Corporation, Society* or *Company* . . . in *London;* which Companies may hold their *Courts,* keep their *Records,* hold

disputations; and in matters concerning their *Societie*, may dissent, divide, break into Schismes and Factions, sue and implead each other at the *Law*, yea wholly breake up and dissolve into pieces and nothing, and yet the *peace* of the *Citie* not be in the least measure impaired or disturbed; because the *essence* or being of the *Citie*, and so the *well-being* and *peace* thereof is essentially distinct from those particular *Societies*; the *Citie-Courts*, *Citie-Lawes*, *Citie-punishments* distinct from theirs. The *Citie* was before them, and stands absolute and intire, when such a *Corporation* or *Societie* is taken down.[4]

In addition to these arguments, which are largely pragmatic ones, drawn from the analysis of social organizations, Williams claims that the practices that follow the joining of civil and religious authority are antithetical to "Jesus Christ, the Prince of Peace." "That the blood of so many hundred thousand soules of Protestants and Papists, split in the Wars of present and former Ages, for their respective Consciences, is not required nor accepted by Jesus Christ the Prince of Peace."[5] It is, in fact, antithetical, according to Williams, for one to imagine that Jesus Christ would support the kind of persecution, banishment, torture, and death that occurs as part of the accepted regime of state-churches.

Setting Jesus Christ, as the Prince of Peace, against the theory and practice of established churches is a dangerous argument for Williams. After all, does not, the voice of the established church rightly interpret the Scripture? It was just at this point that the Reformers broke open the sealed authority of the Pope to interpret officially the meaning of Scripture. Williams turns to this Protestant principle about the priority and norm of Scripture itself to make his point. Williams grants that his critics can turn to Moses and the prophets to justify their claim to power over the society. But he goes on to argue that one cannot find justification for such a model of civil government in Jesus, who is, after all, the center of Scripture, the very Word of God to a Christian people. That turn to Jesus, by Williams, to argue for civil liberty from established church doctrine is an important piece in the broader story that one needs to hear in order to understand the *why* of historical Jesus research.

Another important figure is the famous Dutch jurist Hugo Grotius (1583–1645), considered by some to be the founder of modern international law for his works, *Mare Liberum* (*Freedom of the High Seas*, 1609), and *De jure belli ac pacis* (*Concerning the Law of War and Peace*, 1625, definitive ed. 1631). He is also considered by some to be the founder, or major precursor of Deist thought. To the question of how Europe would find a new framework for public discourse to deal with a rapidly changing world, Grotius provides important direction.

Grotius knew first hand, the serious wounds that religious certainty inflicted on civil society. Condemned to life in prison in 1618, (following the Synod of Dort, convened by the Dutch political party aligned with "strict" Calvinists), because of his published support of a moderate Calvinist movement of Remonstrants (Dutch followers of Jacobus Arminius) and arguments on behalf of religious toleration, Grotius escaped in 1621 by hiding himself in a chest, which was then carried out of the prison by friends, and escaped to France, where his career flourished.

In the introduction to his 1609 *The Freedom of the Seas*, Grotius makes a move that is fascinating, not for the originality of his turn to God, but for the originality of what he draws from the biblical text. Grotius connects the reality of God as "the founder and ruler of the universe, and especially . . . the father of all mankind" to obligations inherent within the human family.

> The law by which our case [the right of the Netherlands to engage in trade with the East Indies] must be decided is not difficult to find, seeing that it is the same among all nations; and it is easy to understand, seeing that it is innate in every individual and implanted in his mind. Moreover, the law to which we appeal is one such as no king ought to deny to his subjects, and one no Christian ought to refuse to a non-Christian. For it is a law derived from nature, the common mother of us all, whose bounty falls on all, and whose sway extends over those who rule nations, and which is held most sacred by those who are most scrupulously just.[6]

But what exactly is the specific law of nature from which Grotius argues that the high seas are the "common property" of all humanity?

> I shall base my argument on the following most specific and unimpeachable axiom of the Law of Nations, called a primary rule or first principle, the spirit of which is self-evident and immutable, to wit: Every nation is free to travel to every other nation, and to trade with it.
>
> God Himself says this . . . through the voice of nature; and inasmuch as it is not His will to have Nature supply every place with all the necessities of life, He ordains that some nations excel in one art, and others in another. Why is this His will, except it be that He wished human friendships to be engendered by mutual needs and

resources, lest individuals deeming themselves entirely sufficient unto themselves should for that very reason be rendered unsociable.[7]

It is from this "decree of divine justice," inferable from nature, that Grotius argues his case that Spain and Portugal cannot deprive the Netherlands of its natural right to trade with the peoples of the East Indies.

While contemporary readers may find it odd that an argument about a trade dispute would begin with a discussion of God and the laws of nature, Grotius' text helps us realize at least three things about the cultural world of seventeenth-century Europe: 1) that there was no established international forum for bringing such disputes, 2) that religious language was still very much a language of diplomacy and political power, and 3) that God, as the ground of Truth and fount of all human reason, was the most basic common assumption from which to build an argument about the relations between peoples and states.

Yet more interesting is that while Grotius implicitly affirms the reality of "Christendom," his God is not particularly Christian. He avoids speaking in Trinitarian terms, and he avoids speaking of the Christ. He does not deny these formulations; indeed, Grotius was a well respected Christian theologian. But with respect to public discourse, Grotius realized that particular Christian claims were no longer effective in achieving persuasion across competing religious groups. Instead, Grotius affirms a God who is the father of all humankind, and whose rules, accessible to reason, must be followed by Christian and non-Christian alike.

Grotius insists that the divine natural law, accessible to all persons by virtue of reason, applies to nations as well as persons. Moreover, from that divine natural law one can discern the most fundamental moral responsibilities of nations toward one another. Thus, the realm of international relations, while obligated to attend to natural law is *not* obligated to one particular faith. Within this broader logic, Grotius affirmed that nations should insist upon belief in God, but tolerate all other differences, including those of Jews and Muslims.

While the institution of official, or established churches was clearly a political development, one needs to recognize again that established churches also justified their existence as official churches *theologically*. While Lutherans, Calvinists, and Anglicans disagreed with Rome over indulgences, and over a range of ecclesiastical issues focusing on authority of Scripture and authority of the papacy, on celibacy, on monastic life, on the number, and interpretation of the sacraments, and so on, the Reformers did not deny doctrines associated specifically with the revealed truth of the Trinity, the dual nature of Christ, the atonement, the inspiration of the Scriptures, and the reality of Jesus' miracles. They interpreted these truths differently than Rome, and with an emphasis on the priority of the Scriptures, but they affirmed these truths nonetheless. In fact, it was precisely because the official church (be it the Lutheran, the Calvinist, the Anglican, the Catholic, and so on) possessed, by the grace of God, truths that transcended human reason, that it should guide and govern the content of public discourse on behalf of the Christian state.

At this point, one can begin to see the cultural, the political, and the religious matrices that will give both tenor and content to what will become the quest for the historical Jesus: the simultaneous calls for a new discourse of reason—a call implicit, for these early voices, in biblical revelation itself—and for a public discourse open to, and tolerant of a broad diversity of religious voices.

CHAPTER

2

Locke, Hume, and the
Shifting Loyalties of Reason

In this chapter I continue to explore the cultural, political and intellectual context that shapes the emergence of historical Jesus research, as begun in the hidden work of Hermann Samuel Reimarus (1694–1768). Reimarus' lengthy writings on the historical Jesus were gathered together by him under the title *Apology or Defense for Rational Worshippers of God*. Written in the context of the German Enlightenment, or *Aufklärung*, the *Apology* opens with an appeal for rational religion and for the toleration of Deism in Germany. It is that appeal for present-day toleration that frames Reimarus' attempt to situate the biblical texts generally and the figure of Jesus specifically within a historical and naturalistic framework. In order to understand what Reimarus was up to in his analysis of the biblical texts, we need to discuss several major thinkers who shaped his passion for interpreting Jesus in a historical and decidedly non-supernaturalistic way.

Lord Herbert of Cherbury (1583–1648) is often considered the founder of Deism. He was encouraged by Grotius to publish his first major work *De Veritate* [*On Truth*] in Paris in 1624. In that book, he proposed a theory of human knowledge in explicit contrast to claims of revelation. In a second book, *De religione Gentilium [Pagan Religion]* (London, 1645), he articulated what became known as the "Five Articles" of English Deism:

1. a belief in the existence of the Deity
2. the obligation to reverence such a power
3. the identification of worship with practical morality
4. the obligation to repent of sin and to abandon it
5. divine recompense in this world and the next[1]

For Cherbury, these articles provided the centerpiece of all religions, including Christianity in its origins.

In many circles, Deism is still often treated only as a kind of misguided theology, too influenced by the mechanistic worldview arising out of early scientific thinking. Thus, the discussion of Deism is frequently reduced to a kind of technical debate between the defenders of modern "reason" on the one hand and the defenders of "revelation" and tradition on the other. While partially true, such presentations often fail to ask the question "why": Why the suspicion about "revelation"? Was the suspicion due only to the arrival of a new approach to knowledge? To continue the argument of the previous chapter, no.

The suspicion about revelation was fueled both by growing concerns about the power of established churches over public, civil discourse, and by an emerging recognition of the need for a new framework for public life. The combination of the warring, fragmented religious communities of post-Reformation Europe and the new cultural demands of an emerging public realm had effectively broken up the stability and authority of the classical theological framework. While the Peace of Westphalia had sought to stabilize the religious and political situation, there is evidence that it actually *increased* the religious zeal and intolerance of many communities, by specifically linking theological identity to political identity and stability. Writing about one hundred years after Cherbury, John Clarke, translating the work of Grotius in 1819, laments the consequences of the Peace of Westphalia:

> How is it that the generality of Christians in one country are zealous for Calvinism, and in another country are zealous for Arminianism? It is not because men have any natural disposition more to the one than the other, or perhaps that one has much more foundation to support it from Scripture than the other; but the reason is plain, *viz.*, because they are the established doctrines of the places they live in; they are by authority made the rule and standard of religion, and men are taught them from the beginning; by this means they are so deeply fixed and rooted in their minds, that they become prejudiced in favour of them, and have so strong a relish of them, that they cannot read a chapter of the Bible but it appears exactly agreeable to the received notions of both of them.

To understand Deism correctly one needs to recognize its concern for public life. The Deist critique of the Trinity was not primarily grounded in metaphysical concerns but in practical ones. Because the established Christian churches defended their authority to govern not only the church but the public life of the nation based on their possession of truths that transcended reason, such as the Trinity and the divinity of Christ, Deists argued for a model of God that would not authorize such sweeping public power. As a movement, Deists—or Freethinkers, as some preferred to be called—were not all of one mind. Many, if not most, viewed themselves as Christians. They differed from orthodox Christianity by claiming, minimally, that even if Christian revelation transcended reason, it could not contradict reason. Some went further and argued that reason should function normatively, discrediting any claim of revelation that did not square with the principles of human reason. At the heart of the Deist movement, however, was the conviction that public discourse needed to be established on a clear, epistemological footing other than revelation. While Christian theology had anchored the public authority of the church in its guidance and control of public life in Western Europe for over a thousand years, the new situation was calling forth new models of both faith and reason.

Locke and the Christian
Impulse to Toleration

While John Locke (1632–1704) was a Christian, his empirical approach to human understanding was informed by aspects of Deist thought. He acknowledged that there were truths that transcended human reason, for example, but he claimed that there could be no supernatural truths that contradicted human reason. He affirmed the reality of Jesus' miracles as empirical evidence of Jesus' divinity, but he also argued with respect to other miraculous claims that it fell to reason to discern whether a miracle had in fact occurred. In these, and other ways, Locke sought to interpret the supernatural claims of Christianity in such a way as to maximize the importance of human reason for authentic faith.

It was not by coincidence that John Locke's most famous treatises, *A Letter on Toleration*, was published in 1689. Only a year after the "Glorious Revolution" of 1688 in which the Protestant William of Orange, of the Netherlands, had overthrown James II, who had sought to claim the Divine Right of Kings and quite possibly to reestablish Roman Catholicism in England, we see Locke thinking about the structure of a civil society and the role of religion in it. In the *Letter,* as well as in his *Essay concerning Human Understanding* and *Two Treatises of Government* (published in 1690!), we see Locke moving toward a new and coherent interpretation of civil society. In contrast, however, to the top-down authority, implied in Robert

Filmer's defense of the Divine Right of Kings, Locke argued from the bottom-up, from the gathering of human beings into a society. For our purposes I will focus on Locke's *A Letter on Toleration*.

One can hear in Locke's *Letter* themes similar to Roger Williams' appeal to Parliament in 1634, as discussed in the previous chapter. But now, one hundred and fifty years after Williams, these concerns are coming not from the margins of the colonies, but from the newly emerging center of intellectual life. Locke wrote his *Letter* in Holland, the land of Grotius, to which he had fled for safety in 1685 from allegations of treason against James II. He addressed it to a close friend, Philipp van Limborch, the leader of the Remonstrant movement in the Netherlands. Within a year, the *Letter* (composed in Latin) was translated into English, French, and Dutch. In it, Locke expresses the heart of his project as a Christian reformer. He opens: "Honoured Sir,"

> Since you ask my opinion about mutual toleration among Christians, I reply briefly that I regard it as the chief distinguishing mark of a true church. For however much some people boast of the antiquity of places and names, or of the splendor of their ritual; others of the reformation of their teaching, and all of the orthodoxy of their faith (for everyone is orthodox to himself); these claims, and others of this kind, are more likely to be signs of men striving for power and empire than signs of the church of Christ.[2]

Locke argues that toleration is the "chief distinguishing mark of a true church," because the ethic of toleration does not strive for "power and empire." In this opening salvo, Locke uses the traditional theological topic of the "marks" of the church against the claims of established churches that do not practice toleration of other religious positions. Such churches, implies Locke, do violence both to the true church and to public life.

Specifically, Locke is concerned that established churches have used the political arm of the state to coerce religious belief and silence public discourse. Given the furor, and viciousness, of these disputes over public—and not merely ecclesiastical—authority, Locke insists that the civil power and the ecclesiastical power must be kept separate.

> The toleration of those who hold different opinions on matters of religion is so agreeable to the Gospel and to reason, that it seems monstrous for men to be blind in so clear a light.[3]

Locke uses the language of the "gospel" as did Williams, as the model of an original, un-diluted Christianity, but he adds that toleration is agreeable not only to the gospel but to "reason." Indeed, he says it is "monstrous for men to be blind" such that they miss the clear "theological" *and* "rational" importance of toleration. Such blindness, and the corruption that attends it, claims Locke, is masked by pretenses to purity and truth.

> But that some may not mask their persecution and unchristian cruelty with a pretence of care for the commonwealth and observance of the laws; and that others, in the name of religion, may not seek license for their immorality and impunity for their misdeeds; in a word, that none may impose upon himself or others, either as a faithful subject of his prince, or as a sincere worshiper of God; I regard it as necessary above all to distinguish between the business of civil government and that of religion, and to mark the true bounds between the church and the commonwealth.[4]

While not attacking the notion of established churches, per se, Locke focuses on limiting the church's power over public discourse. Like Williams, Locke argues that the civil magistrate has no competence in religion, because, as Locke argues, "the care of souls is not committed to the civil magistrate."[5] Even if it were, Locke continues, the power of the magistrate is that of "compulsion" whereas "true and saving religion consists in the inward persuasion of the mind."[6] In addition, even if the external force of civil laws and punishments *could* change people's minds, argues Locke, it would not enhance the salvation of souls:

> For there being but one true religion, one way to heaven, what hope is there that most men would reach it, if mortals were obliged to ignore the dictates of their own reason and conscience, and blindly accept the doctrines imposed by their prince, and worship God in the manner laid down by the laws of their country?[7]

If the civil power has only the power of external force, which is incapable of shaping inward belief, according to Locke, then ecclesiastical power must be limited to the power of persuasion. Here we find Locke's famous definition of the church as "a free and voluntary society." "No man is bound by nature to any church or assigned to any sect, but he voluntarily joins the society in which he believes he has found true religion and the form of worship that is acceptable to God."[8] Locke's view of the church as a society within a society is analogous to Williams' view, discussed in the previous chapter.

Perhaps more importantly, Locke's formulation of the "voluntary" character of the church fits well with his view of civil society developed in his Second Treatise on Government. According to Locke, people move from a "state of nature" into civil society not by fear of Thomas Hobbes's (1588–1679) war of all-against-all (*Leviathan*) but by free choice. The sum of Locke's three pieces is a vision of an expanded civil society. While churches, like other institutions, says Locke, must be able to exercise leadership over their members, including excommunication, he is clear on the limits of ecclesiastical power.

> The arms by which the members of this society [church] are to be kept within their duty are exhortations, admonitions, and advice. If by these means offenders will not be reclaimed, and those who go astray brought back to the right path, nothing further remains to be done but that such stubborn and obstinate persons, who give no ground to hope for their reformation, should be separated and cast out from the society. This is the last and utmost force of ecclesiastical authority.[9]

Nor does the orthodox claim of possessing the "true faith" establish a right for one church to use the force of the magistrate against another church. In the following example, Locke picks up the continuing hatred among Calvinists that had sent a young Grotius to prison for life:

> To explain the matter by an example, let us suppose two churches at Constantinople, one of Remonstrants, the other of Anti-remonstrants. Will anyone say that either of these churches has right to deprive the members of the other of their liberty or property (as we see practised elsewhere) because they are dissenters, and differ from it in doctrines and ceremonies, or to punish them with exile or death, while the Turk in the meanwhile silently stands by, and laughs to see with what cruel torture Christians persecute Christians? But if one of these churches has a power to ill-treat the other, I ask which of the two is it, and by what right? No doubt it will be answered that it is the orthodox church which has this power over the erroneous or heretical. This is to use great and specious words to say nothing at all. For every church is orthodox to itself and erroneous or heretical to others.[10]

Far from giving orthodox voices rights over dissenters, Locke argues that "because every church is orthodox to itself" civil society cannot establish *the* true religion. Toleration, argues Locke, is not a nicety but a necessity for public life and discourse.

In Locke's *Letter* one sees that the practice of religious coercion helped forge Locke's conviction of the inviolable character of the individual conscience. While it is common in theological circles to note that in the modern period faith becomes a private affair, divorced from the public sector, it is *not* very frequently noted that one important reason for that inward orientation stemmed precisely in order to free, and protect, the *public sphere* from the autocratic control of religious authorities. If the human conscience must not be forced, as Locke argued, then the civil power must cease to be the military arm of the church.

Locke's *Letter on Toleration* raised eyebrows throughout the political and religious establishment of Europe. Attacks on his work by Jonas Proast (1640–1710), who was an Anglican clergyman and Oxford educated academic, caused Locke to issue a *Second* and *Third Letter* in response. A central problem for Proast was Locke's questioning the public enforcement of religious participation by the civil authority.

Proast argued for the right and necessity of civil force to compel religious participation. He claimed that Locke's statement that the gospel had prevailed in the "first ages of Christianity" by "its own beauty, force, and reasonableness," was inaccurate. Instead, said Proast, the reasonableness of the early church was supported by miracles "til . . . Christianity had prevailed to be received for the religion of the empire."[11] Since we are no longer living in an age of miracles, says Proast, the truth of the gospel requires the aid of the state against the sinful inclinations of the people. While such a theological argument sounds bizarre to most twenty-first-century Western readers, it was by no means an unreasonable position in the late seventeenth century. Proast, in fact, spoke for more clergymen of his day, inside of England and out, than did Locke, and his position enables us to better grasp the *theo*-logical argument of the established churches.

Proast sees the church's capacity to use the magistrate's force to compel Christian compliance to the Anglican Church as a fundamental element of God's divine providence reaching back to Constantine. For him, and for many, religious "dissent," especially public dissent was a form of outright disobedience, and thus the use of force to compel obedience to God's law was an obvious entailment of both true religion and a just state. Locke's final lines take aim at Proast's fundamental argument, which had aligned divine "miracles" with the "force" of the magistrate. Such an argument, says Locke, "will shew nothing, for your cause, but the zeal of a man so fond of force, that he will, without any warrant from Scripture, enter into the counsels of the Almighty; . . . as may best suit his system."[12]

A more virulent attack was launched by religious authorities against Irish dissenter, John Toland's (1670–1722) *Christianity Not Mysterious*, published in 1696. Deeply influenced by Locke, Toland went beyond Locke's more nuanced understanding of the relation between reason and revelation. Insisting, for example, that revelation conform to natural reason, he writes: "Thus all the doctrines and precepts of the New Testament (if it be indeed divine) must agree with natural reason and our own ordinary ideas."[13] The notion of testing the divinity of Scripture—"if it be indeed divine"— was a question Locke himself didn't raise. It drew a quick response from Irish clergy. Peter Browne, a cleric, in a widely circulated condemnation of the book in Ireland, makes plain the public, political issues beneath his own theological critique of the book.

> The world is at this time so disposed for the reception of all discourses that seem to set up reason and evidence in opposition to the revealed and mysterious that nothing less than the interpositions of authority can stop this current of infidelity and profaneness which threatens to overwhelm the nations.
>
> How far men in power, according to the several stations, are obliged to intermeddle in point of conscience, I shall not inquire. But sure I am, in point of policy, it is become no less than necessary. For the writers of this strain have given broad hints that they are as little friends to our government as our religion. . . .
>
> Their numbers grow formidable, they begin to speak out their infidelity and profaneness as plain as some of them to treason. They are secretly forming themselves in clubs and cabals, and have their emissaries into all parts, which are supported by contributions. And I make little doubt but that their design is at length to show us that all dominion, as well as religion, is founded in reason.[14]

According to Browne, Toland's text is not simply evidence of theological heresy but of treason against the government; Toland, claims Browne, is no reformer, but a revolutionary. The works of such writers, he argues, should be banned from public consumption. And they were. The Irish House of Commons condemned the book and ordered it burned. They also ordered the arrest of Toland, who escaped to England and then to Europe, where he spent the rest of his life on the fringes of society.

Toland's 1696 language that revelation must square with "natural reason and our own ordinary ideas" would be expanded by others, who, like Matthew Tindal, began to challenge the *universal* character of Christian truth by bringing the religious experience of other peoples—increasingly known through trade and travel narratives—to bear on the question of Christian authority over public discourse. In *Christianity as Old as the Creation, or the Gospel: a Republication of the Religion of Nature* (1730), Tindal invited his readers to consider that three-hundred million Chinese could not be excluded from the truth of the gospel. Suggesting that aspects of Confucianism could correct those aspects of the Mosaic law which were overly harsh, Tindal said that Christian revelation—in order to be universally true—needed to seek the truth in all religious traditions. Otherwise, it could not be a truth "as old as the creation." His more subtle point? A genuinely *Christian* society would be a religiously open and tolerant society. Its authentic content would be the ethical teachings of Jesus, which were fully in keeping with the natural law.

From the late seventeenth to the mid-eighteenth century, one sees Christians, like Locke, as well as a variety of Deists, including Toland and Tindal and others, addressing important questions of civil society by challenging the traditional theological arguments that supported the logic of established churches. These took a variety of forms: arguments that Jesus understood himself as Messiah, concerned primarily with the ethical behavior of his followers (Locke); or that the resurrection was questionable due to the contradictions in the Gospel narratives (Peter Annet, 1693–1768); or that the miracles could not be used as evidence of the truth of the Christian religion (Thomas Woolston, 1668–1733); or that the apostles perverted the original gospel of Jesus (Thomas Chubb,1679–1747), or that the early church did so (John Toland, 1670–1722); or that early-church arguments from prophecy as a proof of Jesus' identity were faulty, along with the notion that Jesus thought of himself as a temporal savior (Anthony Collins, 1676–1729); or that early Christian expectations of an imminent *parousia* were wrong (Matthew Tindal, 1657–1733).[15] Whether the issue involved the basic vocabulary of reason and revelation (Locke), or that reason provides criteria by which to test revelation (John

Toland), or even far more specific claims about Jesus and the early church, the issue was not *merely* a theological one. Instead, these new theological arguments were aimed at criticizing the theological underpinnings of established churches, and thereby opening a new realm of public discourse.

While twenty-first-century readers may need to squint at first, as it were, to see—to understand—how issues of public life, and the governance of civil society, were actually being raised by theologians who challenged the traditional doctrines of Christian faith, I hope the reader's eyes are becoming accustomed to the light I am trying to shine on these issues. How, in fact, could the situation be otherwise? European life and culture had been so deeply steeped in Christian Platonism that no new science (Newton, 1687), or model of economics (Smith, 1776), or shift in political philosophy (Smith, 1689; Jefferson, 1776) could undo by itself or together the centuries-old assumption that Christian prelates should govern not only their churches but the civil society of Christian nations as well. By Christian Platonism I mean the articulation of Christian theology within the classical worldview of Plato and the Platonic school extending to the philosopher Plotnius in the third century CE. Expressed most notably in the thought of St. Augustine in the late fourth and fifth centuries CE, the synthesis known as Christian Platonism would frame the development of Christian orthodoxy throughout the Middle Ages into the Reformation period. Just as change needed to occur within the church itself during the Reformation, so in this new modern period change would have to come from within the church and from theological critiques of Christian claims to truth and power.

David Hume: The End of Miracles and Revelation as Public Arguments

Because both monarchs and state-established clergy defended their civil authority as embedded in Christian tradition and divinely established by God and God's revelation in Christ and Scripture, eighteenth-century critics of the altar-and-throne alignment turned increasingly to both rational and historical critiques of divine revelation, miracles, and a high Christology in order to leverage an understanding of public space not seen since Athens and the Roman republic.

During his lifetime, David Hume (1711–76) was best known as a historian. Over time, however, his philosophical works—which, while building on Locke's empiricism, ultimately challenged

Locke's own assumptions—became the basis of his intellectual reputation. Deepening Locke's empiricist approach, Hume argued that there were no "self-evident" propositions of unchangeable truth. A truly empiricist approach, he argued, must resist the siren call of "certainty" and recognize "probability" as the proper domain of human knowledge.

Hume rejected Baruch Spinoza's (1632–77) and Gottfried Leibnitz's (1646–1716) assertions of a distinction between two kinds of human knowledge: necessary truths of reason (e.g., Euclid's geometry) and probable truths of history and scientific observation. While acknowledging the truth of tautological statements (A=A), Hume argued that all claims to factual knowledge about the world were inevitably probabilistic and based upon the relation of cause and effect as known through experience and custom, thus shifting philosophy in the direction of what he called a "mitigated skepticism." Hume rejected a pure, or totalizing skepticism—the idea that we could know nothing (except the truth of the claim that we could know nothing) as inherently contradictory and unrealistic. His notion of a "mitigated skepticism," however, according to which "the wise man proportions his belief to the evidence," was aimed as a sharp critique at attempts to provide rational grounds for religious beliefs.[16]

In one of his *Political Essays*, "On Parties in General," Hume discussed religion at some length under the heading of "factions."[17]

Religions, that arise in ages totally ignorant and barbarous, consist mostly of traditional tales and fictions, which may be different in every sect, without being contrary to each other; and even when they are contrary, every one adheres to the tradition of his own sect, without much reasoning or disputation. But as philosophy was widely spread over the world, at the time when Christianity arose, the teachers of the new sect were obliged to form a system of speculative opinions; to divide, with some accuracy, their articles of faith; and to explain, comment, confute, and defend with all the subtilty of argument and science. Hence naturally arose keenness in dispute, when the Christian religion came to be split into new divisions and heresies: And this keenness assisted the priests in their policy, of begetting a mutual hatred and antipathy among their deluded followers. Sects of philosophy, in the ancient world, were more zealous than parties of religion; but in modern times, parties of religion are more furious and enraged than the most cruel factions that ever arose from interest and ambition.[18]

Insofar as "priestly power" stands opposed to liberty, and does so based upon "subtilty of argument," Hume's sharpened critique of both "innate truths" and *a priori* foundational certainty carries forward the social-political project of Deist thought: an increase of liberty and the critique of Christian power. Small wonder that the German philosopher Immanuel Kant later credited Hume for "waking me from my dogmatic slumbers."

In *An Enquiry concerning Human Understanding*, Hume discusses the limits of human knowledge:

> The utmost effort of human reason is to reduce the principles, pro-
> ductive of natural phenomena, to a greater simplicity, and to resolve
> the many particular effects into a few general causes, by means of
> reasonings from analogy, experience, and observation. But as to the
> causes of these general causes, we should in vain attempt their dis-
> covery. . . . These ultimate springs and principles are totally shut up
> from human curiosity and enquiry. Elasticity, gravity, cohesion of
> parts, communication of motion by impulse; these are probably the
> ultimate causes and principles which we shall never discover in na-
> ture; and we may esteem ourselves sufficiently happy, if, by accurate
> enquiry and reasoning, we can trace up the particular phenomena
> to, or near to, these general principles.[19]

For Hume, these limits of understanding function to ground the humility of the knower and to curb claims of ultimate truth.

Hume recognized, too, the political danger in making public the theological implications of his thought. He left his devastating critique of miracles out of his initial *Treatise of Human Nature* (1737) for fear of public reaction. As he prepared the manuscript for publication, he wrote to a friend, Henry Home:

> I . . . inclose some *Reasonings concerning Miracles*, which I once
> thought of publishing with the rest, but which I am afraid will give
> too much offence, even as the world is disposed at present. . . . I am
> at present castrating my work, that is, cutting off its nobler parts; that
> is, endeavoring [that] it shall give as little offence as possible. . . . This
> is a piece of cowardice, for which I blame myself, though I believe
> none of my friends will blame me.[20]

His caution did him no favors. When he applied for a profes-sorship in Scotland, following the publication of the *Treatise*, he was turned down on account of his religious views. Hume scholar Stephen Buckle believes the rejection wounded Hume deeply. By

1748, he had mastered his fears, however, and he included the treatise on miracles in his *Enquiry concerning Understanding*. There it fits, along with the subsequent chapter on the notion of Providence, within Hume's overall argument about the probable character of human knowledge.

Hume's famous treatise *Of Miracles* warrants more in-depth attention here not only for its deepening criticism of Christian claims to possess supernatural truth, and hence supernatural authorization for governing public life and morals, but also for the way these arguments will resurface in our discussion of Reimarus' critique of the Gospels in chapter three.

Contemporary Roman Catholic scholar, Francis Schüssler Fiorenza points out in *Jesus and the Church* that the church of the eighteenth century turned to miracles and to the story of the empty tomb of Jesus as "evidences" of supernatural action in history, and thus, as evidence of the church's claim to possess supernatural truth.[21] While Locke had been willing to consider the miracles as evidence of Jesus' divinity, Hume argues forcefully against such an argument.

In the opening paragraph of the treatise, Hume invokes the work of Dr. John Tillotson (1630–94), Archbishop of Canterbury, who had argued in a 1684 piece entitled "Discourse against Transubstantiation" against the *real presence* of Christ in the Eucharist. Hume, seeking the cover of the former Archbishop, uses Tillotson to suggest the kind of proof that he will make against all claims to miracles.

> It is acknowledged on all hands, says the learned prelate [Tillotson], that the authority, either of the scripture or of tradition, is founded merely in the testimony of the apostles, who were eyewitnesses to those miracles of our Savior, by which he proved his divine mission. Our evidence, then, for the truth of the *Christian* religion is less than the evidence for the truth of our senses; because, even in the first authors of our religion, it was no greater; and it is evident that it must diminish in passing from them to their disciples; nor can any one rest such confidence in their testimony, as in the immediate object of his senses.[22]

What Hume applauds about Tillotson's argument is that it shifts the grounds of authority from divine assertion to human testimony. Once the authority of a text shifts to human testimony, according to Hume, one is operating in the region of "probability," and here, the "wise man . . . proportions his belief to the evidence."[23] Such is the case when one is dealing with any probable argument, and human testimony to miraculous events is certainly of that type.

Hume begins by arguing that there are reasons to attend seriously to testimony. Nonetheless, he adds, "our assurance in any argument of this kind is derived from no other principle than our observation of the veracity of human testimony, and of the usual conformity of facts to the reports of witnesses."[24] In other words, there is no principle of certainty that operates with respect to testimony, but only the weighing of probabilities.

> Were not the memory tenacious to a certain degree; had not men commonly an inclination to truth and a principle of probity; were they not sensible to shame, when detected in a falsehood: Were not these, I say, discovered by *experience* to be qualities, inherent in human nature, we should never repose the least confidence in human testimony. A man delirious, or noted for falsehood and villany, has no manner of authority with us.[25] (Hume's emphasis)

For the sake of argument, Hume is more than willing to grant a "certain degree" of good will to reports of testimony. Apart from our own "experience" of that good will and inclination to truth, Hume says we would not give testimony any epistemological weight at all. If one raised the objection to Hume the fact that a person is "noted for falsehood" generally, is no proof that such a person is lying in any particular instance, Hume would concur. His emphasis falls on how we, as persons, inevitably interpret testimony, and the degree of authority we give it in varying cases. Thus, "we entertain a suspicion concerning any matter of fact, when the witnesses contradict each other; when they are but few in number, or of doubtful character; when they have an interest in what they affirm."[26] He is really talking about how we, in the context of public discourse, balance trust and doubt. In our experience such factors, claims Hume, diminish the likelihood that a particular testimony is accurate and true.

Moving his argument to the topic of the treatise, Hume says that suspicion is necessarily heightened when one claims that a miracle, or a "violation of the laws of nature,"[27] has occurred. By such definition, there "must," he says, "be a uniform experience against every miraculous event, otherwise the event would not merit that appellation."[28] Because the "laws of nature," are established, says Hume, only by "firm and unalterable experience,"[29] such laws constitute a "proof against a miracle, . . . as entire as any argument from experience can possibly be imagined."[30]

Hume concludes Part One of his treatise by echoing a Christological theme similar to the eucharistic one with which he opened the argument.

> When anyone tells me, that he saw a dead man restored to life, I immediately consider with myself, whether it be more probable, that this person should either deceive or be deceived, or that the fact, which he relates, should really have happened. I weigh the one miracle against the other; and according to the superiority, which I discover, I pronounce my decision, always rejecting the greater miracle. If the falsehood of his testimony would be more miraculous, than the event which he relates; then, and not till then, can he pretend to command my belief or opinion.[31]

For Hume, again, the issue is not whether a miracle "happened." By situating the issue of miracles within the wider discussion of how we, as people, make judgments about probable matters, his argument actually goes to whether the claim of a miracle is so certain that one could morally require intellectual assent to such a claim (e.g., the resurrection of Jesus) by others. In other words, that one person believes a miracle has occurred does not mean that anyone else will be persuaded by that person's testimony.

In Part Two of his treatise, Hume presents three basic reasons why he believes no miraculous event has ever actually been established on "so full an evidence" of testimony, which he allowed as a possibility at the conclusion of Part One.

> For *first*, there is not to be found, in all history, any miracle attested by a sufficient number of men, of such unquestioned good-sense, education, and learning, as to secure us against all delusion in themselves; of such undoubted integrity, as to place them beyond all suspicion of any design to deceive others; of such credit and reputation in the eyes of mankind, as to have a great deal to lose in case of their being detected in any falsehood; and at the same time, attesting facts performed in such a public manner and in so celebrated a part of the world, as to render the detection unavoidable: All which circumstances are requisite to give us a full assurance in the testimony of men.[32]

Notice that Hume insists on more than one observer of any miracle in order for it to approach the bar of knowledge. Why? Because for miracles to count as "facts performed in . . . public manner" they have to be observed by multiple witnesses. Moreover, these witnesses must be learned, possess unquestioned integrity, and noble in the "eyes of mankind" so as to be utterly trustworthy. These are high bars, indeed, but Hume argues that the utterly exceptional category of "miracle," warrants that kind of uncommon scrutiny. To his knowledge, that bar has never been cleared. Hume proceeds to discuss his second argument against miracles, and it involves the process of reasoning about events.

> *Secondly.* . . . The maxim, by which we commonly conduct ourselves in our reasonings, is, that the objects, of which we have no experience, resemble those, of which we have; that what we have found to be most usual is always most probable; and that where there is an opposition of arguments, we ought to give preference to such as are grounded on the greatest number of past observations.[33]

Here the criteria of probability and analogy are set forth, and in such a way as to make any claim for a *supernatural* event virtually impossible. Hume acknowledges, of course, that people do believe in miracles, and offers as explanation that the "passion of *surprise and wonder*, . . . being an agreeable emotion, gives a sensible tendency towards the belief of those events." However, Hume loses patience with stories of wonder when they are joined to "the spirit of religion," or, in other words, to claims that *must* be believed by the faithful. In such cases, there is "an end of common sense," and testimony, he says, "loses all pretensions to authority."[34] A third problem with miracles arises with respect to standards of civilized and educated peoples.

> *Thirdly.* It forms a strong presumption against all supernatural and miraculous relations, that they are observed chiefly to abound among ignorant and barbarous nations; or if a civilized people has ever given admission to any of them, that people will be found to have received them from ignorant and barbarous ancestors, who transmitted them with that inviolable sanction and authority, which always attend received opinions.

Hume's third reason recapitulates implications of the first and second points, specifying however, the ancient and epic strangeness of such cultural stories. In those stories, "battles, revolutions, pestilence, famine and death, are never the effect of those natural causes, which we experience." Instead, "Prodigies, omens, oracles, judgements, quite obscure the few natural events, that are intermingled with them."[35] Hume attributes such stories to the "propensity of mankind towards the marvelous," but he retains a deep suspicion toward that inclination itself. Staging the rhetorical question as to why such events do not happen in our own day, Hume levels a moral critique: "But it is nothing strange, I hope, that men should lie in all ages. You must certainly have seen enough of that frailty."[36] In other words, Hume goes to the contemporary *experience* of being lied to about something, in order to surface a moral suspicion about antiquity. He then goes further and alludes to the parable of the sower, as if to pinpoint the target of his attack: "Be assured, that those renowned lies, . . . arose from like beginnings; but being sown in a more proper soil"—namely, the soil of ignorance—"shot up at last into prodigies almost equal to those which they relate."[37]

While Hume does not return to the case of a "dead man restored to life"—the most illustrative case for which would be the resurrection of Jesus—which he posed at the conclusion of the first part of his treatise, his invocation of that central miracle to Christian faith invites the reader to apply the criteria discussed in part two of the treatise to such a case. At least one reader who seems to have done so is Hermann Samuel Reimarus.

As Hume nears the end of his treatise he seems to bow to the distinction between *faith* and *reason*. "Our most holy religion is founded on *Faith*, not on reason."[38] Hume's point, however, is not complimentary; in effect, he severs the miraculous language of faith from reason. By doing so, he argues that those "who have undertaken to defend it [the *Christian Religion*] by the principles of human reason," are, in fact, "dangerous friends, or disguised enemies" of the faith.[39] A shrewd argument, this final passage seems to privilege faith's distinctly separate character. Anyone paying attention to the argument, however, would recognize that by separating faith from reason Hume has tied the former to ignorance.

Hume's real target is not the simple believer in divine authority—who has already been dismissed as either ignorant or as a well-intentioned believer—but the rational defender of the faith. Insofar as it was the *rational* defense of Christian doctrine that enabled state churches to argue that *all* persons were obliged to honor the dictates set forth by Holy Writ, Hume's concluding assertion that the Christian religion is "founded on *faith*, not on reason," undercuts the universality of experience required for just laws. Faith, understood as a "gift," cannot rightly be commanded of all subjects or citizens. Hume's argument has demonstrated not that all claims to miracles are false, but that it is reasonable to assume that all claims to miracles are probably false. We are almost ready to begin our discussion of Reimarus and his scandalous writings. But first, we turn to a brief discussion of Thomas Jefferson to see even more clearly the political trajectory of Locke's and Hume's and, yes, Reimarus' concern.

Interlude

Jefferson's Jesus and the Religious
Conflicts of a New Civil Society

Why write about Thomas Jefferson (1743–1826) in a book about the historical Jesus? Albert Schweitzer never mentions Jefferson in his book on the quest. If he had, he would have included Jefferson's more "amateurish" work in his chapter entitled, "The Lives of Jesus of the Earlier Rationalism."[1] As F. Forester Church acknowledges in his introduction to *The Jefferson Bible*, Jefferson's "was a search not so much for the historical as for the intelligible Jesus."[2] But Jefferson's voice is helpful to the conversation at hand with regard to two things: 1) his attention not only to Locke's views, but to Hume's, as discussed in the preceding chapter, and 2) his pivotal role in the development of the disestablishment of religion, first in Virginia, but also in the Bill of Rights appended to the Constitution of the United States.

While Jefferson may have been an amateur historian, he penned the most significant sentence in the political theology of the eighteenth century. Sent to King George III, head of the Church of England, the second paragraph of the Declaration of Independence would reorient Christian theology for centuries to come. "We hold these truths to be self evident, that all men are created equal, that they are endowed by their creator with certain unalienable rights, that among these are life, liberty, and the pursuit of happiness."

Jefferson and his contemporaries achieved in the political life of the new nation what so many in Europe longed for, the official separation of church and state. Separating the power and interests of the church from the state was the horizon toward which early interest in the historical Jesus strained. It is that political achievement, therefore, more than any particular historical account of Jesus which answers the major question of the first quest: should

41

the established church govern public discourse? While other important *theological* issues remain as part of this first quest (and recall that I am using, for custom's sake, the range of Schweitzer's book to define the first quest), it is this political achievement, which would be slowly enacted throughout Europe in varying ways, that fundamentally resolves the historic question that drove initial interest in the historical Jesus.

Jefferson and Hume

While Jefferson was obviously influenced by the political philosophy of John Locke; he had also read David Hume.[3] In a letter of August 3, 1771, to Robert Skipworth, Thomas Jefferson recommended "Hume's Essays" in a list of works under the heading of "Religion."[4] And, in a letter to his nephew, Peter Carr, on August 10, 1787, Jefferson sounds distinctly like Hume in suggesting that his nephew think carefully on the subject of religion. After encouraging Carr to read the Bible "as you would read Livy or Tacitus," or in other words, as ancient historians, Jefferson cautions:

> But those facts in the bible which contradict the laws of nature, must be examined with more care, and under a variety of faces. Here you must recur to the pretensions of the writer to inspiration from god. Examine upon what evidence his pretensions are founded, and whether that evidence is so strong as that its falsehood would be more improbable than a change in the laws of nature in the case he relates.[5]

He then supplies a biblical example from the book of Joshua—a text used against Galileo.

> For example in the book of Joshua we are told the sun stood still for several hours. Were we to read that fact in Livy or Tacitus we should class it with their showers of blood, speaking of statues, beasts, &c. But it is said that the writer of that book was inspired. Examine therefore candidly what evidence there is of his having been inspired.[6]

Jefferson's ease with Hume's language of probability, laws of nature, and fitting one's interpretation to the "evidence," suggests that by this point Jefferson had adopted Hume's, and not Locke's, view of miraculous claims.[7] In the same letter, he also encourages his nephew, when reading the New Testament, to "keep in your eye" two contrasting interpretations of Jesus:

1. of those who say he was begotten by god, born of a virgin, suspended and reversed the laws of nature at will, & ascended bodily into heaven

2. of those who say he was a man of illegitimate birth, of a benevolent heart, enthusiastic mind, who set out without pretensions to divinity, ended in believing them, & was punished capitally for sedition by being gibbeted according to the Roman law which punished the first commission of that offense by whipping, & the second by exile or death in furcâ [on a two pronged instrument of punishment][8]

Jefferson, in 1786, was thinking not only about Jesus but also about the separation of church and state, and he had been doing so at least since the time of the Declaration itself. While the separation of church and state was not on the minds of all the delegates to the Second Continental Congress of 1776, one needs to remember that the Church of England was established only in the colony of Virginia, Jefferson's home state. In October of 1776, with the revolution barely underway, Jefferson submitted a bill to the Virginia legislature on the "Disestablishment of the Church of England in Virginia."

Later in 1779, while serving as the United States Minister plenipotentiary to the King of France, Jefferson had a bill "Establishing Religious Freedom," which he had actually drafted in 1777, introduced into the Virginia legislature. Jefferson's emphasis on "establishing" religious freedom was no mere word play; he intended to move Virginia past the language of "toleration," appropriate for nations with established churches, and to the positive affirmation of religious freedom.[9] The Virginia bill's five major points sum up Jefferson's position:

1. that it would be "sinful and tyrannical" for government to compel anyone to provide financial support to a religion contrary to his or her beliefs
2. that because "our civil rights have no dependence on our religious opinions," there should be no religious test for holding public office
3. that religious establishment tends to "corrupt the principles" of the "religion it is meant to encourage" when it offers "worldly honours" based on the external profession of belief
4. that magistrates should not adjudicate questions of religious opinion, but should interfere only when religions violate the public peace
5. that because "free argument and debate" constitute the essential "weapons" of truth in civil society, they should not be "disarmed" by "human interposition"[10]

Jefferson's bill Establishing Religious Freedom in Virginia became law in Virginia in 1786 and elements of that bill entered into both Article Six of the U. S. Constitution in 1787, which eliminated religious tests for public office, and the First Amendment, which guaranteed both the free exercise of religion and that Congress would pass no law establishing religion.

Jefferson's Jesus

Thomas Jefferson credited several conversations with Founding Father, physician, and humanitarian Benjamin Rush (1746–1813) in 1798 as the beginning of his interest in writing a work on the surpassing wisdom of Jesus. The severe wounding of Jefferson's public reputation in the Presidential election of 1800, during which he was accused of being an atheist, may have moved him to think through his religious views. Historian Edward J. Larson, whose *A Magnificent Catastrophe: The Tumultuous Election of 1800, America's First Presidential Campaign* also documents the "supposed scandal regarding Jefferson's religion,"[11] states that while Jefferson "may have been a Deist at one time, by 1800 he probably was a Unitarian."[12]

In 1803 Jefferson made good on his 1798 promise to write a work about Jesus. Called *Syllabus of an estimate of the merit of the Doctrines of Jesus, compared with those of others*,[13] Jefferson divided the work into three sections: "Philosophers," "Jews," and "Jesus." In a letter to Rush, Jefferson described the *Syllabus* "as the result of a life of inquiry and reflection, and very different from the anti-Christian system imputed to me by those who know nothing of my opinions. To the corruptions of Christianity, I am indeed opposed; but not to the genuine precepts of Jesus himself."[14]

In his letter to Rush, Jefferson described his portrait of Jesus in five summary points. In his first two points, Jefferson notes that Jesus, like other great figures such as Socrates and Epictetus, "wrote nothing himself," and that the learned of his time, "entrenched in power and riches," had opposed him out of fear of losing "their advantages."[15] This point, in particular, places Jesus in a political context. Influenced perhaps by Hume's critique of testimonies about miracles, Jefferson says in his second point that the work of "committing to writing of his life and doctrines fell on the most unlearned and ignorant men," working only from "memory," and "not till long after the transactions had passed."[16] Jefferson's third, fourth, and fifth points are especially illuminating:

> 3. According to the ordinary fate of those who attempt to enlighten and reform mankind, he fell an early victim to the jealousy and *combination of the altar and the throne*, at about 33 years of age, his reason

having not yet attained the maximum of its energy, nor the course of his preaching, which was but of 3 years at most.[17] (emphasis added)

Jefferson focuses on the political character of Jesus' death, portraying him as a reformer caught and victimized by the "combination of altar and throne," of church and state. He presents Jesus as a figure taking sides against the powers of the status quo, his ethical teaching having only persuasive force. There are no miracles here, no signs of divine power or kingship; in fact, Jefferson goes out of his way to say that Jesus' life was cut short and that his teaching had not yet reached its full maturity.

Like Hume, therefore, Jefferson goes beyond the earlier Deist argument that revelation must be normed by reason. He simply does away with revelation. His fourth point reiterates the unreliable character of the Gospels he discussed in his second point.

> 4. Hence the doctrines which he really delivered were defective as a whole, and fragments only of what he did deliver have come to us mutilated, misstated, and often unintelligible.[18]

Instead of viewing Jesus as a divine figure incapable of error, Jefferson views Jesus as a flawed but heroic figure of surpassing wisdom—a wisdom largely destroyed by Christian teaching:

> 5. They have been still more disfigured by the corruptions of the schismatising followers, who have found an interest in sophisticating and perverting the simple doctrines he taught by engrafting on them the mysticisms of a Grecian sophist, frittering them into subtleties, and obscuring them with jargon. . . . Notwithstanding these disadvantages, a system of morals is presented to us, which, if filled up in the true style and spirit of the rich fragments he left us, would be the most perfect and sublime that has ever been taught by man.[19]

Jefferson acknowledges to Rush that this initial work, completed in 1803, was partial and incomplete. It was not published. And Jefferson would continue to think about these issues.

When one speaks today of *The Jefferson Bible*, what is meant is Jefferson's production in 1820 of another private work, *The Life and Morals of Jesus,* in which Jefferson literally cut out from the New Testament Gospels those sayings and teachings that he felt were authentic to Jesus' ethical teaching, mixing texts with one gospel from those of another as he saw fit. He describes his sorting criteria as follows:

We find in the writings of [Jesus'] biographers matter of two distinct descriptions. First, a groundwork of vulgar ignorance, of things impossible, of superstitions, fanaticisms and fabrications. Intermixed with these, again, are sublime ideas of the Supreme Being, aphorisms, and precepts of the purist morality and benevolence, sanctioned by a life of humility, innocence, and simplicity of manners, neglect of riches, absence of worldly ambition and honors, with an eloquence and persuasiveness which have not been surpassed. These could not be the intentions of the groveling authors who related them.[20]

Jefferson remains consistent with his 1803 production in insisting—in Humean fashion—on the vulgarity and unlearned character of much of the gospel material. What strikes a new note is his greater insistence in the 1820 work on retrieving what seems utterly and morally true in the "eloquence and persuasiveness" of Jesus.

Critics of Jefferson's *Bible* frequently mock Jefferson's naiveté in taking a scissors to the Bible; but they miss the fact that Jefferson's *cutting* of reason from revelation mirrors Jefferson's *wall of separation* dividing church and state. Like the freedom of the new republic, which, by revolution, had to be cut away from the allied British interests of altar and throne, Jesus' wisdom stood out more clearly when cut away from biblical "fanaticisms and fabrications." Church is surely correct in saying that Jefferson's "was a search not so much for the historical as for the intelligible Jesus."[21] Nonetheless, in arguing that Jesus was killed because he "fell victim to the jealousy and combination of the altar and the throne," Jefferson finds a Jesus who is sympathetic to political reform and fit for the recent history and actual challenges of the new nation.[22]

Schweitzer would doubtless dismiss Jefferson's *Life* as utterly characteristic of the period of "older rationalism": "it is wholly unhistorical. What it is looking for is not the past, but itself in the past."[23] But Schweitzer's own narrow historicism is itself quite naïve. What one begins to see across these interests in a rational, ethical, and finally historical Jesus is the attempt to create a new cultural space in which the established church did not control public discourse. By keeping his eye on the narrowly *historical*, Schweitzer missed the *historic* question that Jefferson, Madison and company answered at least on this side of the Atlantic.

Like Reimarus, who never published his *Apology*, and like Hume, whose *Dialogues on Natural Religion* was completed around

1751 but published only posthumously in 1772, Jefferson did not allow *The Life and Morals of Jesus* to be published during his lifetime. From the 1750s to the 1780s, attempts to free civil society from the entrenched interests of established religion—even in the relatively open space of the new continent—remained a life-threatening, high-risk endeavor.

CHAPTER 3

Reimarus and the Critique of Ecclesiastical Power

Near the conclusion of Albert Schweitzer's 1906 classic, *Von Reimarus zur Wrede*, translated by William Montgomery as *The Quest of the Historical Jesus* (1910), Schweitzer critiques the modern confidence underlying the Quest:

> We modern theologians are too proud of our historical method, too proud of our historical Jesus, too confident in our belief in the spiritual gains which our historical theology can bring to the world. The thought that we could build up by the increase of historical knowledge a new and vigorous Christianity and set free new spiritual forces, rules us like a fixed idea.[1]

The quest for the historical Jesus reveals the sin of modern pride. Yet, in this passage, and in many others like it, Schweitzer seems either utterly unaware or unwilling to acknowledge that the quest may have stemmed less from modern pride than from a serious theo-political challenge to the church's control of public discourse. Martin Kähler's 1896 work *Der sogenannte historische Jesus und der geschichtliche, biblische Christus* [*The So-Called Historical Jesus and the Historic Biblical Christ*] at least acknowledges this when, near the end of his book, he writes that part of the issue of the quest had been the "right and freedom of literary criticism."[2] But Kähler seems not to recognize any significant issue here. He fails to ask which institutions were preventing publication or denying that right and freedom, and on what grounds.

What Schweitzer and Kähler both gloss over by their general acknowledgment of the critique of "dogmatism," is that the quest for the historical Jesus played a significant *theological* role in freeing public discourse from the control of established churches. In this chapter and the next, we will examine portions of the work of

Hermann Samuel Reimarus, considered by Schweitzer and others to be the founding figure in the quest for the historical Jesus. In this chapter, we will attend principally to Reimarus' arguments about Jesus and his disciples in order to understand the motives of his work; in the chapter that follows we will explore the publication of various "fragments" from Reimarus' lengthy, unpublished manuscript *Apologie oder Schutzschrift für die vernünftigen Verehrer Gottes* [*Apology or Defense for Rational Worshippers of God*], by German playwright and philosopher Gotthold Ephraim Lessing (1729–81).

If Hume had been slow to publish his criticisms not only of establishment Christianity but of Deism, even in the relatively free space of Britain's constitutional government, Reimarus was effectively silenced in Germany. He never published his *Apology*. If Hume had, in his own words, "castrated himself" by not publishing the tract on miracles in his *Treatise*, Reimarus writes that he "martyred" himself by not publishing the *Apology*. I draw these parallels because what Reimarus (1694–1768) accomplished in historical discourse is analogous to what Hume accomplished in philosophy, namely, the emergence of a prophetic voice, sharply critical of the assumptions undergirding political and religious power of the era.

Writing probably in the 1760s, according to historian Charles H. Talbert, Reimarus states in the *Apology* "that in order not to become a martyr of his convictions he suffered a martyrdom of another sort caused by his silence."[3] Reimarus knew of what he spoke; according to Talbert:

> Reimarus . . . knew what had happened to J. Lorenz Schmidt, a German Deist who had published his translation of the Pentateuch together with notes of a rationalist bent in 1735. . . . Not only was he arrested initially because of his publication but also he was forced to live the last ten years of his life in obscurity under assumed names. Offered asylum by the Duke of Brunswick, he died in 1751 in humiliation in Wolfenbüttel.[4]

Reimarus had read John Toland's *Christianity Not Mysterious* (1696), and, in Charles Talbert's words, "could hardly have missed" Toland's critique of establishment religion. As Toland put it:

> And such is the deplorable condition of our age, that a man dares not openly and directly own what he thinks of divine matters . . . if it but very slightly differs from what is received by any party, or that is established by law; but he is either forced to keep perpetual silence, or to propose his sentiments to the world by way of a paradox or

under a borrowed or fictitious name. To mention the least part of the inconveniences they expose themselves to, who have the courage to act more above-board, is too melancholy a theme, and visible enough to be lamented by all that are truly generous and virtuous.[5]

A popular and well-published scholar, Reimarus, like Hume, had a good reputation to protect. In his public views he seems to have basically agreed with the reigning liberal theology of Christian Wolff (1679–1754), who had been deeply influenced by Gottfried Wilhelm Leibnitz (1646–1716), and, through Leibnitz, by Locke.[6] Wolff held, in a way similar to Locke, that revelation could be above reason but could not contradict it. While Wolff argued that reason established the criteria for evaluating the genuineness of revelation,[7] he also affirmed God's power to work miracles by virtue of God's infinite character. Wolff, thus, held that revelation was not inconsistent with a natural theology.[8] Reimarus agreed with this view publicly, but not in the *Apology*, where he argued strongly, and in ways similar to Hume, against miracles and that natural theology should replace revelation—a view that would have placed him directly at odds with the Lutheran established church.

Relation to Deism

The final version of the *Apology*, the entirety of which has never been translated, comprised two hand-written volumes. The first volume, containing the preface and books one through five, focused mainly on the Hebrew Bible, while the second volume contained three books dealing with Jesus followed by three books on the disciples and the early church.[9] The first book of volume one, however, is noteworthy for the way it established the overarching concern of the work. It was an appeal to German authorities for religious toleration for Deists.

Read apart from his concern for a widening of religious and public discourse, Reimarus seems little more than a willful heretic. If, however, one attends to the deeper influence of Deism on Reimarus, with its public concerns for freedom of conscience and expression, then one sees Reimarus' criticism—even at its most scandalous—as the expression of a much nobler, critical spirit. The moral insistence by Christian Deists, like Locke, that the conscience cannot and must not be forced helps explain the felt bitterness that one senses in Reimarus' unpublished work. Years later in his 1862 essay on Reimarus, D. F. Strauss attributed much of the tone of Reimarus' *Apology* to the absence of freedom in German public life.

That Reimarus had to keep these views locked in his breast and could be frank and honest only to unresponsive paper, with the exception of a few confidants who were scarcely his equals; and that he had to be silent about the activities of a [Johann Melchior] Göze and other zealots, even having to listen to their sermons and participate in ceremonies that he abhorred as delusion and superstition . . . could only contribute to an embittered disposition toward the church and Christianity, turning it into the most bitter resentment. Hence the sharp tone of his discourse, which in places rises to a sort of fanaticism of reason that can wound faint spirits, while it yet gains respect from a person with deeper insight, because of its zeal for truth and morality, its source, even as on occasion its incorrect understanding may call forth a smile.[10]

A Historical Argument

As later noted by Schweitzer, Reimarus' arguments were not merely rationalistic but historical. Reimarus seeks to interpret Jesus within the orbit of first-century Jewish thought. Just as importantly, however, and in parallel with Hume, Reimarus interprets both Jesus' activity and the biblical accounts naturalistically. He treats them, as Jefferson encouraged his nephew to do, as any other historical text, placing the accounts and actions of the narrative within a probabilistic logic. In the section, "Intention of Jesus and His Teaching," for example, Reimarus places the words, actions, and rituals of Jesus in their ancient Hebraic context, in order to demonstrate that Jesus did not understand himself either as a God-Man or as a member of the Trinity; nor did he understand his own death in the context of salvation by atonement.

Reimarus' point in underscoring a historical and naturalistic reading of Jesus and the apostles, is stated at the outset of the fragment, "Concerning the Intention of Jesus and His Disciples, Part One":

Since nowadays the doctrine of the trinity of persons in God and the doctrine of the work of salvation through Jesus as the Son of God and God-Man constitute the main articles and mysteries of the Christian faith, I shall specifically demonstrate that they are not to be found in Jesus' discourses.[11]

Why emphasize this discrepancy between official church teaching and Jesus? For at least three reasons: *First*, by showing that doctrinal claims such as the God-Man do not go back to Jesus,

Reimarus can demonstrate a rift between what Jesus taught and what the apostles taught about him. *Second*, insofar as Reimarus shows that Hebraic titles such as the "Son of God" or phrases such as "the Father and I are one" did not intend any kind of hypostatic union between Jesus and God so much as a profound yet natural intimacy of spirit, he can argue that the Trinitarian claim about Jesus as the God-Man was not just a later claim made about Jesus, but one that misrepresented his teaching. And *third*, he can argue that the development of those doctrinal claims to transcendent mystery occurred in the context of the apostles' self interest.

Keeping in mind Reimarus' opening concern for the toleration of Deists, one sees how he uses his inquiry into the historical Jesus to raise questions about whether the truth claims of revelation can stand up to rational, historical inquiry. Reimarus' intent is to show that the claims of revelation—of the Trinity, Jesus as a divine man, the inspiration of Scripture, and the divine miracles—cannot stand up to critical inquiry, and thus, should not be imposed on all German citizens—hence, the principle of toleration. Moreover, one does not need to ask whether Reimarus actually "believed" what he was writing about Jesus and the Disciples; it is enough to see that he was trying to demonstrate that a very alternative reading of Jesus, based on public reason and historical methodology was both possible and perhaps more plausible than the claims of revealed Truth.

Taking the Gospels, including the Gospel of John, at face value, Reimarus shows that Jesus intended neither a new religion nor even a coming kingdom of God beyond the nation of Israel. Jesus, he says, preached a gospel of repentance as preparation for the coming kingdom of God, which he [Jesus] would usher into time. Jesus, according to Reimarus, understood himself as the Messiah, and by this term and its corollary, the kingdom of God, he intended only the conventional meaning of these terms, namely, the liberation of Israel from the power of Roman occupation. Thus, Reimarus concludes: "I do not wish to deny that Jesus appropriates all the advantages that accrue from the designation of exceptional prophet, king and beloved of God and which correspond to the contemporary Jewish idea of the Messiah; still, it all remains within the bounds of nature."[12] In other words, according to Reimarus, there is no divine revelation in the story; it can all be grasped by historical reason.

Reimarus makes two important claims about Jesus. First, Jesus' teaching, according to Reimarus, was the most eloquent expression of the natural, moral law.

One need but examine the beautiful Sermon on the Mount [Matthew 5–7], that most explicit of all Jesus' speeches, and he will be thoroughly convinced that Jesus' sole intention is man's repentance, conversion, and betterment, insofar as these consist of a true inner and upright love of God, of one's neighbor, and of all that is good. Accordingly when he elsewhere explains the moral law better than had ever been done, or castigates the hypocrisy of the Pharisees, or defends his own neglect of the ceremonies of the law, it shows the most intimate connection with his main teaching. . . .

Thus the goal of Jesus' sermons and teachings was a proper, active character, a changing of the mind, a sincere love of God and of one's neighbor, humility, gentleness, denial of the self, and the suppression of all evil desires. These are not great mysteries or tenets of the faith that he explains, proves, and preaches; they are nothing other than moral teachings and duties intended to improve man inwardly and with all his heart, whereby Jesus naturally takes for granted a general knowledge of man's soul, of God and his perfections, salvation after this life, etc. But he does not explain these things anew, much less present them in a learned or extravagant way.[13]

Second, Reimarus argues that Jesus did not usher in the kingdom of God. On this point, says Reimarus, Jesus was mistaken, and Jesus' final words from the cross, "My God, My God, why have you forsaken me," should be read as evidence of Jesus' own recognition of his failed eschatological hope.

He began to quiver and quake when he saw that his adventure might cost him his life. Judas betrayed his hiding-place, and pointed out his person. He was taken the night before the fourteenth of Nisan, and after a short trial was crucified, before the slaughtering of the Passover lambs in the temple had begun. He ended his life with the words, "*Eli, Eli lama sabachthani?* My God, my God, why hast thou forsaken me?" [Matt 27: 46]—a confession which can hardly otherwise be interpreted than that God had not helped him to carry out his intention and attain his object as he had hoped he would have done. It was then clearly not the object or intention of Jesus to suffer and to die, but to build up a worldly kingdom, and to deliver the Israelites from bondage. It was in this that his hopes had been frustrated.[14]

While Reimarus, thus, affirms that Jesus was a great moral teacher, he denies both that Jesus was literally divine and that he died for the sins of the world.[15]

Having undercut incarnational, Trinitarian, and salvific language with respect to Jesus, Reimarus attacks the basic notion of Scripture, and especially the New Testament, as divine revelation. The evangelists, argues Reimarus, held themselves out as "reporters" or historians of the life of Jesus; they nowhere suggested that they were vehicles for divine revelation. More importantly, according to Reimarus—and perhaps more damaging for the liberal theology of Wolff—the New Testament accounts of the resurrection are contradictory, and, therefore, cannot be true. Going much farther, Reimarus reads these contradictions not as mere historical missteps but as evidence that the evangelists lied about the resurrection. The disciples themselves, he argued, removed the body from the grave and disposed of it.[16]

Assuming the worst about the apostles, Reimarus claims that they turned Jesus' message about a temporal kingdom of God that would rescue Israel from Roman occupation, into a strangely different teaching:

> that Christ or the Messiah was bound to die in order to obtain forgiveness for mankind, and consequently to achieve his own glory; that upon the strength of this he arose alive from death out of the tomb upon the third day as he had prophesied, and ascended into heaven, from when he would soon return in the clouds of heaven with great power and glory to judge the believers and the unbelievers, the good and the bad, and that then the kingdom would come in glory.[17]

Based on this formulation of the early church's new narrative about Jesus' identity and mission, Reimarus then argues that the new Christian narrative depends upon the factual character of the resurrection: "Now everyone will readily acknowledge, as do the apostles, that Christianity depends entirely upon the truth of the story of the resurrection of Jesus from the dead."[18] If we recall that Hume had also considered the "resurrection of a dead person," in his treatise on miracles, it is both possible and helpful to read Reimarus' discussions of the resurrection and the character of the apostles as a thoroughgoing application of the probability logic that informed Hume's work.

A Humean Take on the Miracle of the Resurrection

Knowing that the resurrection "cannot be proved by reason,"[19] Reimarus sets about demonstrating that the evangelists' "reports" regarding the "guarding of the tomb" and the resurrection are so fragmentary and so contradictory, that the historical probability of the resurrection could not stand up in a public forum:

> Witnesses who differ so greatly in the most important points of their testimony would not be recognized in any secular court as valid and legal . . . to the extent that the judge could rely upon their story and base his decision upon it. How then can anyone want the whole world and all mankind to base their religion, faith, and hope of salvation at all times and in all places upon the testimony of four such varying witnesses?[20]

Running parallel to Hume's arguments against miracles, Reimarus insists that the resurrection requires more "public" affirmation:

> But what is even more significant: in all the forty days that Jesus is supposed to be resurrected and walking among them they do not tell a single one of us any word of his being alive again so that we might go see Jesus and talk with him. . . . My goodness! Why not in the temple, before the people, before the chief priests, or at least before the eyes of any Jew at all? Truth cannot hide or crawl away, and especially such a truth that is familiar to us and that we are supposed to believe.[21]

The multiple contradictions among the evangelists' reports and their lack of public evidence deepens the improbability of an already very improbable event, leading Reimarus to conclude that "suspicion logically falls upon them [the apostles]," that they had "stolen the body at night."[22] In contrast, writes Reimarus, "all reasonable people," including "the entire Sanhedrin, and all the chief priests and scribes" had properly "warned us" of the disciples' "deception."[23]

Like Hume, Reimarus finally asks the reader to make a judgment about the probability of the truth of the evangelists' reports. Occurring at the conclusion of a lengthy analysis of nine contradictions among the resurrection narratives, Reimarus asks:

> Reader, you who are conscientious and honest: tell me, before God, could you accept as unanimous and sincere this testimony concerning such an important matter that contradicts itself so often and so obviously in respect to person, time, place, manner, intent, word, story?[24] . . .
>
> Certainly even if we had no other stumbling-block about Jesus' resurrection, this single one, that he did not allow himself to be seen

publicly, would itself be enough to throw all its credibility aside, because it cannot agree in all eternity with Jesus' intention in coming into the world. It is foolishness to sigh and complain about mankind's disbelief if one cannot furnish men with the persuasive evidence that the matter demands, based on a healthy reason.[25]

Reimarus' argument seeks to shift the notion of religious truth *away from* the burden then required of all citizens to believe in the dogmatic claims of a state church and *toward* a burden requiring legally established churches to argue their truth claims based on public reason. Time and again one sees Reimarus drawing the conclusion that one cannot force or compel religious belief based upon such weak evidence.

But Reimarus is not done yet. Lest one argue, as Hume had considered in his treatise, that the *character* of the apostles constituted a proof of the resurrection, Reimarus goes further than impugning the apostles for lying in their "composition" of a new story of Jesus' mission, and for stealing the body of Jesus.[26] Two other aspects of Hume's hermeneutics of suspicion are picked up in Reimarus' view of the apostles: 1) that miracles gain currency among the poor and ignorant, and 2) that most reports of miracles coincide with the teller's self interest. Near the end of his work, Reimarus says he will inquire into "the real object of the apostles in inventing and building up their new doctrine."[27] He begins by noting the apostle's social location.

> The apostles were chiefly men of the lower class and of small means, who gained their livelihood by fishing and other trades. . . . Now when they resolved upon following Jesus, they entirely forsook their trade and all connected with it, hearkened to his teaching, and went about everywhere with him. . . . Here we do not require deductions or inferences as to what may have induced the apostles to forsake all and follow Jesus, because the evangelists distinctly inform us that they entertained hopes that the Messiah would establish a kingdom, or become kind of Israel, and seat himself upon the throne of David. . . . Indeed, they already sat upon them so firmly in their imagination, that they began to dispute, rather prematurely, among themselves as to who should have the first place and the greatest power next to Jesus.[28]

Virtually from the outset, according to Reimarus, the apostles followed Jesus out of self-interest: seeking their own wealth and power as a consequence of Jesus establishing his kingdom of God. In the wake of his death, they invented a "new doctrine" about Jesus in order to preserve their now-established way of life, "because it is much more probable that men should continue to act from exactly the same motives by which they have undeniably and invariably been actuated before, than that they should abandon them and take up others."[29]

Reimarus imagines the apostles considering their options in the wake of Jesus' death. He imagines them remembering that when Jesus traveled "there were many Marthas who put themselves to a vast deal of trouble and pains to prepare delectable dishes for him,"[30] and that many "benevolent women" provided him "not only with food, but also with money."[31] Moreover, they remembered that the multitudes had not only run after Jesus, but that they "themselves had also been to some extent honored . . . because they were the confidential disciples."[32] In the wake of these and other calculations, concludes Reimarus, the apostles decided to steal the body and lay the basis for their claim of the resurrection.

Reimarus consistently ascribes the basest motives possible to the apostles in order to extinguish any argument for the truth of the resurrection based on the character of the New Testament witnesses. That the apostles set out to fool "the crowds" and "the multitudes," engaging in the false reasoning of miracles and prophecies, is apparent to Reimarus:

> The unerring signs of truth and falsehood are clear, distinct consistency and contradiction. This is also the case with revelation, insofar as that it must, in common with other truths, be free from contradiction. And just as little as miracles can prove that twice two are five, or that a triangle has four sides, can a contradiction lying in the history and dogmas of Christianity be removed by any number of miracles.[33]

If one has not read Reimarus previously, these are shocking statements; small wonder that their publication caused such a stir. Yet, if one recalls, at heart, Reimarus' resentment over the church's control of public discourse, then these arguments take on a different cast. Drawing on the image of a court room, and on the idea of evidence needed to convict someone of guilt, Reimarus argues that far from presenting a compelling case for their miraculous, supernatural quality, the Christian Scriptures can be read more intelligibly as being written by frauds. If that is even remotely the case, by what standard of justice can any single form of the Christian faith be imposed as law upon all citizens?

A Different Kind of Allegory?

In this all too brief presentation of Reimarus' views, there is a final concern that merits attention. While it is difficult to imagine a more scandalous reading of the New Testament—and in Luther's Germany, no less—it is vital to remember that for Reimarus the far greater scandal was how the contemporary church used its wealth and power to silence public discourse. It is worth considering, therefore, whether Reimarus considered his treatment of the apostles and the early church as an allegory of the corruption of the Lutheran state church of his own time.

In the fragment, "The Intention of Jesus and His Teaching," Reimarus explained a distinction between what he called Jewish allegory and the abuse of allegory that occurs at the hands of the early Christians. He shows that statements which describe Jesus as "Son of God" are allegorical in a Jewish sense. The predicate, or intention of such a saying, according to Reimarus, was to highlight Jesus' holiness and wisdom, and thus his closeness to God. The comparison of such a statement would be to other human and holy figures such as Abraham or Moses or David—conventional figures of holiness and wisdom. It would be unthinkable, says Reimarus, to imagine in Jewish thought that such a symbolic statement might mean that Jesus was a God-Man. Such an allegorical interpretation "deviates completely from all rules of [Jewish] allegory,"[34] because the symbolism of Jewish allegory always operates within the range of natural and human comparisons. Reimarus defines allegory as follows:

> An allegory is created when, instead of taking the subject that really is in his mind, one takes a different subject as the counterpart and applies to it the same predicate that was applied to the actual subject.[34]

Assume for a moment that "the subject that really is" in Reimarus' mind in writing *The Apology* is a critique of the established church's preoccupation with its own power over civil society in the eighteenth century. Yet, instead of directly denouncing the contemporary church, he uses the early church allegorically as "the counterpart" of the contemporary church and "applies to it the same predicate that was applied to the actual subject," that is, the church's preoccupation with its own power over civil society. Because the narrative would seem to be about the early apostles, the real indictment of the text would now be somewhat hidden from view. What, therefore, appears at first glance to be a scandalous indictment of the early church is actually an indictment of the scandalous church of his own time.

My warrant for this suggestion comes from Reimarus' conclusion of his treatment of the apostles and their intentions. He turns to the story of Ananias and Sapphira from Acts 5 as a defining story of the early church, yet in telling the story he combines language of his contemporary German culture with that from the ancient past. After recounting how both characters have fallen dead at the apostles' feet, Reimarus comments:

> I will not inquire what became of the money laid at the apostles' feet, for although it was not the whole fortune of Ananias and Sapphira, it is very apparent that the apostles did not restore it to the heirs, but considered it a good prize and kept it. How is it possible in a town or state possessing any sort of law or order that two well-known persons, a man and his wife, should die in a room in broad daylight, be put out of the way, and buried in two or three hours without any inquiry being made as to the manner by which they lost their lives?

Reimarus is clearly treating the *Acts* text as a thoroughly naturalistic, historical report that is open to skepticism. Yet, is something else going on here? Directly prior to these passages, Reimarus noted that "civil discipline was also at that time in a very bad state among the Jews." Several lines further, he adds:

> The apostles felt themselves at liberty to utilize this carelessness and confusion, *and in the midst of one state began to erect another state*, in which religion and opinion, possessions and their appropriation, and consequently the behavior of their adherents no longer depended upon the injunction or prohibition of the laws, but on the beck and call of the apostles, and by them was used against the injunction or prohibition of the laws, under the pretext that one must obey the law of God before the law of man.[36] (emphasis added)

The language of "civil discipline," of one "state" being erected alongside another, of divine law superseding the "law of man": the conjunction of these terms suggests that Reimarus was, perhaps, writing a kind of allegory here, in which the activities of the early church are presented as a precursor to Reimarus' contemporary, established church with its interests of power and social control over the masses.

The final lines of Reimarus' fragment on "The Real Intention of the Apostles" satirize what is perhaps the most celebrated New Testament text on community. In the passage below, Reimarus first completes his skeptical analysis of Peter's Pentecost speech and the conversion of three thousand to the faith, and then takes on the vision of Acts 2.

> The motive which swayed the remainder [of the Pentecost crowd] was not the miracle, but the sweet prospect of enjoying the common wealth which was being so liberally distributed to all, that they ate and drank together, and wanted for nothing as we see by the following: "And they devoted themselves to the apostles' teaching and fellowship, to the breaking of bread and the prayers. . . . And all who believed were together and had all things in common; and they sold their possessions and goods and distributed them to all, as any had need. . . . There was not a needy person among them, for as many as were possessors of lands or houses sold them, and brought the proceeds of what was sold and laid it at the apostles' feet; and distribution was made to each as any had need" [Acts 2:42, 44–45; 4:34–35].
>
> Behold the real reason of the conflux—a reason which operates and has operated at all times so naturally, that we need no miracle to make everything comprehensible and clear. This is the real mighty wind that so quickly wafted all the people together. This is the true original language that performs the miracles.[37]

In this final paragraph, indicting the Acts community of greed, Reimarus blends the past tense with the present—"a reason which operates and has operated" and "this is the true original language that performs the miracles." It is a scandalous indictment; yet he means to point to a far greater scandal—the use of the "miraculous" New Testament and other claims of transcendent Truth to hold centuries of people in intellectual bondage.

Conclusion

Schweitzer's primary interest in Reimarus was that the latter had drawn on historical arguments to identify eschatology as the central motif in Jesus' own preaching and sense of mission. My interest lies in understanding the wider orbit of Reimarus' writing in order to better see what his interest in Jesus was really about. What was historic about Reimarus is that he sought to situate Jesus and his disciples, as well as all of Christian Scripture, in a historical—that is to say, in a naturalistic—worldview that required no divine or Platonic revelation in order to be intelligible. Yet, Reimarus made that contribution to historical criticism out of a deeper set of values and commitments than mere fidelity to the facts. He turned to historical analysis in order to refute a legalized supernaturalism that was being used to justify the established church's control over German public discourse. One need not agree with Reimarus' interpretation of Jesus in order to appreciate his contribution to the development of historical criticism. As we will see in the following chapter, Lessing, while publishing fragments from the *Apology*, disagreed strongly with Reimarus' specific interpretations. So, why did Lessing publish those very interpretations?

CHAPTER

4

Lessing and the Public Staging of the Reimarus Fragments

Enter the playwright and German philosopher and translator of Shakespeare, Gotthold Ephraim Lessing. A figure synonymous with the German Enlightenment, or *Aufklärung*, Lessing was approached by Reimarus' daughter, Elise, after her father's death with a copy of Reimarus' *Apology*.[1] At the time, Lessing was serving as the librarian at Wolfenbüttel, a position offered him in 1769 by the Duke of Brunswick. Lessing had received an exemption from censorship from the Duke in 1772, on the provision that he not attack religion, and in 1773 had begun to publish a series of pieces under the heading *Contributions to Literature and History from the Ducal Library at Wolfenbüttel*.

In 1774, Lessing published the first of seven excerpts or "fragments," as he called them, from Reimarus' *Apology*—a project that would ultimately test the limits of the Duke's exemption. The remaining "fragments" were published between 1774 and 1778, under the name "Unknown" or "Anonymous"—in order to protect the Reimarus family[2]—and with the disclaimer that he had been "quite unable to discover how and when it [the manuscript] came to our Library."[3] Lessing knew, of course, that some would assume that such heretical documents from the Wolfenbüttel library would have been authored by J. Lorenz Schmidt,[4] who died in Wolfenbüttel in 1749, utterly estranged from the German Church.

In this chapter I view the publication of the *Fragments* through the analogy of a dramatic production. Lessing doesn't so much publish the *Fragments* as stage them, masking the identity of the author of the *Fragments* in mystery and using the public forum itself as a theatre. Publishing the *Fragments*, therefore was merely the opening act of Lessing's drama. By publishing the fragments, Lessing sought to generate a public debate about them. If one or more of the fragments generated controversy, then Lessing, as the librarian of the Wolfenbüttel collection, could offer commentary on the documents. He used subsequent attacks by German church officials—aimed both at the "unknown" author and at himself for publishing the fragments—to create an additional role for himself, that of an articulate, "moderate" voice at once critical of the Unknown's positions and suggestive of an alternative position at odds with representatives of the official church.

In the first fragment, entitled "On the Toleration of the Deists" and taken from the opening of Reimarus' *Apology*, the "anonymous" author argued that Jesus had taught a religion both rational and practical, and that anyone who sought to follow Jesus' ethical teaching should be considered Christian. Insofar as both Jews and pagans were tolerated in Lutheran Germany, rationalist Christians should be tolerated as well.[5]

While this first fragment attracted little public attention at the time, it highlights the fact not only that Reimarus' historical criticism sought to expose an abusive situation in eighteenth-century Germany, namely, the silencing of authentic religious voices, but also that Lessing shared this fundamental concern.[6] In this opening section of his *Apology*, Reimarus had also hinted at his deeper argument, pointing out that the natural religion of Jesus was corrupted by apostles who developed a completely different religious system in their search for wealth and power. The effect of Reimarus' critique was to question the origins of the Lutheran Church's authority over and control of public discourse. Insofar as the Lutheran Church both silenced and persecuted the rational and ethical followers of Jesus' teaching, suggested Reimarus, it continued to participate in that process of corruption.

In 1777, Lessing published five more fragments, each ratcheting up the stakes of the emerging debate. We will first summarize Reimarus' arguments in these *Fragments* and then discuss Lessing's response to them. The first of these was entitled, "Of the Decrying of Reason in the Pulpit." This text raises the temperature of the debate because it antagonized those clergy—and there were many by this point—who disparaged "reason" in contrast to God's "revelation" in Scripture. Reimarus argues that if reason was the only tool by which one could prove the truth of the Christian faith, pastors were foolish to criticize the use of it.

The second of the five documents was called "The Impossibility of a Revelation which All Men Can Believe on Rational Grounds." If the previous *Fragment* challenged the clergy's dismissal of reason, the next challenges the clergy's closely held belief that God granted a final and definitive revelation in Christ for the entire world. In one portion of his argument, Reimarus asks his readers to see that this universal vision of the truth of Christian faith was responsible for the murder of forty million men in America by the Spaniards. Reimaurus argues that the claims to revealed religion, or special revelation, are prone to manipulation and abuse, as evidenced by the catastrophic results of such spiritual politics of empire. In contrast to revealed truth, Reimarus argues for a salvation through nature: "*quod ubique, quod semper, quod ab omnibus*" — a natural religion for all places, for all times, and all people.[7]

The third of these 1777 *Fragments* examined the accuracy of a particular text. Called "The Passage of the Israelites through the Red Sea," Reimarus goes beyond the previous critique of a universal revelation, and, through a close reading of the text, argues that there is no way that the *Exodus* story — that "six hundred thousand men of war, besides their families and stuff, all passed through the Red Sea in a single night" — could be historically accurate. Henry Chadwick summarizes: "If the Israelites moved in a column, ten deep, the length of the column would have been one hundred and eighty miles, and they would have taken nine days to cross as a minimum figure."[8]

The fourth argued "That the Books of the Old Testament Were Not Written to Reveal a Religion," largely on the grounds that the Hebrew Bible does not refer to immortality of the soul, which was a crucial belief not only for Christians but for Deists.

The fifth *Fragment* published that year, "On the Resurrection Narrative," studied the inconsistencies among the different evangelists, and concludes from their lack of consensus that they were not simply mistaken about it, but that they lied about the resurrection. At the end of the fifth *Fragment*, Lessing added a commentary on the group as a whole, and in the opening paragraph of that commentary he defends the "public" presentation of these documents.

> And now enough of these fragments. Any of my readers who would prefer me to have spared them altogether is surely more timid than well instructed. He may be a very devout Christian, but he is certainly not a very enlightened one. He may be wholehearted in his upholding of his religion; but he ought also to have greater confidence in it.

In effect, says Lessing, we need more exercises like this. His commentary continues:

For how much could be said in reply to all these [Reimarus'] objections and difficulties! And even if absolutely no answer were forthcoming, what then? The learned theologian might in the last resort be embarrassed, but certainly not the Christian. To the former it might at most cause confusion to see the supports with which he would uphold religion shattered in this way, to find the buttresses cast down by which, God willing, he would have made it safe and sound. But how do this man's hypotheses, explanations, and proofs affect the Christian? For him it is simply a fact—the Christianity which he feels to be true and in which he feels blessed. . . .

In short, the letter is not the spirit, and the Bible is not religion. Consequently, objections to the letter and to the Bible are not also objections to the spirit and to religion. . . .

Therefore while much may depend upon these writings [the Bible], it is impossible to suppose that the entire truth of the religion depends upon them. . . . The written traditions must be interpreted by their inward truth and no written traditions can give the religion any inward truth if it has none.[9]

With these comments, Lessing distances himself from Reimarus, saying essentially that Reimarus' arguments, even if true, do not touch the heart of Christian faith. In this way, Lessing paints Reimarus as something of an "enthusiast," who had gone too far in his critique. And yet, Lessing leaves the door open that Reimarus' critique of revelation and the resurrection narratives might, in fact, *be true*. As part of his public staging of the *Fragments*, Lessing's "commentary" becomes, in effect, another voice, or character, in the public theater, offering a more modest proposal than that offered by the mysterious Unknown. Yet, Lessing does not defend the literal truth of Scripture, nor does he defend the idea that divine revelation is necessary for those who have no rational knowledge of Christ. Instead, he calls his audience to attend to the "inward truth" of a religion accessible to all people, which he identifies with the "spirit" of genuine Christianity, not the "letter."

By publishing the selected fragments of Reimarus' *Apology*, and suggesting they might, in part, be true, Lessing sought to arouse debate—prompting his audience to question the theologically indoctrinated assumptions that governed public as well as private life. In fact, from a number of his own responses to questions and concerns about the *Fragments*, it seems as if Lessing agreed with a significant percentage of Reimarus' critiques about prophecies, miracles, and so on. While disagreeing with Reimarus—"how much could be said in reply to all these objections and difficulties"—and therefore defending religion as such, Lessing hoped to persuade his readers that Reimarus' fundamental concern for the toleration of Deism was itself very sensible.

In his commentary on the fifth fragment released in 1777, "On the Resurrection Narrative," Lessing *disagrees* with Reimarus about the evangelists and their resurrection narratives. The fact that the Gospels disagree with one another on details of the resurrection does not mean that the evangelists lied, or were intentionally deceptive. After all, the evangelists were not the same people as those who witnessed the resurrection.[10] They could have been mistaken, argued Lessing, or forgot something, and so on. Interestingly enough, while Lessing defends the resurrection narratives against Reimarus' critique, he doesn't do so on grounds of their inspired or revealed character, but on purely naturalistic, or public, grounds. In correcting Reimarus, Lessing appears more conciliatory towards Christian tradition; but that appearance was also part of Lessing's overall dramatic strategy. Anyone paying careful attention to his arguments could see that his own stance was far from orthodox.

The publication of the five *Fragments* in 1777 brought forth the kind of response for which Lessing had hoped. J. D. Schumann, a pastor from Hanover, published a reply to the publication of the five fragments called, *On the Evidence of the Proofs of the Truth of the Christian Religion*, defending both the miracles of Jesus and biblical prophecy as "historically" true. In 1777, Lessing composed his own essay, "On the Proof of the Spirit and of Power" in response to Schumann. In this, one of Lessing's most famous theological writings, Lessing did not deny that miracles happened, nor did he deny that prophecies could be fulfilled. The difficulty, said Lessing, was the difference between the personal experience of a miracle or a fulfilled prophecy—which, he said, is itself immediately convincing—and the story of a miracle or a fulfilled prophecy that happened to others and which one hears about only through historical reports.

> If I had lived at the time of Christ, then of course the prophecies fulfilled in his person would have made me pay great attention to him. If I had actually seen him do miracles; if I had had no cause to doubt that these were true miracles; . . . then I would have believed him in all things in which equally indisputable experiences did not tell against him.

Lessing acknowledges Schmidt's use of Origen's (185–253 CE) testimony that miracles were still occurring in the third century, but then adds:

> But I am no longer in Origen's position; I live in the eighteenth century, in which miracles no longer happen. . . . The problem is that this proof of the spirit and of power no longer has any spirit or power, but has sunk to the level of human testimonies of spirit and power. The problem is that reports of fulfilled prophecies are not fulfilled prophecies; that reports of miracles are not miracles.

The gap that Lessing identifies between the convincing power of immediate perception to the more doubtful situation of a reader encountering reports of miracles and revelations is an experiential and a historical one. The historical problem arises, for Lessing, not only because of the passage of time per se, but because the modality of experience changes—that is, from immediate experience to reports of experience—and "the times" change as well. In thinking about this distinction in Lessing's essay, Edward Schillebeeckx points out that some commentators believe that Lessing's distinction was informed by the philosophical positions of Gottfried Leibnitz, or Baruch Spinoza.[11] Here, for example, is Spinoza on the difference between truths of history and the innate truths of reason. "Natural Divine Law," he said,

> does not depend on the truth of any historical narrative whatsoever. . . . The truth of a historical narrative, however assured, cannot give us the knowledge nor consequently the love of God, for love of God springs from knowledge of him, and knowledge of him should be derived from general ideas, in themselves certain and known, so that the truth of a historical narrative is very far from being a necessary requisite for attaining our highest good.[12]

Liebnitz, for his part, put the distinction this way: "The original proof of necessary truths comes from the understanding alone, and all other truths come from experiences or from observations of the senses."[13] Because it deals with reports of human experience, and not human experience itself, historical reason is always probable, not certain. Schillebeeckx, however, sees Lessing making a different distinction: "what mattered [to Lessing] was the antithesis between 'truths from the past,' concerning which we can be historically informed, and 'truths lived out' here and now, something that we are now going through ourselves."[14]

The point at issue is not the shifting terrain of our experience over against the Enlightened terrain of immutable, rationally evident truths; but it is a contrast within the sector of what we call 'factive experience': on the one hand of facts handed down from the past — which we may scrutinize for their historical accuracy . . . on the other, of here-and-now events, lived out by the self, which possess an intrinsic evidential function.

Lessing used the distinction to argue that because he lives in a time that no longer *experiences* miracles, that the assertion of miracles in ancient times inevitably takes the form of report by others, and is thus a less powerful, less convincing claim than if one experienced miracles personally. By this argument, Lessing does not deny the reality of miracles, but he focuses on the fact that because they no longer occur, miracles-as-reports are not immediately convincing. He then turns this argument toward another. Insofar as the report of a miracle is a historical claim, which might be affirmed or doubted on historical grounds, it is not the same kind of claim as an article of the Christian Creed. "Who will deny—and I do not do so—that the reports of these miracles and prophecies are as reliable as historical truths ever can be?—But then, if they are *only* as reliable as this, why are they suddenly made infinitely more reliable in practice?"[15] Finally, he focuses the argument: "If I have no historical objection to the fact that this Christ himself rose from the dead, must I therefore regard it as true that this same risen Christ was the Son of God?"[16]

Even if one grants that miracles such as the resurrection of Jesus occurred, argues Lessing, that admission would provide no warrant for the creedal claims of the church. They are different kinds of truth claims.

But to make the leap from this historical truth [the claim of the resurrection] into a quite different class of truths, and to require me to revise all my metaphysical and moral concepts accordingly; to expect me to change all my basic ideas on the nature of the deity because I cannot offer any credible evidence against the resurrection of Christ—if this is not a "transition to another category," I do not know what Aristotle meant by that phrase.[17]

By arguing in this way, Lessing cannot be accused of doubting the miracles of Christ by church officials or the public at large. But he uses that affirmation to skewer the church's rationale for wanting to affirm the historical reliability of the miracles, namely, that they would produce evidence in support of the supernatural truths by which the church governed public discourse. Thus, in replying to Schmidt, Lessing puts before the public a more cogently convincing argument than Reimarus had against ecclesiastical authority.

Certainly, the most famous, oft quoted lines from Lessing's essay are the following: "If no historical truth can be demonstrated [by reason alone], then nothing can be demonstrated by means of historical truths. That is: *accidental truths of history can never become the proof of necessary truths of reason*" (emphasis added).[18] While many theologians look to this text to argue that Lessing was putting historical-criticism in its place, it is vital to see that Lessing was actually arguing that truth claims based upon miracles and revelation should not be binding on human reason, and, implicitly therefore, on the public.

> But since the truth of these miracles has completely ceased to be demonstrable by miracles still happening now, since they are no more than reports of miracles. . . . I deny that they can and should bind me to the very least faith in the other teachings of Christ.[19]

The most vocal critic of Lessing himself was the pastor of the Lutheran Church of St. Catharine in Hamburg, Johann Melchior Göze (1717–86). He criticized Lessing publicly for upsetting the simple faith of the masses, and claimed that in publishing the *Fragments*, Lessing had intended to attack Christianity. If the *Fragments* had to be published at all, Göze argued, they should have been published in Latin, the language of the learned, and not in German where the fragments wreaked havoc in the public realm. This argument that Lessing had endangered the public peace—used, as we have already seen, against the English Deists—was among the most dangerous for those, like Lessing, who argued in support of rational religion. Lessing responded by accusing Göze of "Romanizing," that is, of using papal tactics of intimidation. For his part, Lessing sought refuge in the figure of Luther: "The true Lutheran does not wish to be defended by Luther's writings but by Luther's spirit; and Luther's spirit absolutely requires that no man may be prevented from advancing in the knowledge of the truth according to his own judgment."[20] Lessing's point in citing Luther was, of course, not simply to claim the authority of tradition to protect the rights of individual conscience, but to protect the right of the person to speak in the public arena—as Luther himself had dared to do. It was just this anxiety about public speech that Göze sought to en-flame not only in circles of the church but in political circles as well. Historian Marilyn Chapin Massey cites the following passage in which Göze "draws a parallel between biblical criticism and politi-cal criticism:"[21]

> [Lessing] believes that he does the Christian Religion and our Savior a service, and promotes the honor of both, when he serves as a mid-wife in publishing the most scandalous pamphlets directed against both. Does Mr. Lessing not see—or does he not want to see—*the logical consequences of this principle*? What would he reply to someone who says: The system of government practiced by the best and most just rulers does not deserve allegiance until every conceivable—however stupid—objection against the system and every conceiv-able libel and insult directed against the person of the ruler, has been set out in print, and placed in the hands of the mass of his subjects; until his most virtuous and benevolent actions have been provoked into defending the honor of their Master, his system of government and his actions?[22]

As we have seen in similar accusations discussed in previous chapters, Göze's remarks basically accuse Lessing of inciting mass disobedience, and hence rebellion against the established authori-ties of church and state. In the ensuing months, Lessing wrote no fewer than eleven responses to the pastor, which he published as *Anti-Göze*.[23]

In 1778, Lessing published one final fragment, the most ex-plosive yet. In "On the Intentions of Jesus and His Disciples," Reimarus argued that the "intentions" of Jesus were very different from the intentions of his Disciples. While Jesus sought to establish a political "kingdom of God" and died in despair on the cross, the disciples, said Reimarus, sought their own self interest and turned Jesus' political expectation into a spiritual reality that would secure them their own financial well-being.[24] By July of 1778, the Duke of Brunswick had heard and read enough. On July 13, he informed Lessing that henceforth his religious writings would need the ap-proval of the censor.

When the Duke of Brunswick informed Lessing that he would need to seek the censor's approval for future publications touching upon religion, Lessing vowed to his brother Karl that he would return to his "former pulpit, the theatre," and there "play the theo-logians a still more annoying trick than ten fragments."[25] His new play, *Nathan the Wise* was written the following year (1779), and it was, as Henry Chadwick puts it, "a plea for the toleration of all religions (except the intolerant)." Because Lessing saw this play as carrying forward the publication of the *Fragments*, it is worth considering more closely. Chadwick summarizes the characters and basic plot.

> The main characters are Nathan the Jew, Saladin the Moslem, and the Knight Templar who represents Christianity of the type Lessing would wish to encourage. Nathan is the model of tolerant charity. Saladin is runner-up. The Knight Templar, though a fine character, is a Christian and has to learn as the play proceeds to appreciate the virtue of religious indifferentism and the vice of anti-Semitism. The message of the play is that all men should treat one another as brothers, irrespective of their religious allegiance. Men are men before they are Christians, Jews, or Moslems. They have one and the same God as their universal Father.[26]

Set in Jerusalem during the period of the Third Crusade (1189–92 CE), the play connects religious violence, specifically here the violence of the Crusades, to claims of superiority among the major monotheistic traditions. At the heart of the play, in Act Three, Lessing places a story that challenges and undercuts the claim of religious superiority—and thus, of cultural predominance—among any of the three monotheistic traditions.[27] The Sultan poses the following question to Nathan: "Since you are a man so wise, tell me which law, which faith appears to you the better?" Nathan responds: Sultan, I am a Jew." And the Sultan responds: "And I a Mussulman; the Christian stands between us. Of these three Religions only one can be the true."[28] The story Nathan tells in response to the Sultan's question exploits the ambiguity in the word "true." Nathan begins:

> In days of yore, there dwelt in east a man
> Who from a valued hand received a ring
> Of endless worth: the stone of it an opal,
> That shot an ever-changing tint: moreover,
> It had the hidden virtue him to render
> Of God and man beloved, who in this view,
> And this persuasion, wore it. Was it strange
> The eastern man ne'er drew it off his finger,
> And studiously provided to secure it
> For ever to his house. Thus—He bequeathed it;

First, to the MOST BELOVED of his sons,
Ordained that he again should leave the ring
To the MOST DEAR among his children—and
That without heeding birth, the FAVOURITE son,
In virtue of the ring alone, should always
Remain the lord o' th' house—You hear me, Sultan?

S. I understand thee—on.[29]

In the last lines from Nathan one sees that the ring itself renders the one who wears it as favored before God and the human community. The ring, therefore, functions as a symbol of what each of the major religions claim to enact: the special, and preferred, bonding of human persons to God and to one another.

The ring finally comes to a father with three sons whom he loves profoundly. As his death draws near, the father, unable to decide to whom to give the ring, calls in the most eminent craftsman in the land, and commands him to make two rings, identical to the first, such that no one will be able to tell the original ring from the newly crafted ones. And so, as death approaches the father invites each of the three sons to meet with him privately. At each meeting he bestows his blessing and a ring. And having met with all three, he dies. And the father no sooner dies than each of the sons appears before the others—each wearing a ring and claiming to be the new head of the household.

Because the father cannot be brought forward to answer the question as to which son is more beloved, or which is the authentic ring, there is no way to tell the authentic from the forgery. The Sultan, listening to this story is not very satisfied.

S. The rings—don't trifle with me; I must think
That the religions which I named can be
Distinguished, e'en to raiment, drink and food,

N. And only not as to their grounds of proof.
Are not all built alike on history,
Traditional, or written. History
Must be received on trust—is it not so?
In whom now are we likeliest to put trust?
In our own people surely, in those men
Whose blood we are, in them, who from our childhood
Have given us proofs of love, who ne'er deceived us,
Unless 'twere wholesomer to be deceived.
How can I less believe in my forefathers

Than thou in thine. How can I ask of thee
To own that thy forefathers falsified
In order to yield mine the praise of truth.[30]

The ambiguity of history, of course, lays behind Nathan's caution that our religious "histories" are family histories, as it were—what H. R. Niebuhr in the 1950s called "internal history"—namely, a tradition of meaning that is neither objective nor certain.[31] Nathan argues that while accepted as true within the religious community, religious narratives are inclined toward the community's self interest. The Sultan begins to come around.

> S. By the living God,
> The man is in the right, I must be silent.[32]

Nathan is not yet finished. Not only are religious claims to truth ambiguous, but religion should not have sway over the civil law. In fact, the three brothers in the story seek remedy by presenting their cases to the local judge. As each supplies his "testimony" before the judge, none of the brothers blame the "Father." Instead, each one accuses the others of forgery, of faking their claims to favored status. Capturing the vulnerable underbelly of religion—its inclination to hate its neighbor, while claiming to possess the truth of God—Lessing's "judge" sends their three appeals packing for lack of any evidence to substantiate their claims. Being a fair judge, he does not intervene in the religious dispute or attempt to solve it by insinuating his own religious views to settle the matter (and thus a good judge by Locke's standards as well as Lessing's). Instead, he lectures them to attend far more carefully to the ethical norms at the heart of their faiths, and so, to the common good of humanity.

> N. The judge said, If ye summon not the father
> Before my seat, I cannot give a sentence.
> Am I to guess enigmas? Or expect ye
> That the true ring should here unseal its lips?
> But hold—you tell me that the real ring
> Enjoys the hidden power to make the wearer
> Of God and man beloved; let that decide.
> Which of you do two brothers love the best?
> You're silent. Do these love-exciting rings
> Act inward only, not without? Does each
> Love but himself? Ye're all deceived deceivers,
> None of your rings is true. The real ring

Perhaps is gone. To hide or to supply
Its loss, your father ordered three for one. . . .

And (the judge continued)
If you will take advice in lieu of sentence,
This is my counsel to you, to take up
The matter where it stands. If each of you
Has had a ring presented by his father,
Let each believe his own the real ring.
'Tis possible the father chose no longer
To tolerate the one ring's tyranny;
And certainly, as he much loved you all,
And loved you all alike, it could not please him
By favouring one to be of two the oppressor.
Let each feel honoured by this free affection.
Unwarped of prejudice; let each endeavour
To vie with both his brothers in displaying
The virtue of his ring; assist its might
With gentleness, benevolence, forbearance,
With inward resignation to the godhead,
And if the virtues of the ring continue
To show themselves among your children's children,
After a thousand thousand years, appear
Before this judgment-seat—a greater one
Than I shall sit upon it, and decide.
So spake the modest judge.[33]

Lessing's judge does not dispute either the question of a final judgment or the nature of eternal life; instead, he highlights the ethical conventions of the respective religious traditions as the most enduring and persuasive public warrants for their claim to superiority.

Equal to, if not *more* important than, the play's message of religious toleration are the images of a judge lecturing the brothers (that is, the religions) on the limits of their public authority. At least in the world of the play, suggests Lessing, religious authorities do not have sway, and it is *that* message, more than toleration, that makes the play such a dangerous one for church authorities.

That the moral voice of *Nathan the Wise* is a Jew, and not a Christian, is also significant. For a German Lutheran audience, Lessing's use of Nathan may well suggest that Christians have, in Lessing's view, lost their moral authority as a result of oppressing the religious others in their midst. Nathan's wisdom is a necessary antidote to Christian power. While perhaps heavy-handed from a literary perspective, Lessing's use of the Crusades functions to remind Lessing's eighteenth-century audience of the very real impact that religious truth claims have had upon European history. Small wonder that church officials prevented any performance of the play prior to Lessing's death in 1781.

Nathan the Wise continues Lessing's critique of Germany's religious-and-political life of the eighteenth century. In fact, the play illuminates more clearly than the publication of the *Fragments* themselves the kind of dramatic strategy at work in their release and in Lessing's commentary. While Lessing chose a less radical stance toward the Christianity of his day than Reimarus, it was a strategic stance, and one that proved ultimately as revolutionary. With Reimarus' help, Lessing produced a drama that the German people would not forget—one that would inspire others, including David Friedrich Strauss.

CHAPTER 5

Strauss, Jesus, and the Scandal of Democracy

By the late eighteenth century, armed political revolutions had occurred in North America and in France. In the latter, victory for the "Rights of Man" had turned to terror. While Thomas Paine blamed the convulsion of violence in France on centuries of priestly rule, there was no doubt that the specter of bloodlust confirmed many European monarchs' and prelates' worst fears that Plato had been right in claiming that democracies were prone to mob rule. This was especially true in the politically and religiously fragmented German states, where a primary political result of the Peace of Westphalia (1648) had been to slow any movement toward either political unification or a coherent policy of religious toleration.

Claiming to extend and export the values of the French Revolution, Napoleon's army invaded northwestern Germany in 1806 and occupied several German states until 1815.[1] The incursion of France onto German soil had a two-fold effect. On the one hand, it brought to Germany an ideology of revolutionary freedom which had a lasting effect on those like poet Heinrich Heine (1799–1865), who was raised in the area and who would later call for neutralizing "the power of religion" in German politics; on the other, it reinforced German calls for restoration of the monarchy to resist the French encroachment.

In her book, *Christ Unmasked: The Meaning of the Life of Jesus in German Politics* (1983), Marilyn Chapin Massey has argued persuasively that *The Life of Jesus Critically Examined*, published in Tübingen in 1835 by David Friedrich Strauss (1808–74), needs to be read and interpreted in light of the tension between revolutionary calls for increased political and religious rights, on the one hand, and the conservative defense of the German monarchy and orthodox religion on the other. Massey describes the contours of that instability:

The formal political organization of Germany from 1815–1848, the German Confederation, which was established at the Congress of Vienna in 1815, was headed by Austria, Germany's leading Catholic power. It did not constitute Germany as a united nation, nor did it foster broad-based representative government. This confederation met in assembly at Frankfurt. Representation was by aristocrats appointed by the kings of its thirty-nine states, and its policies, which were controlled by [Klemens von] Metternich (1773–1859), the chancellor of Austria, consistently favored restoration [of the monarchy].[2]

Massey goes on to quote Ernst Troeltsch, who wrote of the religious-intellectual mood of the period:

The spirit of rationalism had already faded and changed itself in part into a democratic opposition, in part into a capitalistic enterprise. . . . But the old relationships of power and class had only been weakened, not eliminated [by the cultural forces of rationalism and humanism]. From behind [the façade of an altered culture], the power structure of a military-bureaucratic monarchy forced itself into the foreground. This structure was bound together with the restoration of a dogmatic Christian ecclesiasticism which took every opportunity to establish itself.[3]

The linkage of church and state, or "altar and throne," became a central strategy for those German institutions and interests resisting the widening of public participation in the life and leadership of the culture. That these political and religious positions tended to harden increasingly until the Revolution of 1848 is evident from the comment of conservative political philosopher Julius Stahl (1802–61) who wrote that in the revolutionary confrontation of 1848 only two sides existed: "one for the revolution and the other for the throne and the altar."[4]

To this general sense of dis-ease from 1815–48, add another moment in the French Revolution. In July, 1830, the French Revolution in Paris deposed Charles X and liberalized the French constitution of 1814. Word of this renewed revolutionary experiment reawakened German hopes for constitutional reforms that would strengthen the middle-classes, allow representative government, and ease religious and political censorship. According to Massey, the Prussian government's Restorationist response to the 1830 French Revolution "intensified censorship of the university and press," and clamped down on those individual states that sought to "grant limited constitutions."[5] Massey quotes historian Theodore

Bigler, who argues that the general trend functioning through-out the 1815–48 period became intensified during the mid-1830s. About the role of university theology departments in this period, Bigler writes:

> Since in the midst of changing political conditions after 1815 the the-ology professors continued to play a crucial role in clerical personnel recruitment—by training, examining, and recommending candi-dates for church positions—there resulted an increased attention by the government to the creed and political leanings of prospective appointees to the university, and its policy favored men who could be expected to support the ruling authorities.[6]

Strauss: Biblical Analysis in the Midst of a Philosophical Theology

In the charged environment of the 1830s David Friedrich Strauss be-came enamored with the philosophy of G. W. F. Hegel (1770–1831), which had become enormously influential throughout Germany. A seminary student, Strauss decided to travel to Berlin to study with Hegel in 1831. While Hegel died within weeks of Strauss's arrival, his thought became central to Strauss in the years leading up to the publication of *The Life of Jesus Critically Examined*.

Strauss's Use of Hegel's Dialectic

In the preface to volume one of the first edition of *The Life of Jesus Critically Examined*, Strauss opens by critiquing what he calls the "antiquated systems" of supernaturalism and naturalism/rational-ism.[7] Instead of these out-dated approaches, Strauss argues that a new "point of view" is required: "the mythical." Informed by Hegel's dialectical model of affirmation, negation, and synthesis, Strauss opens with a discussion of supernaturalism, then discusses the critique of supernaturalism by rationalism/naturalism, and fi-nally moves toward his own synthesis of "mythic" narrative.

The first outdated position—itself important but no longer ten-able—is supernaturalism, which affirmed the shaping of Scripture by God:

> In the ancient world, . . . the law of connexion between earthly finite beings was very loosely regarded. At every link there was a dispo-sition to spring into the Infinite, and to see God as the immediate cause of every change in nature or the human mind. . . . He it is who gives the rain and sunshine; he sends the east wind and the storm;

Hegel–A Very Brief Introduction

Reality as such, thought Hegel, could be analyzed as a constant historical and spiritual process. Ultimate Reality (or God) is Spirit, which, in order to know itself and to fully realize itself, must negate itself as Spirit and become finite. The initial affirmation of Spirit and its secondary negation in finitude would result in a third move, or synthesis, which is identical with neither of the first two positions. By this ongoing dialectical process of affirmation, negation, and reaffirmation, Hegel could make sense of both historical continuity and the emergence of the genuinely new. Given the influence of Hegel, history and the analysis of the historical process became crucial for discussions of religion, philosophy, and truth. Just as importantly, insofar as one moment of historical process will be negated, or critiqued, in order to open up a new creative synthesis, the process of "critique" itself plays a crucial role in the development of human consciousness itself and, thus, in the journey of Spirit.

Religion, according to Hegel, functions as a penultimate moment in the journey of Spirit to realize itself. Because religion uses stories of particular figures such as Jesus or Moses to convey spiritual precepts, Hegel discusses religion under the heading of *Vorstellung*, or representation or image. Insofar as the spiritual/conceptual meaning, or *Begriff*, of the representation remains implied within the story or imagery, that meaning is neither as clearly distilled nor as advanced as the conceptual discourse of philosophy. Thus, in the final culmination of history, for Hegel, religion will give way to philosophy, but until then religion helps humanity advance in the direction of the truth.

he dispenses war, famine, pestilence; he hardens hearts and softens them, suggests thoughts and resolutions. And this is particularly the case with regard to his chosen instruments and beloved people . . . : through Moses, Elias [Elijah], Jesus, he performs things which never would have happened in the ordinary course of nature.

Our modern world, on the contrary, after many centuries of tedious research, has attained a conviction, that all things are linked together by a chain of causes and effects, which suffers no interruption. . . . This conviction is so much a habit of thought with the modern world, that in actual life, the belief in a supernatural manifestation, an immediate divine agency, is at once attributed to ignorance or imposture. . . . From this point of view, at which nature and history appear as a compact tissue of finite causes and effects, it was impossible to regard the narratives of the Bible, in which this tissue is broken by innumerable instances of divine interference, as historical.[8]

Strauss's use of Hegel's dialectical structure enables him to honor religious traditions of the past while critiquing and moving beyond them. Tradition is important not because it is permanent but because it is part of the journey of Spirit.

The second out-dated position is the Enlightenment model of rationalism, itself important for negating the supernaturalistic argument. The problem with rationalistic explanations, explains Strauss, is that in seeking the "kernel" of truth in the biblical narrative they discarded the narrative "husk." Strauss sought a way to honor the husk of the narrative and not just the kernel of truth.

The third movement, or synthesis of these two "outdated" movements, according to Strauss, is found in recognizing that the biblical texts are neither supernatural in character, nor narrowly rationalistic, but historical constructions by religious communities taking the form of what he calls legend and myth.

> The result . . . of a general examination of the biblical history, is that the Hebrew and Christian religions, like all others, have their mythi [plural of myth]. . . . If religion be defined as the perception of truth, not in the form of an idea, which is the philosophic perception, but invested with imagery; it is easy to see . . . that in the proper religious sphere it [the mythical element] must necessarily exist.[9]

Strauss's definition of religion as "the perception of truth . . . invested with imagery" comes directly from Hegel, and he fuses that language of "imagery" with the language of myth.

Strauss knew that his discussion of biblical narrative as myth would raise eyebrows. Early in *The Life of Jesus Critically Examined*, Strauss explicitly acknowledges that his use of the loaded term "myth" is controversial and prone to dismissal by the public:

> The assertion that the Bible contains mythi is, it is true, directly opposed to the convictions of the believing Christian. For if his religious view be circumscribed within the limits of his own community, he knows no reason why the things recorded in the sacred books should not literally have taken place; no doubt occurs to him, no reflection disturbs him. But, let his horizon be so far widened as to allow him to contemplate his own religion in relation to other religions, and to draw a comparison between them, the conclusion to which he then comes is that the histories related by the heathens of their deities, and by the Mussulman of his prophet, are so many fictions, whilst the accounts of God's actions, of Christ and other Godlike men contained in the Bible are, on the contrary, true. Such is

the general notion expressed in the theological position: that which distinguishes Christianity from the heathen religions is this, *they* are mythical, *it* is historical.[10] (emphasis added)

Myth, in the common mind, acknowledges Strauss, occurs inevitably in the contexts of truth versus falsehood; divine versus human authorship; the factual versus the fictitious; and so on. Strauss responds that such a limited understanding is indicative of a mind "incapable of embracing any but the affirmative view in relation to its own creed, any but the negative in reference to other—a prejudice devoid of real worth," and is simply incompatible with "an extensive knowledge of history."[11] Strauss then suggests a scene that recalls Lessing's *Nathan the Wise*.

> For let us transplant ourselves among other religious communities; the believing Mohammedan is of the opinion that truth is contained in the Koran alone, and the greater portion of the Bible is fabulous; the Jew of the present day, whilst admitting the truth and divine origin of the Old Testament, rejects the New; and, the same exclusive belief in the truth of their own creed and the falsity of every other was entertained by the professors of most of the heathen religions before the period of the Syncretism. But which community is right? Not all, for this is impossible, since the assertion of each excludes the others. But which particular one? Each claims for itself the true faith. The pretensions are equal; what shall decide? The origin of the several religions? Each lays claim to a divine origin.[12]

With this argument, Strauss signals his affiliation with a logic of religious toleration and, implicitly, an expanded vision of allowable public discourse.

We are now in a better position to see what Strauss is up to with the category of myth. We should notice first, that in his definition myth is not linked with falsehood but with the nature of religious truth as such—whether it be "invested" with Christian, Jewish, or Muslim "imagery." In addition, for Strauss, realizing the mythic character of the Hebrew and Christian Scriptures is a peculiarly modern, yet appropriate, way of speaking about the Scriptures due to the vastly improved modern understandings of nature and causality. Given what we know of how the world works, we can no longer simply say that Scripture is historically accurate. By the same token, the fact that one can no longer speak of the Bible as literally, historically true, does not mean that one can dismiss Scripture as false or claim, as Reimarus had, that the evangelists lied about the resurrection.

> This reasoning [about the nature of myth] brings us to the conclusion, that the idea of deliberate and intentional fabrication, in which the author clothes that which he knows to be false in the appearance of truth, must be entirely set aside as insufficient to account for the origin of the *mythus*.[13]

Strauss seeks to *enact* with respect to both Scripture and Christian tradition a *new* synthesis—that of "mythical" interpretation—capable of moving beyond the tired debates between "supernaturalists," on the one hand and "rationalists/naturalists" on the other. His model of interpreting religious claims generally, and the Gospels specifically, through the lens of myth would allow one to continue to speak of the "truth" of Scripture and tradition (in the mode of *Vortellung*, or representation) while also encouraging a reconceptualization of the meaning, or *Begriff*, of those doctrines in language more appropriate for the cultural and intellectual contexts of one's time.[14]

One can see why Strauss was hopeful about his project: By critiquing both supernaturalistic and rationalistic interpretations of the biblical text, Strauss could argue that he had found a path—in sync with the wisdom of Hegel—that could provide a way out of the cultural and religious divide in Germany. The Deism of figures like Lessing had fallen from political favor in Germany, due to the felt political tremors of the French Revolution. In place of rationalism, supernaturalism was once again on the rise in Germany,[15] as German Restorationists sought to unify the fragmented states of Germany through a strong monarchy and religious orthodoxy. For these Restorationists, appeals to Reason, in contrast to appeals to religious tradition and orthodoxy, were viewed as synonymous with Deism and with the American and French Revolutions that flowed from it. Hence, the strategic importance for Strauss to distance himself from Deism, and its rationalism as such. Yet, by critiquing supernaturalism as outdated, Strauss sought to encourage a creative rethinking of Christian traditions, which would appeal to those interested in greater political as well as religious change.

Through careful analyses of particular gospel narratives from the birth of Jesus to his death and resurrection, Strauss shows first, that the assumed supernatural understanding of the text makes no sense, and second, that rationalistic interpretations from the early modern period—trying to salvage a historical core to the stories—also lead to tortured readings of the text. By interpreting the Gospels as mythic texts—as narratives that wrap the early Christian memories and stories of Jesus in their-own-cultural language of significance—Strauss undercut several important theological claims: (1) that the biblical texts were divinely inspired, (2) that the miracle stories were proofs of Jesus' divinity, (3) that the stories and words of Jesus—especially in John's Gospel—should be taken at face value.

What is new in Strauss is the multi-level awareness: (1) that the Gospels were written at some distance from the events of Jesus' life; (2) that they were not eyewitness accounts, and thus, that the names of the Gospels do not correspond to members of Jesus' immediate circle; (3) that most of the gospel material is not historical in any modern, scientific sense but that the Gospels were written and shaped by communities of faith and reflect the language of religious significance available to those communities; 4) and that John's Gospel is virtually empty of historical material. Even more important, however, is how Strauss puts this historical knowledge to work, arguing, in effect, contra Reimarus, that the gospel writers were not historians, but that the stories they told were already largely legendary and mythic in character. While actual history may be entwined with and lay beneath the layer of narrative presented in the gospel, the text itself is surely not a historically accurate report. Instead, the narrative portrayals, argues Strauss, were largely mythical, already affirming Jesus as a sacred figure, using miracles, visions, and stories of resurrection to convey his religious significance. Just as importantly, Strauss's mythic analysis shifts attention away from the dogmatic figure of the God-Man and towards the texts themselves as productions of Christian communities—a move that deeply disturbed conservative theologians and defenders of the monarchy.

Debating Hegel Right and Left

A truly Hegelian position, argued Strauss, would insist on a historical Jesus behind the mythic text, as it were, who lived and died—outside the sacred narrative about him. His *Life of Jesus Critically Examined* demonstrated that the Gospels' mythic portrayal of Jesus was too spiritualized to constitute the radical finitude that Hegel's dialectic required. Thus, one needed to critique the divine-man representation of Jesus in the Scriptures in order to open up the possibility of a genuine synthesis of the infinite (God) and the finite (humanity)—and a reinterpretation of the meaning of the incarnation. Because the transformative *synthesis* of God and finite human being could not occur in *one* human life, but only in all of humanity, according to Strauss, the doctrine of the incarnation, therefore, must not be about the particular person, Jesus, but about humanity as such. The real meaning [*Begriff*] of the Christ, and of Christianity, for Strauss, is that God and humanity have become joined in God's own journey of self-realization. For Strauss, therefore, the reality of the God-Man was a global reality, accessible not through a kind of simple or pure belief in Christian doctrine—which provided a mere starting point for reflection—but through a critique of the divine origins of the Christian Scriptures, doctrines and teaching.

Defenders of the German monarchy, or the Restorationist movement, saw in Strauss's interpretation of the God-Man an affirmation of revolutionary democracy that went counter to Hegel's own view. "Right-wing" Hegelians, like Karl Friedrich Göschel (1784–1862), defended the monarchy and used the intellectual popularity of Hegel, and especially his work, *The Philosophy of the Right*, to justify their position. In that book, Hegel argued:

> This ultimate self in which the will of a state is concentrated is, when taken in abstraction, a single self and therefore is *immediate* individuality. Hence its natural character is implied in its very conception. The monarch, therefore, is essentially characterized as *this* individual, in abstraction from all his other characteristics, and *this* individual is raised to the dignity of monarchy in an immediate, natural fashion, i.e., through his birth in the course of nature.[16]

Göschel argued that Hegel's insistence on "*this* individual" (i.e., the monarch) as embodying the subjectivity and personality of the state demonstrated Hegel's support for the orthodox claim that God became human in one person, Jesus Christ. Writes Massey:

> Göschel concluded that just as the state achieves actual personality in the monarch, the human species achieves it when a head—an individual, namely, Christ as a single person—is given to it. This head is "an *Urmensch*," a real, autonomous individual actualizing personality and providing the conditions of possibility of personality for all humans, singly and collectively. Humans achieve personality as individuals to the extent that they allow "themselves to be penetrated by this single individual [Christ] as the monarch of humanity."[17]

For Göschel, just as the state became actualized in the unique personality of the monarch, so all humanity became fully actualized by allowing "themselves to be penetrated by this single individual [Christ] as the monarch of humanity."[18]

Strauss defended his interpretation of the God-Man as genuinely Hegelian by pointing to an essay Hegel wrote criticizing the Würtenburg Diet of 1815–16 (which, we have seen, moved Germany in a Restorationist direction). Hegel wrote of the Diet:

> The picture of a better and juster time has become lively in the souls of men, and a longing, a sighing for purer and freer conditions has moved all hearts and set them at variance with reality [of the present]. . . . General and deep is the feeling that the fabric of the state in its present condition is untenable. . . .
>
> How blind they are who may hope that institutions, constitutions, laws which no longer correspond to human manner, needs, and opinions, from which the spirit has flown, can subsist any longer; or that forms in which intellect and feeling now take no interest are powerful enough to be any longer the bond of a nation![19]

In addition, Strauss argued from other sections in *The Philosophy of the Right* in which Hegel called for civil reforms such as "trial by jury, a two house parliament system, and public debates among the estates," which limited the claims to absolute power of a hereditary monarch, and which certainly criticized the governing structures of the current Prussian state.[20] Hegel's affirmation in *The Philosophy of the Right* for "circles of association in civil society" as "communities," argues Strauss, underscored a unifying component to public life and public discourse that limited the powers of the monarch to "far more narrow boundaries than [had] been done in Prussia."[21]

What about Jesus' Eschatology?

As with Reimarus before him, Strauss was convinced that the historical Jesus was preoccupied with a future and other-worldly eschatology that could not be maintained intellectually in the modern world of the nineteenth century. Resisting Reimarus' naturalism, however, Strauss found his theological solution once again in Hegel's distinction between *Vorstellung* and *Begriff*. The eschatological vision, which preoccupied Jesus, remained at the level of religious imagery [*Vorstellung*], according to Strauss, because it postponed the actual fulfillment of all things to a hidden future. The fulfillment of all things as concept [*Begriff*] occurred, said Strauss, neither in the distant future, nor in eternity, but in the present—by grasping the truth of the reconciliation of all things. Salvation happens, for Strauss, through *understanding*—an understanding that moves through and ultimately beyond the religious image. Just as this movement goes beyond Jesus to humanity, so it also goes beyond the image of a future place to a consciousness of an eternal present. Writes Strauss, near the end of his work:

> The phenomenal history of the individual, says Hegel, is only a starting point for the mind. Faith, in her early stages is governed by the senses, and therefore contemplates a temporal history; what she holds to be true is the external, ordinary event, the evidence for which is of the historical, forensic kind—a fact to be proved by the testimony of the senses, and the moral confidence inspired by the witnesses. But mind having once taken occasion by this external fact, to bring under its consciousness the idea of humanity as one with God, sees in the history only the presentation of that idea; the object of faith is completely changed; instead of a sensible, empirical fact, it has become a spiritual and divine idea which has its confirmation no longer in history but in philosophy. When the mind has thus gone beyond the sensible history, and entered into the domain of the absolute, the former ceases to be essential; it takes a subordinate place.[22]

Insofar as the completion of the journey of knowledge is not a journey accomplished in actual time, but only in understanding, the meaning [Begriff] of Jesus' eschatological vision was available now—a realized eschatology—available to all persons of genuine understanding.

Early End to a Teaching Career

According to Peter Hodgson, Strauss "expected that the book would be welcomed by serious and enlightened men as a liberation from the fetters of dogmatism and as a basis for the revitalization of the true essence of Christian faith. He was also confident that it would bring him a teaching appointment."[23] In fact, however, the publication of the first volume of the first edition, in the summer of 1835, ended Strauss's teaching career at the age of twenty-seven. The "negative reaction," says Hodgson, "was perfectly extraordinary."[24]

One of Strauss's early critics lamented, as had Pastor Göze about the publication of the Fragments, that Strauss's book had not been published in Latin, which would have protected the people from harm.[25] That same sentiment found a variety of outlets. Schweitzer includes the following in his treatment of Strauss's opponents:

> An anonymous dialogue of the period shows us the schoolmaster coming in distressed to the clergyman. He has allowed himself

to be persuaded into reading the [Strauss] book by his acquaintance . . . and is now anxious to get rid of the doubts which it has aroused in him. When his cure has been safely accomplished, the reverend gentleman dismisses him with the following exhortation: "Now I hope that after this experience which you have had you will for the future refrain from reading books of this kind, which are not written for you, and of which there is no necessity for you to take any notice; and for the refutation of which, should that be needful, you have no equipment. You may be quite sure that anything useful or profitable for you which such books may contain will reach you in due course through the proper channel and in the right way, and, that being so, you are under no necessity to jeopardize your peace of mind."[26]

Besides the pastoral paternalism in the passage, akin to encouraging a child to go back to sleep, the hierarchical, trickle-down theory of truth in the piece, with its emphasis on "proper channels," attempts to reinforce trust in the structures of the official church establishment. Yet, precisely by attempting to buttress the official organs of German Protestantism, the piece also expresses officialdom's anxiety about revolutionary awakenings.

Just as Lessing had been opposed by Rev. Göze, so Strauss had his own most formidable critic, a pietist theologian named Ernest Wilhelm Hengstenberg. Massey writes that Hengstenberg, a dominant theological voice at the University of Berlin, had made a reputation for himself as an enforcer of Protestant orthodoxy and as a friend of the monarchy. In 1830, Hengstenberg had used his editorship of an orthodox newspaper, *Evangelische Kirchenzeitung* (*The Evangelical Church Newspaper*),[27] to accuse two rationalist theologians, Wilhelm Gesenius and Julius Wegscheider, of heresy and had urged civil authorities to move against them.[28] Hengstenberg was encouraged in that attack by a Prussian government official named Ludwig von Gerlach (1795–1877). While the two men ultimately retained their positions, King Friedrich Wilhelm III weighed in on September 23, 1830, declaring: "I consider the influence of theology professors [who] do not feel bound by the dogma of the Protestant Church [as] eternal truths [to be] extremely dangerous for the state."[29] Six years later, on Christmas Day, von Gerlach wrote to Hengstenberg again and urged him to use his newspaper to expose Strauss's *Life of Jesus Critically Examined* and its dangerous implications for the church and all German institutions.[30]

In his attack on Strauss, Hengstenberg sarcastically praised the young theologian for having clarified the rationalist agenda of biblical criticism. Interestingly enough, Hengstenberg uses the political language of "nations" in his condemnation of Strauss. "Two nations are struggling in the will of our time, and two only. They will be ever more definitely opposed to one another. Unbelief will more and more cast off the elements of faith to which it still clings, and faith will cast off its elements of unbelief. That will be an inestimable advantage."[31] Given Hengstenberg's interest in securing an orthodox Germany through alignment with the monarchy, his call for faith to "cast off its elements of unbelief" is nothing short of a call to purify the church and universities of rationalists and liberals, which would therefore purify the public discourse of the nation. According to Massey, Hengstenberg attacked either Strauss or *The Life of Jesus Critically Examined* "in virtually every issue of the *Evangelical Church Newspaper* from 1838–1848."[32]

Hengstenberg's remarks about "two nations" proved tragically prophetic. Hengstenberg was the vocal leader of orthodox Protestantism throughout the 1840s which sided with the monarchy. Historian Theodore Bigler has noted that the failure of official German Protestantism "to side with the people during [as well as after] the Revolution of 1848" eventuated in the alienation of the German people from the church and moved them "to embrace the secular religion of Marxism and National Socialism."[33]

Conclusion

Precisely because of Strauss's detailed level of expertise in handling both biblical and philosophical materials, it is easy to think of Strauss as concerned only about the world of his library, as it were, and not about the wider world of German religious politics. However, as one begins to consider the dialectical form of Strauss's argument, his attempt to find a *via media* between his critique of supernaturalism on the one hand, and naturalism/rationalism on the other, it is difficult to imagine that he is utterly naïve about the dangers surrounding his discourse. While very much like Lessing in seeking both to affirm Christian faith and to limit the power of its doctrinal claims over public life—certainly, at least, over the discourse of scholars—Strauss seems to think that he has found, in Hegel, a genuine way forward. Rather than prove a break against the reemerging politicized orthodoxy, however, Strauss was broken by the interests of altar and throne. Once again, as before, with

Lessing and others, Strauss himself became the scandal. Fired from Tübingen within a month of the first volume's publication, Strauss linked his fate to Lessing's and used the scandal as best he could to advance the right of authors and theologians to publish views critical of established authorities. In concluding the Preface to volume II of *The Life of Jesus Critically Examined*, Strauss, in October of 1835—already fired from his position—identifies himself with Lessing's "scandalous" publication of the Reimarus *Fragments*.

> My work has also been criticized, supposedly from the standpoint of philosophy, by Professor Eschenmayer in a brochure entitled, *Der Ischariotismus unserer Tage* [*The Iscariot of Our Day*]. This monstrous product of the legitimate marriage of theological ignorance and religious intolerance, consecrated by a somnambulent philosophy, is so evidently absurd as to render any word of defense superfluous. Its title, moreover, has become for me the occasion of perhaps too presumptive a reminder—of Lessing, to be specific, who also was once slandered by a Viennese paper as a second Judas Iscariot because he was said to have been paid 1000 Ducats for the publication of the *Fragments* of his unknown author by the Amsterdam Jewish society. . . . And so I want to close the Preface to this second volume of my allegedly shocking work with the words Lessing used to explain why he had not stopped with the publication of the first sample of those bothersome *Fragments*, as I have not with the first part of this book. I am not stopping, he said, "because I am convinced that this scandal is merely a bogey with which certain people would like to frighten away any and every spirit of investigation, because it does not good at all to want to cut out only half a cancer, and because air must be given to the fire if it is to be extinguished."[34]

6

Schweitzer and the Scandal
of Liberal Theology

Readers familiar with Albert Schweitzer's *The Quest of the Historical Jesus* know that when Schweitzer turns his attention to the period of the 1860s and to what he calls the "liberal *Lives of Jesus*," his language shifts dramatically. While he speaks in reverential tones of the "heroic" quest through the period of Strauss, and of its brave honesty in confronting what he calls dogmatic tyranny, Schweitzer turns to the popular work of Ernst Renan's *Life of Jesus* (1863), and the other "liberal *Lives*" of the 1860s, with derision and sarcasm. Here is how he begins his critique of Renan:

> He offered his readers a Jesus who was alive, whom he, with his artistic imagination, had met under the blue heaven of Galilee, and whose lineaments his inspired pencil had seized. Men's attention was arrested, and they thought to see Jesus, because Renan had the skill to make them see blue skies, seas of waving corn, distant mountains, gleaming lilies in a landscape with the Lake of Gennesareth for its center, and to hear with him in the whispering of the reeds the eternal melody of the Sermon on the Mount.[1]

Schweitzer's comparison of Renan's "Life" to artistic "skill" is no complement; Schweitzer is drawing on the Platonic trope that art is a form of lying. In this case, Renan's *Life* is no *real* historical life, according to Schweitzer: it's "art, and worse than that, it's *bad* art." "It is Christian art in the worst sense of the term—the wax image. The gentle Jesus, the beautiful Mary, the fair Galileans";[2] these are all sentimental images, according to Schweitzer, which pander to the most mediocre, low-class, bourgeois art. In this closing chapter of Part One, we'll see how Schweitzer's own proposal for solving the quest is leveraged on his savage critique of Renan and the "liberal *Lives of Jesus*." Against Schweitzer's charges of liberal dishonesty, however, I will argue that he misstates the hermeneutical challenges facing liberal theology and the "liberal *Lives*," and I will argue that Schweitzer's own proposed solution to the quest fails to live up to his own claim that *his* historical Jesus escapes the hermeneutical dilemma of finding oneself, and one's time, in one's study of the past.

The Motives of History

Early on in his first chapter of *The Quest of the Historical Jesus*, Schweitzer acknowledges, albeit vaguely, that the history of the quest has been inspired by different motives.

> The historical investigation of the life of Jesus did not take its rise from a purely historical interest; it turned to the Jesus of history as an ally in the struggle against the tyranny of dogma. Afterwards when it was freed from this *pathos* it sought to present the historic Jesus in a form intelligible to its time. Thus each successive epoch of theology found its own thoughts in Jesus; that was indeed the only way in which it could make him live.[3]

The passage deserves closer examination because it contains Schweitzer's thesis in a nutshell. Schweitzer's acknowledgment that the quest for the historical Jesus emerged in the midst of a wider cultural and theological crisis—that of the "tyranny of dogma"— appears as a lament over the loss of objectivity ("a purely historical interest") from the very beginning. As noted in earlier chapters, however, Schweitzer remains vague on the exact nature of that dogmatic tyranny, providing no real discussion of the broader historical and cultural context in which Deists, rationalists, and historians turned to the figure of a human and historical Jesus as a mode of cultural and theological resistance.

Because Schweitzer offers no deep interpretation of the political and religious battle over dogmatic tyranny, what he means by the phrase "Afterward when it [the 'historical investigation of Jesus'] was freed from this *pathos*" is also utterly unclear. Does the phrase mean: freed from the suffering endured by individual scholars at the hands of both church and society? Does "afterward" refer to the German Revolution of 1848, or the right to publish, which came to Germany in 1850? Or does it refer more widely to the end of the cultural dominance of churches as signaled in the United States by the legal separation of church and state in 1789 and in England by the affirmation of universal religious toleration in 1835? What Schweitzer means by "afterward" is crucial to his argument; there is clearly a divide in his mind between the heroic battle against "dogmatic tyranny" that initiated the quest and the "afterward" when, he argues dismissively, "it [the quest] sought to present the historic Jesus in a form intelligible to its time."

By "afterward," Schweitzer suggests, therefore, a clear point at which the "tyranny of dogma" had passed and a new cultural and theological worldview had opened in which history could again be done objectively and without the meddling of other interests. Yet, while much of his argument hinges on the need for a clear "afterward" in order to condemn the motives of the authors of the "liberal *Lives*" as vehemently as he does, Schweitzer fails to provide such a clear and compelling line of demarcation. "After" what?

Critiquing Schweitzer's Two Phases

While I agree with Schweitzer that there are two phases of the original quest prior to the turn to "thoroughgoing eschatology" at the end of the nineteenth and turn of the twentieth century,[4] I believe they are deeply interconnected rather than clearly distinct. The first phase, I have argued, was primarily about freeing civil discourse from the control of established ecclesiastical bodies. While Reimarus and Lessing offered theological critiques of Christian tradition, they did so in the name of freeing *public* discourse *from* the control of the established church. The political and cultural successes of the first phase, namely: the separation of church and state in the United States, the passage of universal religious suffrage in England in 1835, the Revolution of 1848 in Germany and the subsequent right of publication in 1850—combined with cultural moves in the direction of industrialization and democratization—opened a new space in which biblical scholars and theologians could *encourage* the church to interpret its traditions in the evolving language of a secular civil society.

The emergence of a second phase of historical Jesus studies—the "liberal *Lives of Jesus*" of the 1860s—coincides with the emergence of a liberal theology that sought to engage the church, as well as the newly emerging civil audience; think of Friedrich Schleiermacher's *Speeches on Religion to Its Cultured Despisers*. This newly emerging dual audience presented theologians and biblical scholars with a very difficult and delicate set of choices. The public and theological critiques of revealed Truth, namely, of those claims by which the established churches had claimed the transcendent authority to govern public discourse, as abusive—as tyrannous—led some theologians to wonder how and whether Christian faith could be interpreted in ways that would not justify the former abuses.

Some of those problematic Truths of revealed faith included the Trinity, the divinity of Christ, and the inspiration of Scripture, with miracles and especially the resurrection serving as proofs that the church possessed an authority transcending human reason.

Led by Friedrich Schleiermacher (1768–1834) and Albrecht Ritschl (1822–89), who had both been influenced by Kant and German Romanticism, theological liberals sought to interpret Christian traditions steeped in neoplatonism and Aristotelian philosophy into new philosophical and cultural discourses that focused on human consciousness and human experience. They attempted to synthesize Christian traditions within a newly emerging worldview, a goal Augustine and St. Thomas Aquinas had achieved previously. Precisely insofar as this theological liberalism took hold, one began to see what is called the "turn to the subject" in theology. That phrase, the "turn to the subject," refers to the point at which the disciplines of philosophy and theology began to realize that reality, as such, was in no way "given" transparently to human consciousness, but that human consciousness constructed our perceptions and understandings of reality. The effect of this philosophical shift was huge, even as it took time to settle in and take hold. For theology, this meant one could no longer pretend to see the world with "God's eyes," or pretend to know the "inner life of the Trinity." As Kant pointed out, contrary to the writings of Aquinas and the assumptions of Christian Platonists, one could not, by the use of theoretical reason alone, prove the existence of God, much less know the operations of the divine mind.

In the works of Schleiermacher, who is often referred to as the father of modern theology, one finds a new emphasis on the human person. According to Schleiermacher, when one speaks of the omnipotence of God, for example, one is speaking not with any objective knowledge of God. Instead, one is speaking about the believer's feeling of "absolute dependence." The shift in starting point is from God to human awareness and perception of the sacred. Whereas Christian tradition prior to the Enlightenment started "from above," namely, with a discussion of God and the Trinity, and then proceeded in deductive fashion to speak about creation and redemption, this new movement in theology began by speaking "from below," that is, from human experience, from consciousness, and from experiences of growth, as in the development of consciousness.

While it is frequently noted that theology moves inward in the liberal theology of the nineteenth century, it is much less frequently noted that this inward turn is in the service of a political, or cultural, vision. Far from being discordant with the quest for the historical Jesus, as Schweitzer implies, Schliermacher, Ritschl and others sought to carry out the underlying concerns of the first quest into the area of theology itself.

The problem, of course, is that while civil society now began, in the mid-nineteenth century, to free itself from the power of established churches, those churches continued to have real cultural and political power in those societies. Those ecclesiastical bodies, which retained real influence over the lives and faith of Christians, resisted quite profoundly the loss of that cultural influence. To put it more specifically, rather than adapt their doctrinal teaching to the newly emerging worldview opened up by science and democracy, many insisted more than ever on their affirmation of divine revelation and their possession of a truth beyond human reason.[5]

Given the continuing cultural influence of ecclesiastical institutions, not only in Germany, but throughout Western civilization, the existence of a clear "afterward" to the first phase of the quest — as claimed by Schweitzer — is not so easy to affirm. While civil society would begin to affirm a freedom to publish, the established churches often used their influence to reject the liberal scholarship they found to be heretical. The case of Renan is instructive.

Ernst Renan's book *The Life of Jesus* (1863) created a scandal in Catholic France somewhat similar to the scandal surrounding the publication of Strauss's 1835–36 edition of *The Life of Jesus Critically Examined*. The book became very quickly the most popular book in the history of France up to that time, going through eight editions in only the first three months of publication. The Catholic bishops of France reacted to the work predictably. They were, in Schweitzer's words, "leading the van" in condemning Renan for his naturalistic treatment of the miracles and for his heretical treatment of Jesus. Renan was forced out of his academic position until 1871. At least one of his critics, Amadée Nicolas, encouraged civil authorities, according to Schweitzer, to pursue "the maximum penalties authorised by the existing enactment against free-thought, . . . according to which five years imprisonment could be imposed for the crime of 'insulting or making ridiculous a religion recognized by the state.'"[6]

Clearly, Renan was caught between the newly emerging civil society on the one hand and the continuing power of the church on the other. There is no clear "afterward" — even into the 1860s and 1870s — as Schweitzer would have us believe. Yet, if one might think that Schweitzer would view Renan in the company of those heroes who resisted the "tyranny of dogma," one would be wrong. Schweitzer views Renan and the authors of the "liberal *Lives*" through a very different lens—through the lens of an "afterward" in which they seek to make Jesus fit into a "rational, bourgeois religion." "The works of Renan, Strauss [1864], Schenkel, Weizsäcker, and Keim are in essence only different ways of carrying out a single ground-plan. To read them one after another is to be simply appalled at the stereotyped uniformity of the world of thought in which they move."[7] Why did Schweitzer reach this judgment, and was it a correct one?

Schweitzer's Case

Schweitzer attacks Renan and the authors of the "liberal *Lives*" for being artists and popularizers rather than historians. Schweitzer accuses Renan, and the others, of "dishonesty" and "insincerity" because Renan, like Schleiermacher, turned to the Gospel of John as a historical resource. Within the period of the 1860s, historical scholarship argued convincingly that John was not a resource for reconstructing the historical Jesus. In addition, that same scholarship was becoming more convinced that among the synoptic Gospels, Mark was emerging as the earliest source. What aggravated Schweitzer to no end was not only that Renan, like Schleiermacher, turned to John as a historical resource but also that the authors of the *Lives* of the 1860s used the new research on Mark and Matthew to focus not on Jesus' apocalyptic eschatology, but on Jesus' consciousness, his psychological development, and his social ethic of love. In addition, many of these same liberal scholars kept referring to the Gospel for, what Schweitzer calls, its "spiritualizing" value, its sense of intimacy and higher wisdom. Going for the jugular against these authors of the *Lives*, Schweitzer dismisses them as historians by praising them as literary stylists who use "novelistic devices" to "charm" their audiences.

While one can understand Schweitzer's consternation on this point, one also wishes that he could understand, and have some sympathy for, the priority that liberal theologians were giving to the focus on human consciousness. These liberal theologians were trying to adapt a supernatural, divine-man Christology—a supernaturalism and a Christology that had justified the church's control of public discourse—into a discourse appropriate to a worldview that Schweitzer had praised earlier scholars for fighting for! If these liberal theologies failed to give priority to the latest research on the Gospel of John, it does not necessarily mean they were either dishonest or insincere.

Writing about the work of liberal theology in transposing the supernaturalism of miracles into the language of empiricism, Matthew Arnold wrote in *Literature and Dogma* (1873), that "to pass from a Christianity relying on its miracles to a Christianity relying on its natural truth is a great change. It can only be brought about by those whose attachment to Christianity is such that, they cannot part with it, and yet cannot but deal with it *sincerely*"[8] (emphasis added). In response to Schweitzer's accusation of insincerity, one could well ask: Might not Renan be very sincere about offering to Catholic France an alternative to a supernaturalistic understanding of Jesus? And might not that concern to speak to the Catholics of France have influenced Renan to focus on the Gospel of John, so deeply privileged by the supernatural tradition? Might there not be sincerity in moving from a supernaturalistic conception of Jesus to a historical one, especially if that historical one suggests ethical and political implications about the equality of persons, including the masses, before God? Schweitzer's charge of insincerity is too easy. What of his charge of popularizing?

From the very beginning of his critique of Renan's *Life of Jesus*, and continuing throughout his discussion of the "liberal *Lives of Jesus*," Schweitzer is alarmed by the popularity of these works. Late in his own book, he writes:

> For the last ten years modern historical theology has more and more adapted itself to the needs of the man in the street. More and more, even in the best class of works, it makes use of attractive head-lines as a means of presenting its results in a lively form to the masses.[9]

Running throughout Schweitzer's critique of the 1860s—and his comment would include the seventies and eighties into the nineties!—is a suspicion of "the masses," a suspicion that may go, in part, to the German Revolution of 1848 and to the writings of Marx and Engels, although there is no mention of them in his book.

By the 1850s and 1860s one sees throughout Europe, in both literature and art, a real concern for ordinary people and for peasants. Charles Dickens, for example, published *David Copperfield* in 1850 and *A Tale of Two Cities* in 1859, to name only two of many significant works. Yet, after his death Dickens was derided by some in Britain as a mere popular writer, the "incarnation of Cockneydom," as one novelist who found his works "intellectually lacking" put it. And in France, the painter Jean-François Millet (1814–75) of the Barbizon school, which had its origins in the Revolutions of 1848 and emphasized realism, produced "The Gleaners" in 1857, with its allusions to the Book of Ruth, and "The Angelus" in the years 1857–59. Millet's work was considered dangerous in some quarters. Charged with being a "socialist," Millet wrote in a letter in 1851 that "at the risk of appearing even more socialist . . . it is the human, the frankly human side which moves me most."[10]

Denouncing Renan as an artist, Schweitzer compares him to a "decorative painter" and to poetic and painterly writers such as "Lamartine or Pierre Loti." But Renan's attention to the peasant class in his *Life of Jesus* suggests his indebtedness to more socially engaged painters like Millet. And rather than compare Renan to Loti or Lamartine, why not connect him with the French historian Jules Michelet (1798–1874), who was deeply influenced by the French Revolution of 1830, saw history as a continuing struggle for freedom, and in the 1840s turned away from Christianity toward an almost messianic affirmation of democratic progress? Could it be that in choosing Lamartine and Loti as comparative figures, Schweitzer was already seeking to diminish Renan's stature? Here again, Schweitzer's failure to provide a broader interpretation of the historic questions emerging in public life and civil society raises questions about the adequacy of his more narrow historical reading.

While one might praise Schweitzer's hermeneutic of suspicion for seeing how liberal theology was collapsing into rationalistic, bourgeois culture, one might also see Schweitzer's suspicions as both reductionistic and self-serving. Reductionistic for failing to account for the complexity of the new situation of the church in the midst of—but no longer governing—civil society; self-serving for generating a kind of despair over modern culture that opens too easily onto his own eschatological solution. Thus, while Schweitzer sees only decline and insincerity in moving from the first phase to the second, I believe that liberal theology was much more attuned to the "historic" question of whether the established churches should govern civil society. Deism and the initial critiques of historical Jesus scholarship had participated in this historic project, and liberal theology sought to extend the force of that question to the church's own self-understanding, namely, in its theology. The proposals of liberal theology sought to move Christian theology from an emphasis on those doctrines by which the church had sought to secure its power over civil society, to an emphasis that would enable the church to be both intelligible and credible within the newly emerging society.

Schweitzer's Proposal

In addition to the earlier discussion about the two phases of the quest and the motives that shaped it, Schweitzer, later in the book, argues that there have been three major turning points in the history of the quest. He describes those points using the language of "either/or alternatives," which he, in turn, associated with three specific decades of historical critical research—the 1830s, the 1860s, and the 1890s. Writing of Johannes Weiss's important 1892 work on apocalyptic, "The Preaching of Jesus concerning the Kingdom of God," Schweitzer says:

> He [Weiss] lays down the third great alternative which the study of Jesus had to meet. The first was laid down by Strauss: *either* purely historical *or* purely supernatural. The second had been worked out by the Tübingen school and Holtzmann: *either* Synoptic or Johannine. Now came the third: *either* eschatological *or* non-eschatological![11]

The first two of these three either/or alternatives correspond to the first two moments described in Schweitzer's opening chapter and discussed above, while the third either/or alternative is mentioned only later, as Schweitzer moves toward his own position. Thus, Schweitzer's statement that the initial phase of the quest was undertaken in the struggle against the tyranny of dogma coincides with the first either/or—"*either* purely historical *or* purely supernatural." Schweitzer credits Strauss in the 1830s with laying down the first alternative. Accordingly, Schweitzer's statement that "afterwards," the quest sought to make Jesus "intelligible to its time" corresponds to the 1860s period of the "liberal *Lives of Jesus*," and he credits Holtzmann with laying down the alternative of "*either* the Synoptics *or* the Johannine." In that opening chapter, Schweitzer did not mention a third set of interests or motives that would shape what would become the third alternative, perhaps because he thought the third—eschatological—alternative escaped the problems of motivating interest and became "pure" history.

In closing his criticism of the "liberal *Lives of Jesus*," Schweitzer writes that "the striking thing about these liberal Lives of Jesus was that they unconsciously prepared the way for a deeper historical view which could not have been reached apart from them."[12] That somewhat left-handed compliment is echoed in earlier sections in which Schweitzer praises Strauss for uncovering the essential place of *eschatology* in biblical theology. In light of Weiss's work, Schweitzer presses Strauss's insight about the role of eschatology to a deeper, more foundationalist understanding. "The substratum of historical fact in the life of Jesus is much more extensive than Strauss is prepared to admit. Sometimes he fails to see the foundations, because he proceeds like an explorer who, in working on the ruins of an Assyrian city, should cover up the most valuable evidence with the rubbish thrown off from another portion of the excavations."[13]

Schweitzer goes on to argue that the foundation, the historical substratum, is found in the mind of Jesus himself. Schweitzer criticizes William Wrede (1859–1906), who characterized Mark's Gospel as belonging to the "history of dogma," for not going far enough, that is to say, beyond Mark's theology of the messianic secret, to speak of Jesus himself. "It is quite inexplicable that the eschatological school, with its clear perception of the eschatological element in the preaching of the Kingdom of God, did not also hit upon the thought of the 'dogmatic history'—history as moulded by theological beliefs—which breaks in upon the natural course of history and abrogates it."[14] In other words, eschatology is at the heart of Jesus' identity and self-understanding.

Schweitzer invokes the trope of the Romantic genius in describing the "volcanic force" of Jesus' "incalculable personality," and he claims that in Jesus' decision to go to Jerusalem, "His life at this period was dominated by a 'dogmatic idea' which rendered Him indifferent to all else . . . even to the happy and successful work as a teacher which was opening before Him." Schweitzer's claim to know what grasped the mind of Jesus extends to Jesus' own awareness of predestination, which "goes along with the eschatology."[15] Schweitzer called this model, "thoroughgoing eschatology," because it went further than Weiss's argument about Jesus' preaching of the kingdom of God and it went beyond Wrede's analysis of the messianic secret in Mark.

Schweitzer finds the arguments of the eschatological school convincing in no small part because they are so different from the arguments of liberal theology. What finally demonstrates the superiority of thoroughgoing eschatology over more liberal, non-eschatological interpretations, says Schweitzer, is that "eschatology makes it impossible to attribute modern ideas to Jesus."[16] Schweitzer, in effect, claims that his eschatological understanding of Jesus is superior to that of liberals because it does not attempt to persuade the contemporary masses of bourgeois citizens. He continues:

> Before the advent of eschatology critical theology, was, in the last resort, without a principle of discrimination, since it possessed no reagent capable of infallibly separating out modern ideas on the one hand and genuinely ancient New Testament ideas on the other. The application of the criteria has now begun. What will be the issue the future alone can show.[17]

Schweitzer views eschatology as a principle of dissimilarity—applied not within the field of sayings attributed to Jesus, as would later develop in New Testament criticism, but as a principle that "reveals" the more authentic portrait of Jesus by virtue of being dissimilar from the modern, psychologizing, and socially pandering portraits of the liberals. Schweitzer, for example, views Matt 10:23, the prediction of the Parousia of the Son of Man, as "historical as a whole and down to the smallest detail precisely because, according to the view of modern theology it must be judged unhistorical."[18] That is an odd sort of historical proof. Even assuming Markan priority, the fact that an idea is not a modern one does not prove that it belongs authentically to Jesus.

Schweitzer's eschatological solution not only negates the value of modern historiography when approaching Jesus, it also reaches into, and affirms the "eternal" and the mystical in Jesus' words.

> But in reality that which is *eternal* in the words of Jesus is due to the very fact that they are based on an eschatological worldview, and contain the expression of a mind for which the contemporary world with its historical and social circumstances no longer had any existence.[19] (emphasis added)

He continues:

> They [Jesus' words] are appropriate, therefore, to any world, for in every world they raise the man who dares to meet their challenge, and does not turn and twist them into meaninglessness, above his world and his time, making him inwardly free, so that he is fitted to be, in his own world and his own time, a simple channel of the power of Jesus.[20]

With these words, Schweitzer leads the eschatological retreat of faith from public life.

Having criticized liberal theologians for their artistry and complicity in the development of a modern, bourgeois ideology, Schweitzer, knowingly or not, stakes out the contours of an alternative ideology: faith in an apocalyptic, eschatological Jesus as a rejection of modernity and liberal theology. As we will see in Part II, neo-orthodox theology embraces the apocalyptic, eschatological Jesus precisely because it provides a means of escape from liberal theology's public commitment to human consciousness.

Conclusion

If eschatology is incompatible with modern historical assumptions, as Schweitzer claims, nevertheless it remains compatible with the "end of the century," or *fin de siècle* mindset of *his* time. Schweitzer's emphasis upon the "strangeness" of his eschatological Jesus, his heightened sense of mystical encounter, his higher "tragic" art in contrast to the bourgeois appeals of the "novelistic" historians, and his claim that eschatology has put an end to modern historicizing — all of these elements are perfectly compatible with the world-weariness of other *fin de siècle* authors, articulating their own principles of "discrimination."

Schweitzer's "eschatology" is not as other-worldly, therefore, as he would like his readers to think. His eschatological "other-worldliness" makes perfect sense in a Western cultural environment in which Christian ecclesiastical institutions were losing their power over civil society under the aegis of "separating" the realm and power of the church from the legislative, executive, and judicial powers of the state. With Schweitzer, eschatology becomes the expression of the desire for a religious way out of modernity every bit as much as it is, allegedly, a way into the mind and culture of the historical Jesus.

While many theologians continue to view Schweitzer as the great deconstructor of the quest for the historical Jesus, he was, in fact, at once more certain than Strauss of what could be known about Jesus objectively, and also more certain of the actual content of Jesus' God-consciousness than Schleiermacher. In the end, Schweitzer doesn't believe that the quest for the historical Jesus was a mistake; the liberal scholars, while mistaken, paved the way for the definitive solution of the issue, namely, his own. Unfortunately, Schweitzer's eschatological avoidance of the political and cultural context of historical Jesus research is symptomatic of his eschatological avoidance of modernity at large, from which he ultimately retreats into the mission field. While there are many merits in his argument about the quest for the historical Jesus, the fact that his work was virtually blind to the political, economic, and social pressures surrounding the scholarship of the quest for Jesus argues powerfully for the need to rethink the adequacy of Schweitzer's book as a definitive statement of the first quest.

Part Two

The New Quest

CHAPTER

7

The Christian Retreat
from Public Life

Martin Kähler's *The So-Called Historical Jesus and the Historic Biblical Christ* appeared in German in 1892.[1] The work is taken by many to be the decisive refutation of the quest for the historical Jesus, but I disagree. Kähler's book represents not the end of the first quest, but the beginning of the second.

If one sees the first quest for the historical Jesus as part of a broader debate about the governance of civil society and public discourse, one cannot help but notice the dramatic shift that occurs in the thought of figures like Albert Schweitzer, Martin Kähler (1835–1912), and Karl Barth (1886–1968) at the end of the nineteenth and early decades of the twentieth century. In sharp contrast to the prevailing assumption that Christian authorities should govern the public discourse in the seventeenth and eighteenth centuries, many religious leaders now feared that the rationalism, scientific methods, and democratizing tendencies of the emerging modern period would overtake the church completely. Kähler and Barth go beyond Schweitzer's lament over the decline of the modern period; they attempt to construct, in Kähler's words, a *sturmfreis Gebiet*, an impregnable defense against what they see as an encroaching and aggressive secular culture. In effect, they emphasize the radical separateness of the church (that is to say, the "authentic" church) from the world, and create, rhetorically at least, a new, albeit smaller Christendom—a separate world of faith. In this chapter, I examine the moves by which Kähler and Barth lay the groundwork for this smaller Christendom as well as two important voices, those of the Lutheran Paul Tillich and the Roman Catholic Karl Rahner, who argue for a closer relationship between faith and reason, church and world.

Accusing secular society of seeking to control public space at the close of the nineteenth century, Kähler's late nineteenth-century work virtually acknowledges that the established churches had lost the public debate about the church's divine right to censor and silence public discourse. Kähler's *sturmfreis Gebiet* seeks to salvage the church's internal authority over the faithful not only by keeping "secular" norms and analyses of Scripture and doctrine at bay but also by insisting that an always already known *faith* was the norm of all church discourse. In this way, even if the church could not govern public life it would remain—thanks to the number of Christians in European and American society—a powerful cultural voice within those societies.

To be sure, Kähler does not go to the extremes to which Vatican I (1871) had gone, with its promulgation of papal infallibility, nor to the extremes that emergent Protestant fundamentalism at the turn of the twentieth century had gone with its claims that the biblical text was "literally" true in all its particulars. Nonetheless, those dogmatic and literalistic responses helped shape the contours of a Protestant neo-orthodoxy turning towards faith with no primary foothold whatsoever in human reason. Along with those more conservative movements, Kähler, and Karl Barth, who incorporated Kähler's approach, seeks to minimize and control the impact of modern biblical scholarship generally, and historical Jesus scholarship in particular, on the life and practice of Christian communities. In effect, Kähler and Barth seek to reject liberal theology and reshape the disciplines of both Christian teaching and Christian learning/discipleship in ways commensurate with the church's narrowed range of governance, namely, to the arena of the church itself.

By insisting that the church was under attack from the methodologies of modern science, modern philosophy, and modern historiography, Kähler and Barth justify a defensive posture against any secular learning, including biblical scholarship that challenges the traditional truth claims of Christian faith, arguing that mere human reason could not establish on its own any genuine share in faith, which is itself a divine gift. Historical Jesus discourse, which had critiqued the theology by which established churches defended their right to govern the whole of civil society, is now accused by Kähler of being a new papacy of scholars, in league with modernity's attack on Christian faith. It seems, in his view, that if the former established churches had been in league with the monarchies, so now the newer "liberal" theologies were in league with the democrats and socialists. Kähler seems intent on collapsing both models as entwined with politics, but he seems either unable or unwilling to grasp the difference between an established church's effort to control public discourse and liberal theology's attempt to support a resistance movement opposed to the power of those religious establishments.

It is Kähler and Barth's defensive strategy—one designed to keep Christian faith isolated from what they took to be the acids of modern reason and historical scholarship—that actually lays the basis for the genuinely historic question at the base of the New Quest for the historical Jesus in the 1950s, '60s, and '70s: Is it possible for Christian theology, and Christian churches, to actually address the realities of the human condition in all its diversity and amidst vast processes of cultural change? Put another way, the New Quest will help ask the broader historic question: Can Christian theology actually listen to the voices of human experience, and, if so, to whose voices? In this second quest, while biblical scholars and theologians would not challenge the traditions of the faith—after all, having turned away from public discourse, this New Quest will be an entirely internal debate—they will question and challenge the theological assumptions behind Kähler and Barth's views. Those defending the New Quest will encourage their churches to affirm the importance not only of Jesus' humanity but also of human reason's ability to know something of the core of Jesus' preaching—and these theologians will see this as a vital issue of the legitimacy of Christian theology. Attention to the person of Jesus of Nazareth and his message of the *basileia tou theou*—or the kingdom of God—will, in turn, also call on churches to attend more carefully to the lived experiences of the human community.

Faith Turns Inward—Kähler's Wall of Separation

In his essay, "Martin Kähler on the Historic Biblical Christ," Carl Braaten claims that in attacking the "Life-of-Jesus movement," Kähler recommended a *sturmfreis Gebiet*, an "invulnerable area" where, Braaten writes, "Christ becomes present for believers without the support of objective authorities or the midwifery of historical scholarship."[2] Kähler sought, in Braaten's words, to defend the Christian faith from "any other source outside the preaching from faith unto faith."[3] According to Braaten, Kähler

> frequently referred to the dogmatician as the defense attorney for the simple Christian. One of the tasks of the dogmatician is to preserve the laity from the papacy of scholarship and from the pontification of historical science. . . . His [Kähler's] apologetic concern . . . is

directed more to the threatened faith of the Christian man wholly within the church than to the intellectual doubter on the boundary or outside the church.[4]

We have seen this argument in earlier chapters—the idea that public discourse critical of doctrine and Scripture "threatened" the faith of the simple. We have also seen how that argument was tied to suspicions of political disloyalty and subversion as well. By using such phrases as the "papacy of scholarship" Kähler sought to persuade his readers that the world had been turned upside down by a liberal scholarship that now threatened to silence the church.

Like German Restorationists before him, Kähler linked the instability of this new upside-down religious world to political instability. In an illuminating passage, Kähler compares the work of these "so-called" biblical historians to the English historian Thomas Babington Macaulay, whose popular masterpiece on English history, *History of England from the Accession of James II,* was dismissed by loyalists to the Crown as an inaccurate and biased "Whig" invention. (Locke, of course, was most intimately associated with Whig political theory.)

> There is no more effective method for securing the gradual triumph of a political party than to write a history of one's country like that of Macaulay. Stripped of its historical dress, the bare thesis of the "historian" would arouse too many suspicions. Disguised as history, the historian's theory passes imperceptibly into our thought and convictions as an authentic piece of reality, as a law emanating therefrom. . . . The same is true of dogmatics. Today everyone is on his guard when a dogma is frankly presented as such. But when Christology appears in the form of a "Life of Jesus," there are not many who will perceive the stage manager behind the scenes, manipulating according to his dogmatic script, the fascinating spectacle of a colorful biography.[5]

Kähler uses political discourse as an analogy for what is now an intra-church debate, accusing liberal scholarship of "manipulating" and undermining Christian faith. But while Kähler invokes a political metaphor, he cannot bring himself to admit what the real public concerns of the earlier historical Jesus movement had been about. Why not? Because by Kähler's time the widespread support of universal religious toleration, if not the separation of church and state, had become largely settled issues. Church establishments—

where they existed—had much weaker, if any, direct public authority. Thus, specific church claims to possess a divine revelation that transcended human reason, had been widely rejected as the basis of civil governance. Kähler knows this, and he knows that the "Lives of Jesus" from the 1860s were attempts to defend and support Christian faith within a new public reality that did not privilege Christian revelation. But instead of acknowledging that point, he chooses to view the "Lives of Jesus" as intentionally manipulative of the simple faith "of the many" who do not perceive the deception of the "stage manager."

Small wonder, then, that at precisely this moment in his argument Kähler announces that it is the theologian, himself in this case, who is the hero of this theo-political drama.

> Yet no one can detect the hidden dogmatician so well as a person who is himself a dogmatician, whose job it is to pursue consciously and intentionally the implications of basic ideas in all their specific nuances. Therefore, the dogmatician has the right to set up a warning sign.[6]

In this model of the theologian as neutral referee of intra-church discourse, Kähler tacitly acknowledges that the church—not the society at large—is now the smaller arena within which theological discourse is to be evaluated. And within the church itself, insists Kähler, arguments grounded in secular assumptions, such as historical analysis, have no place and no "authority." While historical Jesus scholarship is linked dismissively to the subversive activity of social revolutionaries, and to the work of German historians such as Karl von Rotteck (1775–1840) who had argued persistently for freedom of the press, Kähler equates his "biblical Christ" with the simple purity of Christian faith.

To support his argument, Kähler drew, in part, on the work of Danish Lutheran theologian Søren Kierkegaard (1813–55), who had argued vehemently that the "probability" of scientific reason and the passionate risk of Christian faith were completely separate. Writing in his book, *Concluding Unscientific Postscript* (1846), Kierkegaard dismissed any attempt to "prove" or ground Christian faith in reason. Such attempts, thought Kierkegaard, would sap the vitality, the "passion," from faith. In fact, he argued, faith "would have in the new certainty its most dangerous enemy. For if passion is eliminated, faith no longer exists. . . . For whose sake is it that the proof is sought? Faith does not need it; aye, it must even regard

While Kierkegaard was largely underappreciated during his lifetime, he became recognized, once rediscovered, as one of the founders of existentialism, a philosophical/theological movement skeptical of cultural institutions and sharply critical of the herd mentality so constantly found in public and political life. In contrast to that herd mentality, existentialists claimed that authenticity could not be conferred by group status, and that each individual had to venture one's own freedom, through decision, in order to become an authentically free person.

the proof as its enemy."[7] Famous for the term "leap of faith," by which he meant not to denigrate reason but to point out the vast difference between the two domains, Kierkegaard underscored the impossibility of moving from rational inquiry to the passion of authentic faith.

One of the key examples that Kierkegaard uses to demonstrate *how little* genuine faith needs the probable logic of historical reason is his dismissal of historical Jesus research. "If the contemporary generation (i.e., Jesus' followers) had left nothing behind except the words: 'We have believed that in such and such a year God showed himself in the puny form of a servant, taught and lived among us, and then died'—that would be more than enough."[8] One could know every detail of the life of Jesus, argued Kierkegaard, and still not have faith.[9] Possessing a rational argument, even one grounded in the probabilities of historical evidence, could not lead one to faith. Authentic faith—not the kind that came with infant baptism in an established religion—confronted one with, in Kierkegaard's terms, an "Either/Or" situation, requiring a radical, existential *decision* on behalf of faith.

It would be Kähler who would use Kierkegaard's "Either/Or" argument for rejecting historical Jesus scholarship. Kähler's framing of that question, and his response to it, has provided the framework for the theological rejection of historical scholarship to this day.

Kähler's argument

To get at the "full reality" of a historical figure, says Kähler, one needs to distinguish between *Historie* (and its adjectival form *historisch*), which attempts to make sense of factual appearances in an objective manner, and *Geschichte*, which attempts to grasp the deeper "meaning" of the event or person being studied. While modern historians engage in *Historie* as they seek the reality of Jesus behind the gospel narratives, which Kähler has argued cannot be done because of the lack of genuine historical resources, the theologian—and the Christian believer—is interested in *Geschichte*, seeking the "full reality" of Jesus that addresses our "inner perception" while also exerting a "permanent influence" upon history.[10]

To be sure, says Kähler, the "appearance" of Jesus in human history was a "historical" event. Yet faith, according to Kähler, is not concerned with the facticity of the historical, but with the "historic" (*geschichtlich*) internalized impact of a person on subsequent history.

> What is a truly "historic figure," that is, a person who has been influential in molding posterity, as measured by his contribution to history? Is it not the person who originates and bequeaths a permanent influence? He is one of those very dynamic individuals who intervene in the course of events. What they are in themselves produces effects, and through these effects their influence persists. . . . Thus, from a purely historical point of view the truly historic element in any great figure is the discernible personal influence which he exercises upon later generations.[11]

Kähler's insistence that the power of the "historic figure" originates *in the person*—that is to say from within themselves—is important for his later Christological claim that *"Christ himself is the originator of the biblical picture of the Christ"* (emphasis Kähler's). The gospel writers, says Kähler, did not invent their portraits of Christ; rather, the power of Christ's person engraved itself on their lives. Thus, the Scriptures are trustworthy because they are the "testimonies" of those eyewitnesses imprinted and sealed by the power of Christ's person.

> Hence, we may conclude that in his unique and powerful personality and by his incomparable deeds and life (including his resurrection appearances) this Man has engraved his image on the mind and memory of his followers with such sharp and deeply etched features that it could be neither obliterated nor distorted.[12]

If one asks, what, according to Kähler, was the impact, the "decisive influence" of Jesus upon subsequent history? His answer is: Faith.

> According to the Bible and church history it [the impact or influence of Jesus] consisted in nothing else but the faith of his disciples, their conviction that in Jesus they had found the conqueror of guilt, sin,

temptation, and death. From this one influence all others emanate; it is the criterion by which all the others stand or fall. This conviction of the disciples is summed up in the single affirmation, "Christ is Lord."[13]

Historical analysis in the scientific mode, argues Kähler in a manner distinctly like Kierkegaard, is not the same as the historic impact of Jesus' person and work. Historical analysis cannot get one to faith, says Kähler, and faith is the only reason one would be interested in Jesus in the first place.

> This brings us to the crux of the matter: *Why* do we seek to know the figure of Jesus? I think rather it is because we believe him when he says, "He who has seen me has seen the Father" (John 14:9), because we see in him the revelation of the invisible God. Now if the Word became flesh in Jesus, which is the revelation, the flesh or the Word? Which is the more important for us, that wherein Jesus is like us, or that wherein he was and is totally different from us? Is it not the latter, namely, that which he offers us, not from our own hearts, but from the heart of the living God?[14]

By arguing that the witness of the biblical Christ originated with Christ, who is himself from the heart of God, outside of all history, Kähler implies that the biblical testimony about Jesus is free from the kinds of "party" bias to which the historical Jesus scholars have all fallen prey. Thus, the only mode of inquiry into the life Jesus that Kähler considers authentic is one that begins and ends in faith, which is quite apart from questions that could be answered by historical methods. Even his own analogy to the power of historic individuals must be surpassed when describing the reality of Christ.

> For me the picture which has the effect of "overpowering" us is precisely that of the Christ grasped by faith, the picture of Christ preached from and in faith, and therefore most emphatically not the picture of an extraordinary human being. No, the picture of Christ which has such an effect is that which bears within itself a dogma, a confession of faith. . . . That is to say, this kind of picture presents the figure of the *Lord*, the Savior of the world, the Redeemer from sin and guilt, God revealed. Not only in its content but in so many words, this picture of the Christ confronts each person with the Either/Or: cornerstone or rock of offense (1 Pet 2:6–7).[15]

By invoking Søren Kierkegaard's Either/Or categories, Kähler digs the moat around his invulnerable space of ecclesial life and practice. Facing an emerging civil society's increasing insistence on openness to public debate, Kähler's response is to withdraw the church from such discourse to a place where religious authority is protected from the questions of historical criticism.

Late in the book, Kähler comes close to acknowledging the wider impulses of historical Jesus research. "Why is it then that scholars repeatedly point out the errors in the traditional text of the Bible? . . . Why do they spend time proving that historical statements in the books do not correspond with the conditions of the time to which the tradition ascribes their origin? They do so chiefly, do they not, to secure the right and freedom of literary criticism."[16] Unfortunately, Kähler provides no follow-up discussion about which authorities are responsible for blocking the freedom of publication. Kähler doesn't pursue the question of "rights" because he doesn't see such public freedom as vital to the spiritual life of persons or communities. Quite the opposite, Kähler recognizes only the threat of such questions to the truth claims of Christian tradition. It never occurs to him to ask whether freedom of publication is not simply a "right" for an individual but a profound need for civil society—in fact, the lifeblood of a genuinely public civil society.

Kähler's solution of an impregnable boundary between faith and civil society sounds somewhat ironically Jeffersonian, returning the insult of the separation of church and state with his theological insistence that historical criticism cannot erode the truths of biblical faith. It is difficult to miss the whiff of resentment against the modern world in Kähler's argument. Karl Barth's neo-orthodoxy would take this separation even farther, insisting not only that neither human knowledge nor experience could in any way prepare a person for faith, but also that the God of Christian faith was in no way immanent to ordinary human experience, but instead radically and Wholly Other.

A Higher Wall of Separation

With the advent of World War I (1914–18), Swiss Reformed theologian Karl Barth who had studied with liberal figures such as Adolf von Harnack decided that liberal theology's affirmation of human reason and European culture had blinded its capacity to speak an authentically challenging Word of God to the world. Liberal theology's God, he argued, was too immanent, too close to human experience, and thus susceptible to being replaced by human experience.

It was, to invoke the language of the great reformer John Calvin (1509–64), idolatry.

If the War provided a *krisis* of faith for Barth's own theological commitments, he used the word *krisis* symbolically to call for a bold, new movement in theology, one that rejected modern liberalism's focus on the achievements of human reason in favor of what he called "dialectical" theology, and what others would call "neo-orthodoxy." In effect, Barth used World War I as a dramatic proof of the arrogance and fallenness of human reason. This insight led him not only to insist on the radical transcendence of God — God as *totaliter aliter*, or "Wholly Other," with its emphasis on the distinctiveness and power of God's Revelation — but also on the theology of original sin.

Barth grasped that the use of reason in public life in the seventeenth, eighteenth, and nineteenth centuries — a reason affirmed by early historical Jesus scholarship — to challenge the established churches' claims to control public discourse, had led to a new situation. But if the claim of divine revelation could no longer function as a warrant to govern and control the discourse of public life, it remained a powerful warrant in the "public" life *of the church*, which remained — for that time at least — the vast majority of Europe's and America's citizenry. What Barth knew was that within the arena of the church itself, the historic teachings of supernatural revelation and original sin were resources that one could use to reject not only

Augustine on the Fall of Reason

Implicit in Barth's attack on the arrogance of modern reason is Augustine's fifth-century rejection of Pelagius (354–420/440 CE), in which Augustine (354–430 CE) argued against Pelagius and his followers that humanity, once fallen through the sin of Adam, could do nothing by itself to return to God. Pelagius argued that Adam's sin had affected only Adam, and that it was unjust to ascribe Adam's sin to all of humanity. Certainly, argued Pelagius, one must agree that on the basis of the gift of human reason (the rational soul) and the gift of the Jewish Law (the commandments) one could, in principle, lead a life without sin. But Augustine denied this. He knew that to agree with Pelagius would allow one to argue that one did not need Christ for one's salvation, and, therefore, that one did not need to belong to the church, a church which had just recently been declared, in 387, the official religion of the Roman Empire. Augustine's argument carried the day, and the views of Pelagius were condemned at the Council of Carthage in 418.

modern reason but also liberal theology. The "bomb" that Barth "threw into the playground of the theologians" was, in effect, the charge of heresy against anyone who argued that human reason, unaided by grace, could lead one to authentic faith.[17] In *The Epistle to the Romans* Barth brilliantly trumpeted the return to revelation as a dramatic return to Truth over against the illusions and falsehoods of modernity. While acknowledging the new reality of the church's reduced sphere of authority, Barth's soaring rhetoric does not so much acquiesce to the new situation as boldly proclaim it as the dawning of righteousness in the midst of a fallen world.

> Men have *imprisoned* and encased the *truth*—the righteousness of God; they have trimmed it to their own measure, and thereby robbed it both of its earnestness and of its significance. They have made it ordinary, harmless, and useless; and thereby transformed it into untruth. . . . If mankind be itself God, the appearance of the idol is then inevitable. And wherever the idol is honored, it is inevitable that men, feeling themselves to be the true God, should also feel that they have themselves fashioned the idol. . . . Against such rebellion there can be revealed only the wrath of God.[18] (Barth's emphasis)

Barth's singular emphasis on the utter incomprehensibility of God and thus, on revelation, raised serious questions even for those who largely agreed with him: Even if one wanted to affirm the decisive significance of revelation for the Christian, didn't one need to affirm some capacity within human nature itself to receive such a Wholly Other revelation? Barth's famous 1934 debate with Emil Brunner wrestled with this very question. Arguing that insofar as human beings were created "in the image of God," and that Christian tradition had long defined this "Imago Dei" in terms of the rational soul, Brunner claimed that theology must affirm at the very least the capacity for human beings to "hear" the Word of God. Without such a capacity, he argued, how would one begin to know that one had been addressed by God? Barth's famous reply was "Nein." There was no such capacity for knowledge of God in human nature. Apart from grace one could not know that God—the true God—existed. There could be no preparation—either through philosophy or historical criticism—for the receipt of this grace which utterly transforms and redirects the life of the person. In his reply, Barth's radical separation between the realms of "nature" and "grace" draws on John Calvin's view that Adam's sin left humanity in a state of "total depravity," with no possible path of return, save by Christ and the gift of justifying grace.

If human knowledge could in no way prepare the human person for faith, then surely, one might think, Barth would turn to institutional Christianity as a reliable refuge from the false gods of the world. No, not categorically. Barth, following Kierkegaard, knew that the church was sinful as well as grounded in grace. In *The Epistle to the Romans*, Barth argues for the inevitable gap between the church as founded in the Word of God and the limitations of the humanity that participates in it.

> The Church is the fellowship of MEN who proclaim the Word of God and hear it. It follows from this situation that, when confronted by the adequacy of the Word of God, human lips and ears must display their inadequacy; that, though men are bound to receive and proclaim the Truth as it is with God, as soon as they do receive it and do proclaim it it ceases to be the Truth; that however true the Theme of the Church may be, as the theme of the Church it is untrue. This is at once the miracle and the tribulation of the Church, for the Church is condemned by that which establishes it, and is broken in pieces upon its foundations.[19]

Barth then discusses the nature of the church as seen in two differing lights—one, the light of human reason, the other the light of faith. He calls the first the "Church of Esau," and the second the "Church of Jacob."

> And so by its Theme the Church is divided into the Church of Esau—where no miracle occurs, and where, consequently, men are exposed as liars, precisely when they hear and speak about God; and the Church of Jacob—where miracle is, and where, consequently, the Truth appears above the deceit of men. The two Churches do not, of course, stand over against one another as two things. The Church of Esau alone is observable, knowable and possible. It may be seen at Jerusalem, or Rome, or Wittenburg, or Geneva. The past and the future can be comprehended without exception under its name. The Church of Esau is the realm where failure and corruption may be found, the place where schisms and reformations occur. But the Church of Jacob is capable of no less precise definition. It is the unobservable, unknowable, and impossible Church, capable neither of expansion nor of contraction; it has neither place nor name in history; men neither communicate with it nor are excommunicated from it. It is simply the free Grace of God, His Calling and His Election; it is Beginning and End. Our speech is of the Church of Esau, for we can

speak of none other. But we cannot speak of it without recollecting that its theme is the Church of Jacob.[20]

Inevitably, argues Barth, the institutional life of the church is enmeshed in the limited structures of human perception and human reason. Thus, the true church is the invisible church—the gift, the grace, of revelation affirmed and lived out courageously in faith.

It is virtually impossible to see Barth's arguments as anything other than a radical erasure of attempts by Christian theologians to interpret Christian faith within the world-view of modernity, and, thus, as a radical rethinking of the ground rules of Christian theology and discourse.

> The Gospel of Christ is a shattering disturbance, an assault which brings everything into question. For this reason, nothing is so meaningless as the attempt to construct a religion out of the Gospel, and to set it as one human possibility in the midst of others. Since Schleiermacher, this attempt has been undertaken more consciously than ever before in Protestant theology—and it is the betrayal of Christ. The man under grace is engaged unconditionally in a conflict. This conflict is a war of life and death, a war in which there can be no armistice, no agreement, and no peace.[21]

In this passage, written during World War I and seemingly inspired by it, Barth draws on the eschatological language of Schweitzer, Kähler and others to paint a vast battle between authentic faith, which comes as a "shattering disturbance," and the rational, historical "constructions" of the liberal theologians. It is as if Barth were arguing that the War itself was simply a manifestation of this deeper, theological conflict.

In passage after passage, Barth critiques the presumption and sinfulness of human reason, and argues that neither reason nor experience can help us "reach up" to God. God remains "Wholly Other," accessible only by His choice to reveal Himself.

Paul Tillich

While Barth's dramatic cry of divine Otherness created a very distinct theological program for an increasingly disestablished but still numerically powerful church, Barth's views were not universally affirmed in the Protestant community. Paul Tillich (1886–1965), writing in his *On the Boundary: An Autobiographical Sketch*, discussed the tragedy of World War I for liberal theology. "World

War I," he writes, "was disastrous for idealistic thought in general. . . . The experience of those four years of war revealed to me and to my entire generation an abyss in human existence that could not be ignored."[22] But Tillich's theological response to the war was different from Barth's. He agreed with his teacher, Martin Kähler, about the historical Jesus and the Christ of faith, but he disagreed with Barth's total emphasis on the "Otherness" of God.

> The foundation of Christian faith is the biblical picture of Christ, not the historical Jesus. The criterion of human thought and action is the picture of Christ as it is rooted in ecclesiastical belief and human experience, not the shifting and artificial construct of historical research. Because I took this position I was called a radical theologian in Germany, whereas Americans call me a Barthian.[23]

Tillich then insists that he does not agree with Barth's "supernaturalism."[24] Instead, he says, he sought to hold philosophy and theology (reason and faith) together. By focusing on the question of the *meaning* of existence, Tillich sought to occupy what he called the "boundary" between philosophy and theology. Because a boundary not only separates but connects what it separates, it proved a fruitful metaphor for exploring how the deep questions about the meaning of life, as posed most profoundly by existential philosophy, could be genuinely "answered" by a Christian theology. In order to genuinely answer the questions about the meaning of life, however, Tillich argued that one had to really listen to the questions. Thus, one needed to pay attention to the sciences, and to the arts, and to philosophy, as well as to movements in culture, such as the socialist Labor Movement "with the so-called dechristianized masses."[25] More than this, Tillich argued that each generation of theologians needed to respond to the questions of their time and place in the *form* of those questions. Thus, one couldn't simply listen to the question and then reply by reciting the ancient creeds; instead, one needed to interpret the language of the tradition in such a way that it was a genuine response to the question. Tillich called this method a correlational approach to theology, and it veered sharply from Barth's view.

Question and answer belong in correlation, just as the "divine-human relationship is a correlation." Tillich explains the correlational work of theology this way:

> Theology formulates the questions implied in human existence, and theology formulates the answers implied in divine self-mani-

festation under the guidance of the questions implied in human existence. . . . This is a circle which drives man to a point where question and answer are not separated. . . . It belongs to man's essential being, to the unity of his finitude with the infinity in which he was created and from which he is separated. A symptom of both the essential unity and the existential separation of finite man from his infinity is his ability to ask about the infinite to which he belongs: the fact that he must ask about it indicates that he is separated from it.

The answers implied in the event of revelation are meaningful only in so far as they are in correlation with questions concerning the whole of our existence, with existential questions. Only those who have experienced the shock of transitoriness, the anxiety in which they are aware of their finitude, the threat of nonbeing, can understand what the notion of God means. Only those who have experienced the tragic ambiguities of our historical existence and have totally questioned the meaning of existence can understand what the symbol of the Kingdom of God means. Revelation answers questions which have been asked and always will be asked because they are "we ourselves."[26]

Because Tillich understands theology as an explanation and defense of Christian faith in response to existential questions arising in philosophy and culture, his theology is called an apologetic theology. Clearly disagreeing with Barth, Tillich writes: "In our day, apologetics does not mean erecting a new principle in opposition to existing intellectual and moral standpoints."[27] Instead, Tillich argued that apologetics needs to seek a "common criterion" between the discourses of modern humanism—including socialistic and atheistic humanism—and Christian faith. That common criterion is what established the conversational boundary between these differing disciplines and viewpoints.

Among the most influential of those boundary engagements, for Tillich, was the one with existential philosophy, especially in the work of Martin Heidegger (1889–1976). Heidegger's 1927 *Sein und Zeit* (*Being and Time*) is a landmark book, one of the most important philosophical works of the century, and certainly one of the most important for theologians. Heidegger sought to return philosophy to an inquiry about the nature of Being, and he proposed to do this by an existential analysis of the creature who asks the question of the meaning of Being. Tillich noted that while Heidegger was an atheist, his existential philosophy was an outgrowth of a humanism suffused with Christian thought:

Much of its [Heidegger's philosophy's] terminology is found in the sermon literature of German Pietism. His interpretation of human existence implies and develops, however unintentionally, a doctrine of man that is one of human freedom and finitude. It is so closely related to the Christian interpretation of human existence that one is forced to describe it as "Theonomous philosophy" in spite of Heidegger's emphatic atheism.[28]

Thus, Tillich sought to identify a common criterion between Christianity and existentialism that would make a genuine Christian response to Heidegger possible, and he found that criterion in the area of *human meaning*. That is why when one reads Tillich's theological works, they read and sound more like the work of an existential philosopher than the work of a traditional Christian theologian: he is responding to Heidegger and other existentialists in the *form* of their questions.

While Tillich greatly appreciated the works of the Christian existentialist Kierkegaard, the influence of the atheist existentialist Heidegger is much more central for understanding Tillich's commitment to a theology reaching out to the world, rather than to a theology in which Christians talk only to one another. It is, therefore, quite important to understand the difference between Barth and Tillich as we go forward. Both theologians affirm the importance of revelation for theology. Barth's radical separation between nature and grace, however, and his anti-Pelagian-like attacks on human reason give Tillich pause. Without naming Barth in particular, he criticizes what he calls "Manichaean tendencies" in theology. Referring to teachings associated with Mani (216–276 CE), which held that reality was divided between rival principles of Good and Evil, light and darkness, and so on,[29] Tillich is suspicious of a radical division between nature and grace. While affirming, with Martin Luther (1483–1546), the "bondage of the will," or what Tillich calls the estrangement of humanity from its essential goodness, Tillich makes an important qualification: "the doctrine of the bondage of the will presupposes the freedom of the will. Only what is essentially free can come under existential bondage."[30] For Tillich, the situation of sin, or estrangement, does not prevent human beings from seeking salvation:

The question of salvation can be asked only if salvation is already at work, no matter how fragmentarily. Pure despair—the state without hope—is unable to seek beyond itself. The quest for the New Being presupposes the presence of the New Being, as the search for truth presupposes the presence of truth.[31]

While Tillich will affirm with Barth the necessity of revelation for bringing one from the point of seeking to actual faith, he also affirms in ways that Barth does not what he calls the "quest for the New Being," or, the search for God. By using the language of heresy, in this case Manichaeanism, Tillich cautions that too radical a separation between God and the world, between revelation and reason, may itself be sinful, and thus, a threat to theology's own credibility.

Karl Rahner

Tillich was not the only major Christian thinker to be influenced by Heidegger. The most influential New Testament scholar of the twentieth century, Rudolf Bultmann, was deeply indebted to Heidegger's existential philosophy. We will discuss Bultmann in the next chapter. Anglican theologian John Maccquarie, who translated Heidegger's major early work, *Sein und Zeit* (*Being and Time*), is also a major figure. For now, however, I want to say a bit more about the preeminent Roman Catholic theologian of the mid-twentieth century, Karl Rahner (1904–84). A student of Heidegger's, Rahner's approach to theology was deeply informed by Heidegger's existential analysis of the structure of human being. Like Tillich, albeit from a Catholic perspective, Rahner draws on Heidegger to disagree sharply with Barth's Either/Or rejection of history and philosophy.

In his first major work, *Hearers of the Word* (1941), Rahner asked about the capacities of a creature who might be able to hear a word from a transcendent God. Recall that Barth had rejected any such capacity in the human person prior to the advent of grace. Rahner thought very differently about the problem. He argued his point in terms of the basic structure of human knowing. The capacity for the mind to reach out and grasp anything, he argued, presupposes a fundamental openness to all of reality, to a horizon that is infinite. By virtue of this *Vorgriff*, this preapprehension of the infinite horizon of being, which Rahner would name more explicitly as God, all human knowing would always already exist within a horizon of grace. Insofar as the human person is created with a capacity for the infinite and his or her search for understanding occurs within the infinite mystery of Being, then philosophy—the quintessential discipline of the search for human meaning—cannot be alien to theology. Rather, Rahner argued, philosophy was, in fact, an independent and distinct presupposition of theology. By presupposition, Rahner does not mean "predetermined," as if every authentic philosophy must lead to religious faith. Nor does he mean that once one comes to faith, and thus, to theology, that one can discard philosophy as mere scaffolding. No, he speaks as a theologian who insists—against Barth—that the independence of philosophy is itself an important gift—a sign of God's grace already present in the world and not simply in the church.

> Since the self-disclosure of God in a personal revelation and as a free act of love can appear only to someone who understands himself and who thus disposes autonomously over himself, revelation presupposes a clearly distinguished, free philosophy as the space of its own possibility.[32]

Rahner simply cannot make sense of Barth's view that there is nothing within human nature itself that opens us to receive faith. As Rahner puts it:

> After all, revelation . . . is heard by a human being who already knows other things besides this revelation. . . . The hearing of a message by someone who already has other knowledge can only be possible . . . in confrontation with this other knowledge . . . ; it is hearing by means of categories already possessed from elsewhere, a reception within previously given horizons.[33]

Not only does theology affirm continuity between itself and philosophy, according to Rahner, it also affirms a synergy between them. By affirming the creativity and independence of philosophy in its exploration of human meaning, Rahner suggests—as was the case also with Tillich's theology—that philosophy can aid the creative ongoing work of theology. As Rahner puts it: "The listeners change the situation of the speakers."[34] The two disciplines remain distinct, insists Rahner, but revelation and, therefore, theology, which reflects on revelation, is not opposed to philosophy or to human thought more generally.

Conclusion and Transition

While I wanted, in thinking about these three chapters of Part Two, to cut to the chase of the New Quest for the historical Jesus, I simply do not think it is possible to make real sense of the historic character of that quest without understanding something of the theological context that would shape it so dramatically. By considering, even briefly, how theology—in its turn toward revelation—began to turn away from the growing influence of secular thought, one can begin to see subtle but important tensions that affirm the goodness and importance of reason, and of the world. It is in that theological tension that the New Quest will begin to emerge.

Also of real importance is not simply the fact of the turn to revelation, to the Otherness of God, but the new sense of space in which this Otherness would be known—the space of existential inwardness. Is it just by chance that at the approximate time that Christendom as expressed in the form of established churches, which had possessed real authority over *public* discourse, has begun to break apart, that Christian theology should turn its authority "inward," to the domains of an authentic church and an authentic self? Thus, one needs to see something of the importance of existentialism in shaping a new twentieth-century discourse of Christian faith—a discourse that no longer governs public life but that seeks to inform and shape the life of Christians in the church.

The tension between the Barthian and Tillichian theologies discussed above is, in some ways, a tension between two existentialisms: on the one hand, there is the distinctly Christian existentialist Kierkegaard who helps Barthians hold the language of faith within the orbit of the church; on the other hand, the atheist Heidegger who helps Tillichians and Rahnerians pull the language of faith toward the world. But what both forms of existentialism will inevitably do—precisely because they ask the question of what constitutes meaningful existence—is to push Christian theology to reconsider what faith, understood as an existential following of Jesus of Nazareth, might mean.

By the mid-1950s theologians and biblical scholars working along the lines of Tillich and Rahner became concerned that the Barthian approach to revelation created too wide a separation between God and the world, and thus between the church and society—a divide that had the feel of resentment. They looked about them and saw a world of science that wasn't going away. In the specter of the atom bomb they continued to see the destructive capacity of human reason, but in the birth of the United Nations, and in research in all areas of medicine, in the social sciences as well as the natural sciences, and in the power of technology and the exploration of space, they saw developments that were also positive and groundbreaking. In the Civil Rights movement taking hold in the mid-to-late 1950s theologians encountered a powerful public theology that entwined both the Exodus liberation narrative and the emancipatory language of the Declaration of Independence—thus drawing on both the biblical and Enlightenment traditions.

By 1958, when the recently elected Pope John XXIII called for the Second Vatican Council it was, he said, to "open the windows" of the church to "allow some fresh air" inside. The openness he sought would be twofold: one, a greater openness with other Christian communions that had over the centuries simply anathematized one another and declared one another anti-Christ; the other a greater openness to the world—to other faith traditions, especially a reassessment of Jewish-Christian relations, and to the modern world itself, to historical biblical criticism, and, for the first time, to the principle of religious freedom. While maintaining a clear sense of Roman Catholic distinctiveness, John XXIII sought to lower the walls separating the church from the world.

Perhaps Barth, Kähler, and company had over-reacted. What if faith, and theology that reflected upon faith, was not an either/or proposition? Theology, at least some theologians argued, needed to listen to the world and to engage the world. Did not God do as much in the incarnation? Might not a return to the question of the historical Jesus help ground a Christian engagement with the world?

CHAPTER 8

Avoiding Scandal
The New Quest

In the previous chapter, we saw that Martin Kähler and Karl Barth established a high wall separating revelation and faith from philosophical and historical inquiry. This separation had the effect of accentuating the radical difference between God and the world, and between the authentic teaching of the church and secular, public reason. The turn to existentialism also had the effect of privatizing revelation, that is to say, emphasizing the way divine revelation addresses the individual person, calling for transformation and commitment.

While sharing in that turn to the existential character of revelation and faith, other theologians including Paul Tillich and Karl Rahner found such an either/or divide not only theologically rigid but also dangerous for the life of the church. While clearly affirming the priority of revelation, these latter theologians sought, with the aid of Heidegger's existential philosophy, to affirm the openness of reason to receiving the message of revelation. In order for faith to speak not only to faith but also to the world, there needed to be some "point of contact," some "common ground" by which the word of God could be received as both challenge and grace for one's life. Thus, while Tillich and Rahner did not seek in any way to reclaim the right of the church to control or govern public discourse, they did seek to show that Christian faith could be both intelligible and persuasive to modern persons and modern culture. By using existentialist philosophy, and in particular Heidegger's, to focus their interpretive methods on the analysis of the human person's own openness to the world and to the future, these theologians sought to pull Barth's supernaturalism back down to earth. In the process, their focus upon humanity, and humanity's openness to receive revelation, inevitably resurrected the question of the historical Jesus, albeit in a very different context from that of the first quest.

Rudolf Bultmann

Rudolf Bultmann stands in the minds of many as the most important biblical scholar of the twentieth century. Bultmann's Yale lectures of 1951, published as *Christ and Mythology,* show Bultmann reflecting on his early career. At that time, he says, theologians were not all sure they could make sense of the eschatological understanding of Jesus uncovered by the work of Strauss and Weiss, Wrede, and Schweitzer. In all of their portrayals, Jesus appeared to be wrong about his expectation for an imminent end of time. If Jesus was wrong in his eschatological expectation about the inbreaking kingdom of God, what sense could Christian theology make of him?

> When I began to study theology, theologians as well as laymen were excited and frightened by the theories of Johannes Weiss. I remember that Julius Kaftan, my teacher in dogmatics in Berlin, said: "If Johannes Weiss is right and the conception of the Kingdom of God is an eschatological one, then it is impossible to make use of this conception in dogmatics." . . . Today nobody doubts that Jesus' conception of the Kingdom of God is an eschatological one. . . . Indeed, it has become more and more clear that the eschatological expectation and hope is the core of the New Testament preaching throughout.[1]

Looking back on his career, Bultmann sees the significance of his own work as that of bridging the fields of biblical study and theology. Indebted to Heidegger's existential philosophy, Bultmann had argued for the possibility of an existential encounter with Jesus. Heidegger had discussed human existence as a "project toward death," in which the existential awareness of death actually enabled human beings to claim responsibility for their lives. Seen in these terms, death awakened human beings not simply to their final "end," but also provoked them to ask about the existential "ends" for which they were living. Eschatology became, in Bultmann's hands, the theological starting place for asking about the *meaning* of human life. From this point on in the twentieth century the topic of eschatology would cease to be an outdated, dusty idea discussed at the very end of a systematic theology. Instead, eschatology became a point of orientation—awareness of our end as a provocation to reflect upon the meaning of life, and thus a provocation to decide to become a Christian.

Bultmann is justly famous for his emphasis on "demythologizing" Scripture. In those same Yale lectures, Bultmann discusses why it is necessary to demythologize Scripture.

> The whole conception of the world which is presupposed in the preaching of Jesus as in the New Testament generally is mythological; i.e., the conception of the world as being structured in three stories, heaven, earth, and hell; the conception of the intervention of supernatural powers in the course of events. . . . This conception of the world we call mythological because it is different from the conception of the world which has been formed and developed by science since its inception in ancient Greece and which has been accepted by all modern men.[2]

The mythological cast to the teachings of Jesus and the New Testament does not exhaust the meaning of these texts; far from it.

> We must ask whether the eschatological preaching and the mythological sayings as a whole contain a still deeper meaning which is concealed under the cover of mythology. If that is so, let us abandon the mythological conceptions precisely because we want to retain their deeper meaning. This method of interpretation of the New Testament . . . I call de-mythologizing. . . . Its aim is not to eliminate the mythological statements but to interpret them.[3]

As with Tillich and Rahner, Bultmann finds in his dialogue with Heidegger the existential category of *meaning* which enables one to link the existential challenge of Jesus' discourse to the existential challenge of preaching today. But Bultmann is not simply a Tillichean.

According to New Testament scholar James M. Robinson, Bultmann turned from liberalism toward Barth's position following his attendance at a 1923 debate between liberal theologian Adolf von Harnack and Harnack's former student Barth that focused on the "content of the gospel." Harnack argued:

> "If the person of Jesus Christ stands at the centre of the gospel, how can the basis for a reliable and communal knowledge of this person be gained other than through critical historical study, if one is not to trade a dreamed-up Christ for the real one?" . . . To this Barth replied: "The reliability and communal nature of the knowledge of the person of Jesus Christ as the centre of the *gospel* can be no other than the reliability and communal nature of the *faith* awakened by God. Critical historical study signifies the deserved and necessary end of

those 'bases' of such knowledge which are no bases since they are not laid by God himself."[4]

Bultmann found Barth's theological argument—itself analogous to the views of Kähler—convincing. Bultmann, thus, also came to believe that historical scholarship and what it could discover about Jesus belonged to the category of knowledge—and very uncertain knowledge at that—but not faith. Yet Bultmann found in Heidegger's existential philosophy a way of holding on to the category of history.[5] What if, Bultmann asked, there was not just one approach to history, that is, an objectivistic view, but a second approach, one that sought a "dialogue with history"? Bultmann makes this appeal in the Preface to his early work, *Jesus and the Word*, published in 1926.[6] There, he differentiates between "an approach to history which seeks by its *method* to achieve objectivity,"[7] and another that seeks a "personal encounter with history."[8] While the former approach, he says, is very helpful for grasping things like the "correct chronological sequence of events," it "misses the true significance of history."[9] In words reminiscent of Martin Kähler's argument, Bultmann claims that these two approaches reflect differing interests:

> Now, when we interpret the Bible, what is our interest? Certainly the Bible is an historical document and we must interpret the Bible by the methods of historical research. . . . But what is our true and real interest? Are we to read the Bible only as an historical document in order to reconstruct an epoch of past history for which the Bible serves as a "source"? Or is it more than a source? I think our interest is really to hear what the Bible has to say for our actual present, to hear what is the truth about our life and about our soul.[10]

Bultmann builds upon, but goes beyond, Kähler and Barth by providing an exegetical approach to better explain the shattering encounter between the Word of God and the individual person. The focus, says Bultmann, will be on the "message of Jesus":

> When we encounter the words of Jesus in history, *we do not judge them* by a philosophical system with reference to their rational validity; *they* meet *us* with the question of how we are to interpret our own existence. That we be ourselves deeply disturbed by the problem of our own life is therefore the indispensable condition of our inquiry. . . . The subject of this book is . . . not the life or the personality of Jesus, but only his teaching, his message.[11]

Here, Bultmann seems to leave open the door to historical research. If we cannot know the "person" of Jesus by historical methods, can we know the "words of Jesus" or the "message" of Jesus by historical methods? Granting Bultmann's point that one will seek to understand Jesus' message by an existential encounter with his words and his teaching, could it be possible to identify the actual words and teaching of Jesus by historical methods?

Because Bultmann suggests throughout the book that some words and some teaching were more likely spoken by the person of Jesus than others, he seems to suggest that there may be a point of contact between the two approaches. But Bultmann's analysis is enigmatic. The arrangement of the text in *Jesus and the Word* operates on both the objectivist and the existentialist tracks. With respect to historical-critical analysis, Bultmann agrees with Johannes Weiss that Jesus was an eschatological prophet who expected the imminent end of the world. Bultmann seems confident in laying out this message of Jesus under three headings: (1) "The Teaching of Jesus: The Coming of the Kingdom," which interprets Jesus' language of the kingdom in his Jewish context; (2) "The Teaching of Jesus: The Will of God," which argues that Jesus' ethical teaching belongs inherently to Jesus' eschatological call to decision; and (3) "The Teaching of Jesus: God the Remote and the Near," which argues for the authenticity of passages calling persons to repent and receive forgiveness of sins.

But even as he presents his historical analysis of Jesus' teaching, Bultmann weaves into his discussion of Jesus' first-century audience existentialist language clearly drawn from the nineteenth and twentieth centuries. Bultmann has barely begun to introduce the centrality of the theme of "the Kingdom of God" in Jesus' preaching when he writes:

> Now is the time of decision. . . . The Kingdom of God . . . involves complete renunciation, brings every man face to face with the ultimate *Either-Or*.[12]

And a few pages later:

> What then is the meaning of "the Kingdom of God"? How is it to be conceived? The simplest answer is: the Kingdom of God is deliverance for men. It is that *eschatological* deliverance which ends everything earthly. . . . Therefore it demands of man decision. . . . This deliverance confronts man as an Either-Or.[13]

Bultmann uses the existential categories of "decision," "meaning," and "Either-Or," to describe the challenge of Jesus' message to his original audience! By this existential anachronism Bultmann paves the way for his argument that Jesus' *eschatological* message also confronts "modern man" with a radical decision about his own life. Sounding distinctly like Barth, Bultmann writes:

> The Kingdom of God, then, is something miraculous, in fact the absolute miracle, opposed to all the here and now; it is "wholly other," heavenly. . . . Whoever seeks it must realize that he cuts himself off from the world, otherwise he belongs to those who are not fit, who put their hand to the plow and look back.[14]

By weaving existential and theological language into his historical argument, Bultmann is clearly seeking to express some continuity between historical scholarship and the language of faith. Yet, in several passages he indicates that that continuity is possible only from the side of God's revelatory grace. In a passage clearly directed against the theological liberalism of the nineteenth century, Bultmann writes:

> The Kingdom of God is not an ideal which realizes itself in human history; we cannot speak of its founding, its building, its completion; we can say only that it draws near, it comes, it appears. It is *supernatural, superhistorical*; and while men can "receive" its salvation, can enter it, it is not *they*, with their fellowship and their activity, who constitute the Kingdom of God, but God's power alone.[15]

Keeping in mind Bultmann's description of two approaches to history, it seems that while the first approach of historical analysis can establish, with sound probability, the teaching of Jesus, the second approach, existential dialogue—as controlled by doctrine—completes the process of interpretation. Put another way, the teaching of the pre-resurrection Jesus is interpreted through a post-resurrection lens.

But has Bultmann underscored continuity between the two approaches or not? Near the very end of the book he adds a further element of mystery. Just as there are two approaches to history, so also, he says, there are two understandings of language. Writing on the topic of sin and forgiveness, Bultmann writes that "Jesus is the bearer of the word, and in the word he assures man of the forgiveness of God." Such a statement, says Bultmann, can become an "*event* of divine forgiveness" for a reader or person of faith only "if we set ourselves free from a commonly held . . . habit of understanding the word only as the natural expression of the speaking individual."[16] Such is the way, says Bultmann, that modern historical study deals with language: it flattens both history and language to a set of factual claims. "But," he continues:

> if we return to the real significance of "word," implying as it does a relationship between speaker and hearer, then the word can become an event to the hearer, because it brings him into this relationship.[17]

Corresponding to the two approaches to history discussed above are two approaches to language. If the reader can shift from reading the texts of Scripture as objects of analysis to reading them with an openness to being questioned and confronted by them, and thus called into new relationship, then, suggests Bultmann, one can *still* experience the forgiveness of God as mediated by the text. One can become a hearer of the Word, but perhaps only in the act of faith and its decision.

But Bultmann isn't finished. The existential understandings of history and language fundamentally shift one's understanding of the human person. The *meaning* of human life, says Bultmann, cannot be analyzed from a distance, as historians seek to understand a person by contextualizing him or her. No, at the existential plane, the possibilities for persons are not closed by history but "stand open"—"that in every concrete situation new possibilities appear, that human life throughout is characterized by successive decisions."[18] And ultimately, by the decision for or against faith.

In each of the three shifts—history, language, and the nature of human beings—one can see Bultmann attempting to work out a model of revelation, that is to say, a model for how Barth's Wholly Other God speaks through Scripture and, perhaps too, how revelation comes to the two churches that Barth called the Church of Esau and the Church of Jacob. Predictably, Bultmann identifies the problematic character in the topics of history, language, and human nature with the modern historian, and in each case separates the inauthentic modern historian from the authentic Christian existentialist. He seems driven to this position by the Either/Or existential language of Kierkegaard as taken up in turn by Kähler and Barth. But does he really need to make such a distinction between the objective and the existentialist approach to history, language, and human nature? Must historical analysis always be objectivistic? Has the historical Jesus become the husk that can be discarded once the existential message of faith has been discerned? Or can there be continuity between the historical Jesus and the existential

Christ of faith? Are not our common assumptions of speaking and hearing also open to moments of wonder? Cannot contextual analyses of human events also lead to amazement rather than dulling predictability? And what of his focus on language as the vehicle of proclamation and meaning?

In his *Theology of the New Testament* (1951), Bultmann tries to resolve the issue by arguing that the *kerygma* (the Greek word for "preaching" or "proclamation"), which Bultmann understood as the proclamation by the early church of Jesus *as the Messiah*, "is the basic and primary thing which gives everything else—including Jesus' own teaching—its special character." Yes, he acknowledges that there is an "implicit Christology" in Jesus' "call to decision" during his ministry, but that is not the decisive thing:

> All that went before appears in a new light—new since the *Easter faith in Jesus' resurrection* and founded upon this faith. But if Jesus' person and work appear to them in the new light of Easter faith, that means that his significance lay neither in the content of what he had taught nor in some modification to the Messiah idea. It does mean, though, that *Jesus' having come was itself the decisive event* through which God called His Congregation (Church). . . . Indeed, that is the real content of Easter faith: God has made the prophet and teacher Jesus of Nazareth Messiah![19] (Bultmann's emphasis)

In other words, Bultmann suggests that while the historical Jesus must be affirmed as the "presupposition" of the early Christian *kerygma* (proclamation), knowledge of Jesus' teaching was not at all primary to the experience of Christian faith. Thus, theology need not explore Jesus as knowable by history but only Jesus Christ as known by faith.[20] This conclusion will trouble his own students and lead to the crisis that generates the New Quest.

Responses to Bultmann and the Focus of the New Quest

It is important to realize that the New Quest for the historical Jesus emerges out of the ambiguities in Bultmann's historical *and* theological analysis. In *Jesus and the Word*, Bultmann went beyond Weiss and the eschatological school of the time by insisting that aspects of the ethical teaching found in the Synoptics were authentic to Jesus, as well as Jesus' preaching on forgiveness and repentance. With respect to both the ethical teaching and the themes of forgiveness, Bultmann argued that both were implied in Jesus' preaching of the eschatological kingdom of God that was beginning to break in to history. Bultmann had, thus, expanded the field of potentially authentic material, while simultaneously expressing ambivalence not only about what history could know with certainty about particulars, but about historical research impacting Christian faith.

In 1953, Ernst Käsemann, New Testament scholar and a student of Rudolf Bultmann, presented a lecture to a reunion of Bultmann students in Marburg, Germany. The title of the lecture was "The Problem of the Historical Jesus."[21] Käsemann begins by acknowledging that historical criticism of the nineteenth century had itself reached the conclusion that it was impossible to reconstruct a life of Jesus based on the Gospels. Moreover, he affirms the importance of faith for grasping the significance and vitality of what can seem to be merely the past.

> Mere history is petrified history, whose historical significance cannot be brought to light simply by verifying facts and handing them on. . . . Only that man is in genuine continuity with past history who allows it to place him in a new condition of responsibility. . . . In theological terms, this means that only in the decision between faith and unbelief can petrified history even of the life of Jesus become once again living history.[22]

What disturbs Käsemann, however, is the question that Bultmann leaves unresolved, namely, whether knowledge about the message and preaching of the historical, that is to say, pre-Easter Jesus is also important for theology. Käsemann believes that such knowledge is crucial for theology and he attempts to demonstrate this by showing that preserving the teaching of Jesus was crucial for the synoptic tradition itself.

> A primary concern of the Gospels is unmistakably the particularity with which the eschatological event is bound to *this* man from Nazareth, to the arena of Palestine and to a concrete time with its special circumstances.[23]

Insofar as revelation occurs within this decisive historical event, as the *kairotic* moment of decision and fulfillment, Käsemann argues that the history of Jesus neither would nor could be set aside:

> Revelation creates *kairos*. . . . Because primitive Christianity experienced the earthly history of Jesus in this way as *kairos*, it wrote Gospels and did not after Easter simply let the life of Jesus go by the board. Easter did not render this experience superfluous; on the contrary it confirmed it.[24]

Thus, says Käsemann, the early synoptic communities affirmed that "out of the isolated encounter with Jesus" came "the presence of the exalted Lord," and thus, the "once" of Jesus' earthly life becomes the "once for all" of faith.[25]

Because the early church did not set aside the historical Jesus as irrelevant to faith, neither, argues Käsemann, should the church today. While stating that one cannot substitute the historical Jesus for the exalted Lord of post-Easter faith, Käsemann insists we cannot "do away with the identity between the exalted and earthly Lord without falling into docetism and depriving ourselves of the possibility of drawing a line between the Easter faith of the community and myth."[26]

What concerns Käsemann is the very real possibility that the language of "revelation" can be used, and perhaps is already being used by some theologians and church officials, to avoid legitimate criticism. Does he mean Barth? I don't know, but by invoking the ancient heresy of "docetism" (from the Greek that means "to seem")—a position which argued for Jesus' full divinity but not his humanity, namely, that Jesus only "seemed" to be human—Käsemann implies that he will not be bullied by Barthian-like charges of heresy.

Käsemann acknowledges the difficulty of sorting out the authentic message of Jesus from the kerygmatic narrative of the Gospels. But he sees even in the rewriting of Jesus' own message by the early church not erasure but critical reframing for a new situation.

> By acting as it did the community bore (and still bears) witness to history as being living and contemporary. It interprets out of its own experience what for it had already become mere history and employs for this purpose the medium of its preaching. It is precisely by this method that the community rescues the facts of the past from being regarded only as prodigies and wonders. . . . To state the paradox as sharply as possible: the community takes so much trouble to maintain historical continuity with him who once trod this earth that it allows the historical events of this early life to pass for the most part into oblivion and replaces them by its own message.[27]

Käsemann believes that while the synoptic communities' own claims of faith covered over most of the historical detail of Jesus' life—and precisely because they so wanted to express his *significance* to them—their efforts to represent the teaching of Jesus contains elements of Jesus' own proclamation. In other words, Käsemann believes that there is demonstrable continuity between the historical Jesus and the Christ of faith, and that one needs to insist on this point theologically, lest faith and the claim of revelation become docetic abstractions. [28]

> It is not only at this point [the early Church] in its history that the community does this. The same process is always being repeated in the course of Church history. Time and again, continuity with the past is preserved by shattering the received terminology, the received imagery, the received theology—in short, by shattering the tradition.[29]

Is Käsemann suggesting that the current moment in the mid-1950s is just such a moment of historic shattering? Perhaps so.

Bultmann's focus in thinking about the early Christian *kerygma* had been the writings of Paul and John. With the Synoptics, however, argues Käsemann, it is not simply that the Proclaimer became the Proclaimed, as in Paul, but that the proclamation explicitly sets out to re-present the past proclamation *of the Proclaimer*. Thus, says Käsemann, the problem of the historical Jesus is not simply a problem of modern historians, but rather it is a problem within the *kerygma* itself![30]

Käsemann sets out to identify several passages that he and other exegetes believe are authentic to Jesus and which indicate something of an implicit Christology in Jesus' words—that is to say, a distinctive sense of his own identity. Pointing to the "first, second and fourth antitheses in the Sermon on the Mount,"[31] Käsemann believes that the contrasting formula "you have heard it said"–"but I say" is one such remarkable formula, embodying "a claim to authority which rivals and challenges that of Moses."[32] While Käsemann believes that Jesus did not refer to himself as the Messiah,[33] he believes that this authentic fragment suggests an *implicit* awareness, or self-understanding, which later the early church would both affirm and interpret in its own more explicit categories of Messiah and Son of God. With respect to the "But I say" formula, Käsemann writes:

> To this there are no Jewish parallels, nor indeed can there be. . . . The unheard-of implication of the saying testifies to its genuineness. . . . Certainly he was a Jew and made the assumptions of Jewish piety, but at the same time he shatters this framework with his claim.[34]

Käsemann goes on to argue that Jesus' shattering of both the Sabbath commandment ("The Sabbath was made for man, not man for the Sabbath") and the law of purification (that it is not what enters a man that makes him impure but what comes out from him) are no small disputes. Rather,

> he [Jesus] is striking at the presuppositions of the whole classical conception of *cultus* with its sacrificial and expiatory system. To put this in another way, he is removing the distinction (which is fundamental to the whole of ancient thought) between the *temenos*, the realm of the sacred, and the secular, and it is for this reason that he is able to consort with sinners.[35]

These passages are the heart of Käsemann's claim for an implicit Christology within the message of Jesus. But when Käsemann talks about Jesus "removing the distinction" between the "realm of the sacred and the secular" he is thinking about more than Jesus and the first century; he is thinking about what is happening in twentieth-century theology in the separation of revelation from reason. Near the end of the essay he writes: "The preaching of the Church may be carried on anonymously; the important thing is not the person, but the message. But the gospel itself cannot be anonymous, otherwise it leads to moralism and mysticism."[36]

At the heart of the New Quest is a dis-ease with the Barthian tilt toward revelation and toward the "mysticism" of an existential analysis that seems docetic to some and Manichaean to others. Käsemann's concern to yoke faith to history is not only a serious call for integrity with respect to Christian origins, but also a call for integrity in the Christian theology of the present.

Bultmann responded to Käsemann's essay in 1960. In that essay, which included some minor concessions, Bultmann included a footnote that the church was the "bearer of the *kerygma*." In language reminiscent of Barth's "Church of Jacob," Bultmann wrote:

> It is self-evident that "Church" here is not an institution but an eschatological happening. It is not the guarantor but itself the object, of faith. It is a scandal, in exactly the same sense as the Cross is a scandal.[37]

Writing in 1964, Käsemann can make no sense of what seems to him an utterly docetic view of the church "suspended between heaven and earth," and he draws from the passage a severe judgment on his former teacher:

> Does it not finally become evident . . . that for Bultmann nothing historical really has any theological substance or meaning? Do we not see instantaneously . . . why the historical Jesus cannot possibly,

on the basic presupposition of this thinking, have any independent significance whatever? . . . For me, to accept Bultmann's interpretation would be to transgress the limits drawn by the Reformation; it would be to surrender the possibility of adopting a posture of radical criticism in the face of ecclesiastical tradition.[38]

Käsemann's profound complaint is that the complete dismissal of the historical Jesus would mean that the church would have no criterion—in Jesus!—for either authenticating its message, or for a critique of the church's claims and practices. This concern for integrity, insists Käsemann, is not merely a modern one, but a concern of the synoptic Gospels themselves:

The earthly Jesus had to keep the preached Christ from dissolving into the projection of an eschatological self-consciousness and becoming the object of a religious ideology. History acquired an eschatological function. The past gave to the present the criteria for discerning the spirits.[39]

Writing as if he were thinking every bit as much about the current climate as about the first and second centuries, Käsemann adds that "theological undertakings . . . become most dangerous of all when they are absolutized." And, pointing to the variety of approaches to Christology in the New Testament, he notes, "This is precisely what the New Testament refrains from doing."[40]

James M. Robinson

In his 1959 book *A New Quest for the Historical Jesus*, James M. Robinson pulls together the work of a variety of scholars (most of whom were Bultmann's own students) who have already picked up on Käsemann's essay. If Käsemann had emphasized the ability of contemporary historical analysis to hear and recognize a distinctive self-consciousness in Jesus—an implied Christology, Robinson offers a complementary existential interpretation of the "self" that should inform one's understanding of both Jesus' "self-consciousness" and the "self-consciousness" of one engaging the message of Jesus. Careful to avoid associating the modern view of the self with the assumptions of the nineteenth century (e.g., personality traits, emotions, and so on), Robinson—clearly indebted to Heidegger and to Bultmann's 1926 Preface to *Jesus and the Word*—writes:

The self [in the contemporary view] is not simply one's personality, resultant upon (and to be explained by) the various influences and ingredients present in one's heritage and development. Rather self-hood is constituted by commitment to a context, from which commitment one's existence arises. . . . Selfhood results from implicit or explicit commitment to a kind of existence, and is to be understood only in terms of that commitment.[41]

Insofar as one understands the self in this existential sense, suggests Robinson, one can see how it enables what Bultmann called a new approach to history—one that enables a dialogue between Jesus' message and the contemporary person. Robinson affirms that Kähler and Barth were right to object to any attempt to provide an "objectively verified proof" of Jesus' saving activity. One cannot move in any natural way from historical analysis to faith. But such a criticism, says Robinson, "does not apply to the modern [existential] view of history and historiography which would be presupposed in a new quest." He continues:

For the objectivity of modern historiography consists precisely in one's openness for the encounter, one's willingness to place one's intentions and views of existence in question, i.e., to learn something basically new about existence and thus to have one's own existence modified or radically altered. Nor can the end result of such historical research be a proven *kerygma* dispensing with the necessity for existential commitment.[42]

Arguing from Bultmann's existential approach to history, Robinson suggests that church officials need not fear the lack of existential commitment (i.e., faith) in the new approach to historical Jesus research. In fact, such new research could correct a current imbalance in the discussions of Jesus. Agreeing with Käsemann on this point, he writes:

The current limitation of New Testament research to the *kerygma* has a significant formal deficiency: it sees Jesus only in terms determined by the Christian encounter and thus obscures formally the concreteness of his historical reality. . . . Research upon Jesus' message would serve formally to draw attention to the flesh of the incarnation.[43]

Underscoring the existential character of the New Quest's historiography, Robinson not only seeks to allay ecclesial anxieties of historical analysis undermining faith, he suggests that the New Quest's approach to history can, by "draw[ing] attention to the flesh of the incarnation," enable the possibility of an existential encounter between Jesus and the lived commitments of modern men and women.

Käsemann and Robinson were not, of course, the only New Testament scholars who sought to argue for an implicit Christology in Jesus' self-understanding. According to Norman Perrin, it was another Bultmann student, Ernst Fuchs, who went farther than Käsemann, or others, in arguing for an implicit Christology in Jesus' self-awareness.[44] Like Käsemann, Fuchs points to the utter distinctiveness of Jesus' claim to authority, but he locates Jesus' implied Christology not simply in Jesus' words but in Jesus' *conduct*. As Perrin comments, insofar as "Jesus' conduct is the actual context of his preaching," Fuchs argues that Jesus' conduct is every bit as powerful—for embodying the kingdom of God—as any words he could have stated. Perrin adds:

> [F]or example, [according to Fuchs] the parable of the Prodigal Son is set in the context of Jesus' (eschatological) table-fellowship with sinners, and defends this conduct by referring to it as a direct exhibition of the will of God. "Jesus dares to assert the will of God, as if he himself stood in the place of God!" Jesus' conduct in regard to sinners actually implies more than would have been involved in an explicit claim to be Son of God or Son of Man.[45]

Fuchs focused on more than the question of Jesus' self-consciousness and the idea of an implicit Christology. He also followed up on Bultmann's understanding of the *kerygma* as a word event, and, along with Gerhard Ebeling, sought to articulate a theology that linked the proclamation (*kerygma*) of the early church to the proclamation of faith in contemporary preaching. Drawing upon Heidegger's existential analysis of the plight of modern persons in the West—that we are lost in the inauthenticity of what Heidegger called "everydayness"—Fuchs portrays Christ, the Word of God, as authentic speech that breaks through the emptiness of our modern illusions. For Fuchs, it is the modern world view that especially needs to be demythologized. In the act of authentic preaching, therefore, the Word of God interprets us, demythologizes us, and calls us to conversion.

Using Christ as the "Word of God" to link the *kerygma* of the gospel to the contemporary practice of preaching, Fuchs and Ebeling provide an institutional avenue through which the Otherness of God could break through the alienation of modern life and re-create the world in the authentic speech of the gospel. Rather than simply reflecting on the text in a way that would help the congregation understand a point of dogma or a moral lesson for everyday life, a preacher's task was to proclaim to the congregation the inbreaking power of the gospel in and for their own lives. Thus, the eschatological word-event of preaching sought to reawaken a vitality of faith with the boldness of a proclamation that the kingdom of God had drawn near—even now in the hearing of the congregation—demanding decision and commitment of one's life.

By developing Bultmann's interpretation of Heidegger for a theology and practice of preaching, Fuchs and Ebeling designate the church as the primary scene of this theological movement. Yet by refocusing the task of preaching to address the question of the meaning of human existence, these scholars also link the proclamation and life of faith more closely to the questions asked of all people. The existential focus of this word event meant that preaching was now a discourse of *meaning* meant to challenge and illuminate the congregation's own grappling with questions of meaning in their life. Faith, in this new model of preaching, would not simply be an affirmation of a Christian doctrine long embedded in the history of Christendom but the testimony of one's whole life as made evident in the range of its decisions and commitments.

Writing in 1963 on the state of the debate about the kingdom of God in the teaching of Jesus, Norman Perrin affirms the importance that existential analysis had made in interpreting Jesus' teaching of the kingdom of God.

> Whatever reservations one may have about the thoroughgoing existentialism of Bultmann and his school, there can be no doubt but that they have done us an invaluable service in directing our attention to the sphere of individual human existence as the sphere in which the Kingdom of God is manifested.[46]

To the extent that Jesus' preaching of the kingdom confronted and invited his hearers into a new relationship with God in the here and now of their world, a contemporary existential analysis of the kingdom of God could also confront a modern-day audience with this same challenge to decision and new relationship.

CHAPTER 9

The New Quest and the Changing Voices of Theology

Writing in 1969, Langdon Gilkey could look back at the breaking up of neo-orthodox theology with some detachment.

> One could sum up the problem thus: Neo-orthodox theology presupposed a stark and real separation between the Church and the world, between belief and unbelief, between the Word of God and the secular. Its religious discourse proceeded on the assumption that its hearers *were* this Church, *had* this belief, and *heard* the Word. But the actual situation was by no means characterized by any such clear and distinct separation: the world was within the Church, belief was saturated by secular doubt, and no one, either in the pew or the pulpit, was sure a divine Word had been heard at all or a divine presence manifested. In such a situation, the theology that was unable to relate itself to ordinary experience was bound to falter—and it did.[1] (Gilkey's emphasis)

But if Gilkey seems more coolly analytical about this theological development in 1969, he acknowledges that he had not been just five years earlier. He quotes an earlier essay, a passage worth sharing here in its entirety:

> No more than five years ago [1959] the "younger theologians" seemed to have a comfortable basis for their task, fashioned by the great theologians of the '20s, '30s, and '40s. . . . We saw ourselves as a generation of "scholastics" whose function would be to work out in greater detail the firm theological principles already forged for us. We knew from our teachers what theology was, what its principles and starting point were, how to go about it, and above all we were confident about its universal value and truth.

The most significant recent theological development has been the steady dissolution of all these certainties, the washing away of the firm ground on which our generation believed we were safely standing. What we thought was solid earth has turned out to be shifting ice—and in recent years, as the weather has grown steadily warmer, some of us have in horror found ourselves staring down into rushing depths of dark water.[2]

As I have argued in the preceding two chapters, several theological currents—including Paul Tillich, Karl Rahner, and the scholars of the New Quest—had sought to correct what they interpreted in Barth's theology as an over-rejection of human experience and the modern, secular world. While still attending closely to revelation, these movements sought to reconnect theology to human experience. By the late 1950s and early 1960s, the call by theologians to reconnect with the world and ordinary human experience had reached a tipping point. What Gilkey describes as the rapidly eroding "certainties" of the previous decades, were not merely intellectual in character but historical and cultural, as well.

The crisis of the nuclear arms race and the space race, the Civil Rights movement in the United States, and the early stages of globalization, along with the emergence of the tragedy of the *Shoah*—to say nothing yet of the challenges that would come in the 1960s, with the assassination of President Kennedy, with resistance to the Vietnam War, the women's movement, the War on Poverty, the Black Power movement and the gay liberation movement, the continuing crisis of the nuclear superpowers, and calls for global justice—all raised profoundly difficult questions about whether the church had anything meaningful to say to the world. As all these global and cultural issues emerged, it became increasingly clear that the church's self-isolation from the public life of the world—what Gilkey refers to as the alleged "real separation between the Church and the world"—was profoundly problematic. It would be in this context of cultural and religious crisis that the research of the New Quest would participate in movements of historic significance.

By the mid-1960s, Norman Perrin could point with some confidence to three major "aspects of the teaching of Jesus" that historians had established "beyond reasonable doubt: the parables, the Kingdom of God teaching and the Lord's Prayer tradition."[3] From these very basic assumptions dramatic theological challenges would emerge, including challenges to the "existential" hermeneutic used by many in the New Quest itself. Over the decade of the

1960s and into the 1970s and 1980s, we see three significant shifts related to the work of the New Quest: 1) the use of eschatological and apocalyptic discourse to confront the church and society, 2) a re-engagement with secular and humanistic culture, and 3) a new theological focus on the kingdom of God as a social and political category. These shifts, at least partially enabled by the New Quest of the Historical Jesus, will open up a new historic question for theology: *whose experience* matters in the work of theology?

Eschatology as Political Critique
of Both Church and Society

Recall that for Ernst Käsemann one of the most important reasons for asking the question of the historical Jesus in 1953 was that Christian faith was in danger of losing contact with the heart of its own *historical* message. By 1962, Käsemann's concerns had become a sharp rebuke. In an essay entitled "On the Subject of Primitive Christian Apocalyptic," Käsemann attacks the church's inward preoccupation with its own set-apartness, or specialness:

> To encourage the Christian community to contemplate its own navel is certainly to render it no service at all. That exodus from established positions which characterizes the Church in its true being has never taken place without apocalyptic hope and warning. Conversely, the necessary step into the freedom of the coming moment at a given point in history has been dictated as often by hope as by despair; moreover, the challenge has often been not specifically Christian but one proceeding from humanity as such. There are historical matters of fact which, though we may shrink from them in the name of a modern dogmatic theology, can only be ignored at our peril, when they ought to be driving us to critical reappraisal.[4]

In this rather stunning paragraph, Käsemann suggests that it is the church, not simply the individual, who is in need of hearing an eschatological, apocalyptic word of warning and of hope. The church, too inwardly preoccupied with the "navel gazing" of existentialist meaning and with the inner purity of "modern dogmatic theology," is in danger of losing, according to Käsemann, its sense of direction, its sense of touch with the world. The church, suggests Käsemann, must listen to "historical matters of fact" and to "humanity as such" if it is to hear again its own gospel clearly. Others were listening.

Roman Catholic theologian Johann Baptist Metz was a student of Karl Rahner's. While profoundly indebted to the range and depth of his teacher's work, Metz argued that the existentialism that dominated the 1930s, '40s, and '50s had made Christian faith too private an affair, generating a model of faith that failed to account for major structural shifts in society, and that failed to account for the political character of the gospel itself.

Opening his 1968 work, *Theology of the World*, Metz urges the church to engage the new secular reality.

> Today's world has become secular, and it would appear that the process is by no means over yet. This universal secularity challenges faith to say what its attitude to it is. Faith can try, of course, to ignore the acuteness of the situation and simply hammer away behind locked doors at its customary practices in theology and piety, as though there had been no day of Pentecost and therefore no need to understand and answer for the ever changing times. A faith that is so unhistorical is not likely to feel threatened. . . . This kind of faith is never stuck for words. It can go on talking with extraordinary superiority about God and the world. But it lacks urgency and the taste of reality and it can suddenly, in the midst of Christianity, descend to mythology.[5]

Like Käsemann, and others, Metz believes that the logic of neo-orthodoxy (in its Catholic as well as in its Protestant form) had turned the church inward and away from history—hence his critique of a "faith so unhistorical." To turn the church around, the church would itself need to face historical reality and hear the eschatological, apocalyptic call of the Spirit of Pentecost announcing the emergence of the gospel in a new world.

The world of modern history, argues Metz, is a world oriented to change and to the future. It is this commitment to the future that provides what Metz calls a "horizon," and what Tillich might have called a common criterion, within which Christian theology can actually engage secular thought. But before Metz uses this horizon of the future to engage the secular world, he first uses it to critique neo-orthodox and existentialist theology.

> This horizon [the future] . . . reveals the world as history, history as final history (*Endgeschichte*), faith as hope, and theology as eschatology.

While Metz builds on the idea of eschatology, so deeply entrenched in biblical studies and in neo-orthodoxy, he uses that eschatological horizon to critique the existentialist theologies of recent decades.

This horizon [the future] characterizes the attempt of theology to sur-
pass and to go beyond the modern transcendental, personalistic, and
existential theology without disregarding its valuable insights. . . . It
has brought the Christian faith into a proper relationship to human
existence and subjectivity. However, this [existential] theology faces
two dangers. On the one hand, this . . . theology tends to limit the
faith by concentrating on the *actual* moment of the believer's personal decision. The *future* is then all but lost. It becomes only another
name for the intractable factors of the present decision. On the other
hand, this . . . theology tends to become private and individualistic.
It fails to bring into sufficient prominence the social and political
dimensions of the believer's faith and responsibility.[6]

If Bultmann had called for demythologizing the Scriptures in
order to make them existentially powerful, Metz now calls for the
"de-privatization" of existential theology "in order to make the
Christian word a *socially* effective word."[7] And he invokes the authority of the martyred Dietrich Bonhoeffer to make his point:

Dietrich Bonhoeffer prophesied it [a new de-privatized and therefore public language of faith] in his own way: "The day will come
on which men will again be called to speak the word of God in such
a way that the world will be transformed and renewed by it. It will
be a new language, perhaps quite unreligious, but liberating and re-
demptive, like the language of Christ, so that men will be terrified
by it, and yet overcome by its strength, the language of a new justice
in truth, the language that proclaims the peace of God towards men
and the approach of his kingdom."[8]

Metz's de-privatized eschatology enables him to read Jesus'
proclamation of the kingdom of God in a new political light. If
the horizon, or common ground, that enables the church to confront and be engaged with the world, is the "future," then the key
Christian terminology for that engagement is not simply eschatology, but more specifically, the coming kingdom of God.

The Christian is moved to flee and to renounce the world not because he despises the world but because he hopes in the future of
the world as proclaimed in God's promises. . . . A faith which is
guided by such a hope is primarily not a doctrine, but an initiative
for the passionate innovating and changing of the world toward the
Kingdom of God.[9]

While Metz preserves neo-orthodoxy's sense of the distinctiveness of the church over against the world, he believes the existentialist interpretation of the gospel has led the church, in Käsemann's words, to contemplating "its own navel." The gospel, insists Metz, is not simply for the church, but for the world, and not simply for individual conversion but for the transformation of society. "The Church is not the goal of her own strivings; this goal is the Kingdom of God."[10] In Metz's political understanding of the gospel, however, this kingdom of God is not simply a Platonic form, but a historical goal.

> These promises [the eschatological promises of the Kingdom of God] stipulate and appeal to us to make them a present reality in the present historical condition and, in this way, to verify them—for we must "veri-fy" them. The New Testament community knew at once that it was called to live out the coming promise under the conditions of what was their "now," and so to overcome the world. . . . Jesus' parables—to mention another biblical detail in this context—are parables of the kingdom of God, but, *at the same time*, they instruct us in a renewed critical relationship to our world. *Every eschatological theology, therefore, must become a political theology, that is a socio-critical theology.*[11] (Metz's emphasis)

While Metz does not turn explicitly to the work of the New Quest in his book *Theology of the World*, his use of eschatology to critique current existential interpretations of theology and to open up the political dimensions of Jesus' teaching of the kingdom of God is a pivotal development.

Both James Cone, in his 1970 book *A Black Theology of Liberation* and Gustavo Gutierrez in his 1971 book *A Theology of Liberation* make more explicit use of the New Quest research. Cone is quite explicit. After quoting several passages from Käsemann's 1953 lecture and citing other New Quest scholars as well, Cone links their work to the task of Black theology:

> Like the theologians of the new quest, black theology also takes seriously the historical Jesus. We want to know who Jesus *was* because we believe that this is the only way to assess who he *is*. . . . Without some continuity between the historical Jesus and the kerygmatic Christ, the Christian gospel becomes nothing but the subjective reflections of the early Christian community.[12]

While Cone takes this historical research seriously, he moves it in a distinctively new direction.

Taking seriously the New Testament Jesus, black theology believes that the historical kernel is the manifestation of Jesus as the
Oppressed One whose earthly existence was bound up with the oppressed of the land. . . . To understand the historical Jesus without
seeing his identification with the poor as decisive is to misunder-
stand him and thus distort his historical person.[13]

Cone turns the understanding of Jesus in Black theology against
the assumptions of "white" theology. Claiming that the "history of
Christendom, at least from the time of Constantine, is a history of
human enslavement,"[14] Cone argues that white scholars continue
to misread Jesus' core message of the kingdom of God:

Jesus' restriction of the kingdom to the poor has far-reaching implications for our understanding of the gospel message. It is interesting,
if not surprising, to watch white New Testament scholars explain
away the real theological significance of Jesus' teachings on the kingdom and the poor. . . . As long as oppressors can be sure that the
gospel does not threaten their social, economic, and political secu-
rity, they can enslave others in the name of Jesus Christ.[15]

Similarly, Gustavo Gutierrez, while appreciative of Metz's approach to political theology, expresses some concern that this new
political theology has emerged in affluent Europe. "This explains,"
says Gutierrez, "the rather abstract level on which the political
sphere is at times treated in Metz's writings."[16] Adds Gutierrez:
"in places like Latin America, things are different. The process [of
political theology] here does not have the characteristics [of secularization and privatization] it exhibits in Europe. Faith, the gospel, the church, have in Latin America a complex public dimension
which has played (and still plays) an important role in support of
the established order."[17]

Arguing against the Christian tendency to interpret Jesus in an
apolitical manner—that being the traditional idea that "Jesus was
not interested in political life; his mission was purely religious"[18]—
Gutierrez turns to the "historical Jesus" to locate the political dimensions of Jesus' life. Discussing the similarities and differences
that Jesus shared with the Zealots, Jesus' stance toward Jewish
leaders, and his execution by political authorities, Gutierrez argues
that Jesus' message transcends the voices and concerns of his context because the gospel he announces "goes to the very root of human existence: the relationship with God in solidarity with men."
He continues:

The Gospel does not get its political dimension from one or another particular option, but from the very nucleus of the message. . . . The life and preaching of Jesus postulate the unceasing search for a new kind of man in a qualitatively different society. . . . More profoundly, the announcement of the Kingdom reveals to society itself the aspiration for a just society and leads it to discover unsuspected dimensions and unexplored paths.[19]

While major works by other liberationists including Leonardo Boff (*Jesus Christ, Liberator*, 1972) and Jon Sobrino (*Christology at the Crossroads*, 1978) would make more extensive use of New Quest research, one sees already the basic pattern. The New Quest's focus on the *message* of Jesus—understood centrally as the proclamation of the kingdom of God and the presence of an implicit Christology—enabled a social and political interpretation of the "hearers of the Word."

The focus on Jesus' teaching of the kingdom enabled new interpretations of Jesus *as the Christ*. The core concern of these new Christologies was not on Jesus' atoning death; rather, this new focus on his teaching emphasized his *solidarity* with the marginalized. Jesus' death and resurrection remained important, but not because of a theology of atonement; rather, Jesus' death was now seen as faithful and courageous consequence of his solidarity with the oppressed. In these new voices, Jesus' message echoes that of the prophets; God's reign, God's will, was for a transformed society, not simply for a "privatized" existential decision of faith.

The Christian Humanism
of Hans Küng

Influenced by the political theologies of the day, but less strident in tone, Hans Küng's *Christ Sein* made an immediate impression upon its publication in Germany in 1974 and in the United States in 1976 when it was translated as *On Being a Christian*. Critical of neo-orthodoxy's too narrow interpretation of the faith, Küng announces that by the time of his writing things have, in fact, already changed within the church itself: "Surprisingly enough, Church and theology have not only—in the end—come to terms with the secularization process, but—particularly in the time since the Second Vatican Council [which ended in 1965]—have even entered vigorously into the swing of it."[20] But this "turn," says Küng, to "the 'world,' to society, to the modern sciences, was overdue."

Even conservative Christians cannot overlook the way in which the Church, particularly in modern times, has increasingly compromised and distorted the Christian message. . . . It thus became more and more remote from the men who were pressing modern history toward greater freedom, rationality, humanity: a Church encapsulated and on the defensive against the modern outlook, outwardly tied up with the ruling powers, inwardly traditionalist, authoritarian and often totalitarian.[21]

Küng sees his work, therefore, as a major attempt to re-situate Christianity within the broad and deep discussions of "humanism," with a particular concern for what, if anything is distinctive about a *Christian* humanism. Like Gilkey, who more forcefully than Metz argued that the neo-orthodox separation of church from society was deeply flawed, Küng calls for a serious re-engagement with the world.

Pure kerygmatic theology has had its day. A scholarly answer to the question about the Jesus of history is again regarded as possible today in a new form and within certain limits: not only in Anglo-Saxon and French exegesis, but also once more in German and indeed—after Ernst Käsemann had given the signal to turn in 1953—in the Bultmann school itself.[22]

Yet, in the same breath, Küng acknowledges Metz's critique of the existentialist readings of Scripture: "However justified the interpretation of all New Testament texts with reference to the 'historicity' of human existence ('existential interpretation') and to the 'decision' of the individual, it must not become so individualistic and introspective as to rule out real history (and thus the 'world,' society, the social relevance of the message, the future)."[23]

What determines for Küng the heart of the Christian message—a message that is, in his view, radically humanistic—is the teaching of Jesus. By arguing that the heart of the Christian message is the teaching of Jesus and not simply his death and resurrection, Küng draws on the findings of the New Quest to shift the centerpiece of Christian theology toward a set of commitments and a way of life and not the imitation of Jesus' death. At the heart of Jesus' message, according to Küng, is his teaching about the kingdom of God. It would be a serious mistake, says Küng, if one interpreted that "kingdom" as aimed only at "man's soul," as if Jesus were to be interpreted "merely as a pastor and confessor." Instead, argues Küng:

"The message of God's kingdom is aimed at man in all his dimensions, not only at man's soul but at the *whole* man in his mental and material existence, in his whole concrete, suffering world."[24] And when one looks to the content of Jesus' message of the kingdom, Küng sounds remarkably like Käsemann when describing Jesus' rejection of legalism.

> It is clear that Jesus did set himself above the law: not only above tradition, the oral tradition of the Fathers, the *halakhah*, but above Scripture itself, the sacred law of God, the Torah, recorded in the five books of Moses. . . . He rejected completely the binding force of oral tradition. In word and deed he attacked the regulations of cultic purity and fasting and particularly the Sabbath regulations.[25]

With other members of the Quest, Küng affirms the authenticity of the "But I say to you" antitheses of the Sermon on the Mount and the "Amen, amen, I say to you" sayings—both of which seem to indicate a claim of authority greater than Moses, and thus an implicit Christology.

If the kingdom of God is not finally about the Law or legalism, however, what is the kingdom of God about? Turning to the Lord's Prayer, Küng underscores the petition, "Your will be done."

> What God wills in heaven is to be done on earth. This then is the meaning of the message of the coming of God's kingdom, it is understood as a demand made on men here and now: let what God wills be done. . . . For many devout people "doing God's will" has become a pious formula. They have identified it with the law. . . . It is precisely this legalistic attitude however to which Jesus give the *deathblow*. . . . Man's relationship to God is not established by a code of law, without his being personally involved. He must submit himself, not simply to the law, but to God: to accept, that is, what God demands of him in a wholly personal way.[26]

As with many of the New Quest scholars, the responsiveness of faith remains framed in largely individual if not directly existential terms. Yet Küng also follows Fuchs's emphasis on Jesus' deeds.

> Jesus' words really were eminently deeds. . . . Theory and practice, for Jesus, coincide in a much more comprehensive sense: his *whole behavior* corresponds to his proclamation. And, while his verbal proclamation substantiates and justifies his conduct, his actual behavior clarifies his proclamation in the light of practice, makes it unassailable: he lives what he says and this gains him the minds and hearts of his hearers.[27]

And this widening of his perspective—indebted to the work of political and liberation theologians in the 1960s—expands the language of the kingdom of God beyond existentialism to social and political structures. According to Küng, Jesus, by "the company he kept," pushed beyond the legalism and social mores of his day.

> Jesus took up an essential positive attitude to all of them [social outcasts] and . . . rejected in principle any causal connection between sin and sickness and also social ostracism. . . .

> Women, *who did not count in society at that time and had to avoid men's company in public.* . . . Children, *who had no rights.* . . . People ignorant of religion, *the numerous small people who could not or would not bother about the law. These "simple" ones are commended: the uneducated, backward, immature, irreligious, those who are not at all clever or wise, the "little" or "lowly," even "least" or "lowest."*[28] (Küng's emphasis)

Faith, or "being Christian," according to Küng, makes sense for one's whole life. "We began this book with the direct question: *Why should one be a Christian*? And the answer is equally direct: *In order to be truly human*."[29] By arguing that Christian faith represents a better understanding of humanism than other contemporary models, Küng has also shifted the eschatological language of the first two-thirds of the twentieth century to wisdom language:

> Christians are no less humanists than all other humanists. But they see the human, the truly human, the humane; they see man and his God; see humanity, freedom, justice, life, love, peace, meaning: all these they see in the light of this Jesus who for them is the concrete criterion, the Christ. In his light they think they cannot support just any kind of humanism which simply affirms all that is true, good, beautiful and human. But they can support a truly radical humanism which is able to integrate and cope with what is untrue, not good, unlovely, inhuman: not only everything positive, but also—and here we discern what a humanism has to offer—everything negative, even suffering, sin, death, futility. . . .

> > *By following Jesus Christ*
> > *man in the world of today*
> > *can truly humanly live, act, suffer and die:*
> > *in happiness and unhappiness, life and death,*
> > *sustained by God and helpful to men.* [30]

Eschatology is still present in Küng's proposal—a profound focus on the kingdom of God as "God's future," a "consummation" that "does not come about either through social (intellectual or technical) evolution or social revolution (of the right or the left)."[31] But the focus of eschatology is turned more decisively toward social critique: "The hope in God's future must serve . . . to criticize the present world and thus to transform society and existence."[32] In this way eschatology begins to blend into visionary wisdom demanding embodiment and practice.

Feminist Theologies of Daly, Radford Ruether and Schüssler Fiorenza

In 1968 Mary Daly published *The Church and the Second Sex*. Indebted to Simone de Beauvoir's *The Second Sex* (1949), the book was a powerful critique of the patriarchal assumptions of Christian discourse. Followed in 1973 by her classic, *Beyond God the Father*, Daly repudiated Christology as *Christolatry*. "I am proposing that Christian idolatry concerning the person of Jesus is not likely to be overcome except through the revolution that is going on in women's consciousness. It will, I think, become increasingly evident that exclusively masculine symbols for the idea of 'incarnation' or for the ideal of the human search for fulfillment will not do."[33] Daly, who understood the Bible as a "culture-bound book" did not find discussions of the historical Jesus helpful. "The problem is not that the Jesus of the gospels was male, young, and a Semite. Rather, the problem lies in the exclusive identification of this person with God, in such a manner that Christian conceptions of divinity and of the 'image of God' are all objectified in Jesus."[34]

While other Christian feminists acknowledged Daly's contributions to feminist philosophy and theology, they did not agree with her assessment on the question of Jesus. Rosemary Radford Ruether's 1983 work *Sexism and God-Talk: Toward a Feminist Theology* asks the question, "Can a Male Savior Save Women?" Radford Ruether acknowledges the problem to which Daly pointed: "A Christology that identified the maleness of the historical Jesus with normative humanity and with the maleness of the divine *Logos* must move in an increasingly misogynistic direction that not only excludes women as representative of Christ in ministry but makes her a second-class citizen in both creation and redemption."[35] Rejecting both "Spirit Christologies" and "Androgynous Christologies," Radford Ruether calls for a "reencounter with the Jesus of the synoptic Gospels, not the accumulated doctrine about him but his message and praxis."[36] Calling for something akin to Bultmann's demythologizing of ancient texts, Radford Ruether says that "once the mythology about Jesus as Messiah or divine *Logos* . . . is stripped off, the Jesus of the synoptic Gospels can be recognized as a figure remarkably compatible with feminism."[37] By this statement, Radford Ruether does not mean to suggest that "Jesus was a feminist" but that

> Jesus renews the prophetic vision whereby the Word of God does not validate the existing social and religious hierarchy but speaks on behalf of the marginalized and despised of society. . . . This reversal of social order doesn't just turn hierarchy upside down, it aims at a new reality in which hierarchy and dominance are overcome as principles of social relations.[38]

By focusing on the message and praxis of Jesus—as modeled in the New Quest—Radford Ruether can argue: "Theologically speaking . . . we might say that the maleness of Jesus has no ultimate significance. . . . Jesus, the homeless prophet, and the marginalized women and men who respond to him represent the overthrow of the present world system and the sign of a dawning new age in which God's will is done on earth."[39]

Also published in 1983, Elisabeth Schüssler Fiorenza's *In Memory of Her* makes more extensive use of the New Quest materials. Reaching back to Elizabeth Cady Stanton (*The Woman's Bible*, 1895), who "conceived of biblical interpretation as a political act," Schüssler Fiorenza rethinks Christian origins and therefore Christian theology through the lens of a feminist hermeneutics.[40] Indebted to Daly's *Beyond God the Father* and to the work of political and liberation theologians, including Metz, Schüssler Fiorenza calls for a "paradigm change" to undo the patriarchal assumptions embedded in both academic scholarship as well as in Christian theology.

> Since paradigms determine how scholars see the world and how they conceive of theoretical problems, a shift from an androcentric to a feminist paradigm implies a transformation of the scientific imagination. It demands an intellectual conversion that cannot be logically deduced but is rooted in a change of patriarchal-social relationships. Such an intellectual conversion engenders a shift in commitment that allows the community of scholars to see old "data" in a completely new perspective.[41]

Her commitment to the critical hermeneutics of feminist studies leads Schüssler Fiorenza to affirm her "primary accountability" to "the women's movement for societal-ecclesial change rather than to the academy" with its patriarchal tendencies.[42] Such a commitment, however, does not involve a wholesale rejection of the academy.

> In my opinion, feminist biblical scholarship and historical bibli-
> cal scholarship share as their common hermeneutical perspective
> a critical commitment to the Christian community and its tradi-
> tions. . . . Feminist historical analyses . . . share both the impetus of
> historical biblical studies and an explicit commitment to a contem-
> porary group of people, women, who, either religiously or cultur-
> ally, are impacted by the traditions of the Bible.[43]

Of particular interest to my argument is that Schüssler Fiorenza draws, in part, on the scholarship of the New Quest to interpret what she calls the Jesus movement. Her very expression "Jesus movement" underscores the *continuity* between Jesus and the early church that is the hallmark of the New Quest: "I am not seeking to 'distill' the most 'authentic' tradition of Jesus-sayings in such a way as to separate Jesus from his own people, Israel, and his first followers. The Jesus movement is not conceivable without Jesus, of course, but it is also inconceivable without Jesus' followers."[44]

Following Perrin's advice that one should situate the message of Jesus contextually before interpreting it, Schüssler Fiorenza situates the Jesus movement as a "renewal movement within Judaism."[45] She then sets about distinguishing Jesus' message from that of John, the Pharisees, and the Essene community. The difference, she says, between Jesus and John the Baptist is not so much a "break" but a "shift in emphasis." "While John announces God's judgment and wrath preceding the *basileia* (the Greek term for kingdom or em-pire) and eschatological restitution of Israel, Jesus stresses that, in his own ministry and movement, the eschatological salvation and wholeness of Israel as the elect people of God is already experien-tially available."[46] Moreover, it is the distinctive way that Jesus and his movement interpret the experiential availability of the *basileia* that distinguishes Jesus from the Essenes and the Pharisees.

> Just as the Essenes and Pharisaic associations, the Jesus movement
> gathered around the table and shared their food and drink. Yet while
> the Pharisees sought to realize Israel's calling as a "nation of priests"
> by carefully observing the ritual purity of the "holy table" and by
> eating their meals "like priests," Jesus and his movement did not
> observe these purity regulations and even shared their meals with
> "sinners." The central symbolic actualization of the *basileia* vision of
> Jesus is not the cultic meal but the festive table of a royal banquet or

wedding feast. This difference in emphasis was probably one of the major conflict points between the Jesus movement and the Pharisaic movement.[47]

Schüssler Fiorenza then takes the festive availability of the *basileia* and moves the discussion of that teaching in a new direction. Noting the "patriarchal culture" in which the Jesus movement was inaugurated, she argues that "it is important to see who the people are for whom the *basileia* is claimed."[48] Schüssler Fiorenza makes an important shift here. If one thinks of Bultmann and the existential interpretations of Jesus' proclamation, one remembers the focus on the "call to decision." Küng, too, interprets the *basileia* as a call to radical following of the "will of God" within a largely modern and secular culture. But Schüssler Fiorenza understands the *basileia* differently. With other liberationist theologians, she brings to the fore what has been hiding in plain sight: "that Jesus claimed the *basileia* for *three* distinct groups of people: (1) the destitute poor; (2) the sick and the crippled; and (3) tax collectors, sinners, and prostitutes."[49] For these groups, the *basileia* is not primarily an existential challenge; it is "good news" announcing God's favor and God's passionate concern for them. And in the following passage, Schüssler Fiorenza links Jesus' proclamation of the *basileia* to the contemporary movement for women's liberation:

> The tensive symbol *basileia* of God evokes in ever new images a realization of the gracious goodness of Israel's God and the equality and solidarity of the people of God. A very similar understanding of equality is expressed in one of the earliest statements of the contemporary women's liberation movement:
>
> > "We define the best interests of women as the best interests of the poorest, most insulted, most despised, most abused woman on earth. . . . Until Everywoman is free, no woman will be free."
>
> Radical feminism has rediscovered the "equality from below" espoused by the Jesus movement in Palestine without recognizing its religious roots.[50]

This linkage between the *basileia* of Jesus and the universal history of women's political and cultural oppression is carried forward by Schüssler Fiorenza in a distinctive way. Interpreting the Jesus movement's proclamation of the *basileia* as a "discipleship of equals," she argues—against the backdrop of Jesus' parables and wisdom sayings—that a model of God as *Sophia*, as the goddess

Wisdom, informs the teaching and praxis of the Jesus movement. So much so, that Schüssler Fiorenza argues that "Jesus probably understood himself as the prophet and child of Sophia."[51]

> To sum up, the Palestinian Jesus movement understands the ministry and mission of Jesus as that of the prophet and child of Sophia sent to announce that God is the God of the poor and heavy laden, of the outcasts and those who suffer injustice. As child of Sophia he stands in a long line and succession of prophets sent to gather the children of Israel to their gracious Sophia-God.[52]

Such an understanding of the Jesus movement's proclamation of the *basileia* lays the basis for a transformed model of the church and its relationship to the world of suffering people.

Gilkey, Metz, Cone, Gutierrez, Radford Ruether, Schüssler Fiorenza, Küng and many other theologians have all utilized the historical Jesus research associated with the New Quest to move the central concern of Christian faith and theology from the neo-orthodox and traditionalist Roman Catholic preoccupation with life *inside* the church to a much more dramatic concern for life and peoples *outside* the church. While it would be wildly incorrect to say that the historical research of the New Quest in any way caused these new theological movements, it is appropriate to point out that the scholarly work of the New Quest provided extremely important supporting arguments that enabled the message of Jesus to be not only heard but proclaimed in both new and profoundly challenging ways.

Conclusion

From the self-isolating rhetoric of Kähler and Barth, who had rejected the quest for Jesus in favor of divine revelation and a safe haven for Christian faith in a newly emerging secular society, the scholars of the New Quest had sought to help pull the church back toward an engagement with the modern world with all its problems and its promise. It is ironic that the scholarship of the New Quest, which had sought to avoid scandal by assuring ecclesial authorities of its orthodox intentions (such as fidelity to the incarnation and the articulation of an "implicit Christology"), gave rise to the most revolutionary, although arguably orthodox, theologies of the twentieth century. Many found these theologies enormously hopeful in expanding the public sensibility of the church. Others, however, were scandalized by the claims of women, of black Americans, of the desperately impoverished poor of Latin America and of Asia, that Jesus' preaching of the kingdom of God had called, in effect, for the systematic transformation of the social, economic, and political structures of the world.

While Vatican II (1962–65), convened by Pope John XXIII, had itself provided both hope and confidence for both Catholic and Protestant theologians alike for a serious re-engagement with the world, a variety of post-Vatican II pronouncements on birth control, on denying ordination to women, and on the errors of liberation theology, combined with the crackdown on theologians such as Küng and Boff confirmed just how limited the Vatican's outreach to the modern world would be. Nonetheless, neither theology nor culture could simply reject or avoid the newly empowered voices. Or could they?

Many Protestants also found these political theologies too radical to affirm, with many in the largely white Baptist and Evangelical community continuing to deny women access to ordination, and to reject calls for economic and political transformation. The rising religious and political power of these latter groups in the United States, along with conservative Roman Catholics, would fuel the revival of Christian fundamentalism as a political force in American politics and set the stage for a Renewed Quest for the historical Jesus.

Part Three

The Renewed Quest

CHAPTER 10

The Turn to Language in Biblical Studies and Theology

In the previous two parts of the book I have argued that the two quests for the historical Jesus discussed so far were themselves part of wider quests of truly historic dimensions. The first quest for the historical Jesus involved a search for an open civil society, free from the authority of the established churches. The "New Quest" involved a search, within the Christian community itself, for a theology connected to human experience and to the modern world. As we move into our discussion of a third quest, it is again important for us to consider the theological and cultural questions surrounding what Robert Funk would call the Renewed Quest, as undertaken by the Jesus Seminar.

By focusing on the Jesus Seminar as a third major quest for the historical Jesus, I do not mean to discount the significant work of other individual scholars on the historical Jesus. What I take to be historic about the Jesus Seminar is the commitment by a significant number of scholars to move outside of both church and academy in order to address a wider, public audience. In its commitment to examine texts outside the Christian canon of the New Testament and in its commitment to draw conclusions without regard to Christian doctrine, the Jesus Seminar veered significantly from the assumptions and practices of the New Quest, even as it built on the accomplishments of that endeavor.

Perhaps more importantly, the Jesus Seminar's commitment to a public audience was shaped by two important developments, one academic, which we will explore in this chapter, and one political, which we will take up in Chapter 11. On the academic side, the social sciences, the humanities (including philosophy and the arts), and theology were undergoing a profound paradigm shift *from* a focus on the human subject *to* a focus on language as the medium in which all experience occurs and within which all experience is both constructed and interpreted. Demonstrating the situated, interpretive, and power-laced character of virtually all human discourse, this turn to language resisted claims of universal understanding or totalizing truth in favor of more contextual analyses of human speech and behavior.

Influenced in part by the later Heidegger's shift to the study of language (as epitomized in his famous phrase, "Language is the house of Being"), philosophers such as Hans-Georg Gadamer (hermeneutics), Richard Rorty (neo-Pragmatism), Jacques Derrida (deconstruction), Kenneth Burke (rhetoric), and Michel Foucault (analysis of power), to name several major theorists, began to influence the direction of biblical and theological studies by turning them toward language. For these theorists, human experience was not available as a kind of "given"; rather, experience was always already interpreted within the web of language. Derrida's phrase, "there is nothing outside the text" pointed anew to the construction of human knowledge and thus also to the impossibility of any univocal, or once-for-all, interpretations of reality.

Often referred to in discussions of "postmodernism," the turn to language functioned to reorient philosophical and theological understandings of truth. From the nineteenth- and twentieth-century model on truth as a totalizing, univocal explanation of reality, to truth as discernible only within absence, hiddenness, and an unstable play of perspectives, the shift to language made truth a moving target. Thus, the study of rhetoric, dismissed in much of the modern period as mere decoration, re-emerges with this new turn to language as a focus on the construction of arguments and the construction of meaning within the multiple audiences and motivations of social and political contexts, even as the discipline of hermeneutics also comes to the fore with its attention on the complex, situated character of all interpretation.

On the political side, which we will take up in the next chapter, the political phenomenon that would shape the project of the Jesus Seminar was the resurgence of Christian fundamentalism as a powerful political force in the United States. While at one level fundamentalism appears to move in the opposite direction of postmodernism's "turn to language," the politicized fundamentalism of the Moral Majority, Christian Coalition and other groups was no mere throwback to the early fundamentalism of late nineteenth and early twentieth century. Here, that tradition, which certainly since the Scopes Trial of 1925 had pursued a more culturally separate course, reappears with rhetorical force, connecting to the moral concerns of Roman Catholics over abortion along with the political aims of Ronald Reagan and the Republican Party in their attempts to wed the interests of fiscal and social conservatives, and using social media and technology to advance an agenda of religious and political establishment. Even as it rejected postmodernism's emphasis on the play of language in favor of its own rigid truth claims and supernaturalism, the newly politicized Christian fundamentalism used all the strategies of the "turn to language" to shape its own religious and political rhetoric.

In this chapter, however, we focus on the turn to language in order to get a handle on when the New Quest ended and when the Renewed Quest began. We will pursue this question in three phases: first, we will look at the way several leading scholars associated with the Jesus Seminar were working on Jesus-related topics prior to formation of the Jesus Seminar in 1985. These scholars, Robert Funk, John Dominic Crossan, Bernard Brandon Scott, and Marcus Borg, were all influenced by the New Quest but were also thoroughly involved in the new turn to language. Secondly, we will turn to the work of significant theologians, University of Chicago theologian David Tracy on the one hand and Yale theologians Hans Frei and George Lindbeck on the other. These theologians crafted major theoretical positions, known as "revisionist" theology (Tracy) and "narrative," or "postliberal," theology (Frei/Lindbeck) that shaped the discipline of theology—certainly in the United States— over the decades of the 1980s and 1990s. In this second section of the chapter we will study their proposals for developing the "turn to language" in theology, and note similarities and differences to the positions of Tillich, with respect to Tracy, and Barth with respect to Frei and Lindbeck. In the third section of this chapter, I turn more specifically to Tracy's and Lindbeck's arguments, as respondents to a 1979 forum in which they rejected—in varying ways—Hans Küng's proposal that the historical Jesus should be the criterion and norm for Christian theology. I will suggest that that conference is a helpful marker for thinking about the end of the New Quest, and for thinking about the beginning of the Renewed Quest.

The "Turn to Language" in Funk, Crossan, Scott, and Borg

It is difficult to assess when the New Quest ended; its theological impact was felt well into the 1980s, as discussed in the previous chapter. The New Quest had proven helpful not only in turning theology toward human experience but also in opening up the diversity of human experience, especially with respect to themes of racial, gender, and economic justice. The conviction that the preaching of the kingdom of God lay at the very heart of the historical Jesus' life and teaching had helped authorize a new set of political theologies identifying with Jesus' social/political message. To the extent that eschatology remained significant for these political theologies, it was in the context of hope for a changed future in the near-term, not in the long-term of eternity. And thus, these theologies sought to ignite a sense of resurrected hope and new life in communities that had suffered systemic injustice. The themes of grace and faith prepared one not so much for the eschatological hereafter but for the realized eschatology that came with a sense of empowerment. As communities of traditionally marginalized persons realized that God—God as Woman, God as Black, God as the Oppressed One—was calling them, encouraging them into a new and different form of empowered transgressive speech, they were no longer content with patience and waiting for the end of history. Instead, God was calling them into history and into the process of making history.

For these theologies the New Quest's turn to experience, as such, was not nearly adequate, as we saw in the last chapter. Rather, the question of *whose experience* called for wider democratization in both church and society. Attempts, for example, by some theologians in the late 1960s through the early 1980s to speak of "common human experience" were contested by feminist theologians, African-American theologians, and a variety of liberationist theologians, on the grounds that such a claim to "common experience" functioned to silence the very real differences of those who suffered under the regime of the "common experience" of white, European males. Under such scrutiny, the rhetoric of existentialism, with its challenge to personal authenticity, also began to appear, if not quaint, at least inadequate to address the newly emerging concerns about power and group consciousness. In addition to the new awareness of social power embedded in language systems, the focus on human "experience" was itself shifting to a new philosophical focus on "language."

The turn to language and to issues of power lay near the heart of the historic question that the Renewed Quest would itself ask as it sought to discern what Robert Funk called the "voice print" of Jesus. In biblical studies and in theology, the language of metaphor and of story or narrative began to appear not simply as a vehicle of delivery but as the organizing structure of the discipline and its interpretive key. Other tropes, including analogy, irony, metonymy, and hyperbole, would follow suit. By turning to such figurative devices, biblical and theological scholars affirmed that language itself was in no sense literal or transparent to experience. Language, instead, was always at a remove from experience, or "presence," as Derrida put it. Robert Funk and John Dominic Crossan were co-chairs of the Jesus Seminar throughout its early work from 1985–93, which culminated in *The Five Gospels*. Both are often associated with the earlier New Quest due to their significant literary analysis of the parables, influenced by the existentialism of Heidegger and the turn to language among post-Heideggarian philosophers.

ROBERT FUNK, in his critically acclaimed work of 1966, *Language, Hermeneutic, and Word of God: The Problem of Language in the New Testament and Contemporary Theology*, extends C. H. Dodd's understanding of parable as metaphor. He uses the language of metaphor to pull together the existentialist and eschatological themes of other biblical scholars and theologians of the New Quest.

> Metaphor seeks to rupture the grip of tradition on man's apprehension of the world in order to permit a glimpse of another world, which is not really a different but a strangely familiar world. Metaphor, moreover, remains temporally open-ended, thus permitting the hermeneutical potential of the vision conjured up to make its own claim upon the future. It is in these senses that parabolic imagery is genuinely metaphorical. It does not look *at* everydayness, but *through* it. It fractures everydayness in the interest of a referential totality of a peculiar order.[1] (Funk's emphasis)

In the language of "everydayness," one can hear Heidegger's critique of conventionality in the human situation; in Funk's arguing for parable's "claim upon the future," one hears Bultmann's eschatological horizon. It will take Funk only a page or two more to claim that the parable presents the hearer with a "choice."

> It is too little to call the parables as metaphors teaching devices; they are that, but much more. They are language events in which the hearer has to choose between worlds. If he elects the parabolic world, he is invited to dispose himself to concrete reality as it is ordered in the parable, and venture, without benefit of landmark but on the parable's authority, into the future.[2]

It is the parable for Funk that pulls together the existential and eschatological dimensions of Jesus' preaching of the kingdom of God into a word event (the word "event" from Heidegger's translation of the Greek *ereigness*) that can challenge the hearer. One can see in this argument how Funk's work was instrumental in the biblical scholarship of the New Quest. But one also finds passages in which Funk is thinking differently. Even in the passage quoted initially, the idea that metaphor "seeks to rupture the grip of tradition" is a provocative way of putting metaphor's turn upon the conventionality of language. It is true that at one level he is thinking of Jesus' critique of the rabbinic interpretation of the law: "Jesus attempted nothing less than to shatter the whole tradition that had obscured the law."[3] And yet, Funk's use of "shattering" language echoes Käsemann's that we saw several chapters back. Funk, along with others in the 1960s, like Harvey Cox in *The Secular City* and Gilkey in *Naming the Whirlwind*, believes that secular culture needs to be creatively engaged. In his treatment of the parable of the Good Samaritan, for example, Funk notes that "the parable draws a narrative picture that is wholly secular: neither God nor his Messiah 'appear.' And the Samaritan responds to the needs of the neighbor without ulterior reasons."[4] Funk's affirmation of the secular continues even as he points to the sacred dimension of the story:

> Nevertheless, it must now also be said that the reign of love—to use a "secular" term—has drawn near for the Samaritan, too, as it were. He has taken up his whole abode in a world where the plight of neighbor, in and out of itself, draws a net of love around the cohumanity of the two.[5]

One can see in these few lines how Funk uses parable to rethink the language of revelation, not as a supernatural phenomenon but as a language event that opens up and discloses an alternative way of being in the world. When he writes of the Samaritan, "He has taken up his whole abode in a world," he means that the Samaritan has entered into the "reign of love," a secular rendering of Jesus' *basileia tou theou*.

Funk's interest in using language and the workings of secular literature to open up the meaning of the parables and of the sacred as a possible dimension of reality (rather than thinking of the sacred in terms of the supernatural) is underscored in his little book, *Jesus as Precursor*. In one provocative chapter after another Funk sets Jesus, his parables, and his teaching of the kingdom of God alongside the enigmatic work of the great contemporary parabolists Franz Kafka, Jorge Luis Borges and other major critical and prophetic writers of the nineteenth and twentieth centuries. Drawing on the work of philosophers like Heidegger and Ludwig Wittgenstein as well as

Philip Wheelwright's writings on metaphor, Funk seeks to explore how understanding the literary character of Jesus' parables actually enables one to understand the sacred dimension to which the parables point.

> It should now be clear why ironic, metaphoric, and parabolic language came so readily to Jesus' lips. These modes of language point beyond themselves, to what cannot be said; they refuse to come to rest in the literal, the particular, the propositional, the casuistic. To criticisms, questions, situations, friendly and hostile, Jesus steadily refused to respond within the horizon of the received world. Instead, he referred his critics and friends, by means of non-explicit language, to the world, the horizon, which was real and ultimate for him—the domain of God.[6]

Funk's literary comparisons help him explore the counter-cultural character of the parables, and thus their capacity to speak to a mid-twentieth-century generation distrustful of conventions and the dead metaphors of tradition.

> To the artist of our time what is taken to be real is illusory; the common world is phony. The tradition merely deceives, reinforces the illusion, because it makes pretentious claims to ultimate truth. The artist forsakes the sanity of the received world and goes in mad search of the really real, which lies beyond the rim of present sight.[7]

Along with the contemporary artist, Funk is concerned that the parables no longer speak to us.

> As the parables were sedimented in the Jesus tradition, their potential as parables was stopped down, their metaphorical impact muted. The potential of the parable to evoke a fresh circumspective apprehension of the totality of what is there—a new world—was reduced to a specified meaning, a point, a teaching. This meaning or teaching could then be attached to the parable as a generalizing conclusion or be divorced from the parable and transmitted as a "truth." . . . The parable is mined for its moral and religious propositions. And the making-present of the reality of God is exchanged for belief in God.[8]

Funk's literary analysis of the parables, therefore, is an exploration of the parable's disclosive power in the face of a tradition too committed to static understandings of dogmatic truth. Nonetheless, Funk knows that whether the parables are a "living tradition" is far from certain. He realizes with philosopher George Steiner that in the wake of the *Shoah* it "is not possible to edit classical texts or write commentaries on scripture . . . without some premonition that these languages no longer speak."[9]

The work of historical and literary analysis of the parables is important, for Funk, precisely to determine whether the Jesus tradition can still speak a powerful and persuasive word. "The fundamental question for the interpreter who wishes to recover the Jesus tradition today is this: is it possible any longer to recover the parable as parable?"[10] In the "Epilogue" to the book, Funk suggests that his book might serve as an appropriate introduction to the discipline of theology:

> If theology is to address the human question, the study of theology ought to begin these days with a study of poetry—not a study of verse, but a study of poiesis in the root sense. Franz Kafka, Jorge Luis Borges, Albert Camus, Henry Miller, Samuel Beckett, Eugene Ionesco and their relatives may be sufficiently strong medicine to induce theology, once the queen of the humanities, to shake off her torpor.[11]

The revitalization of theology will occur, according to Funk, when theology joins "in the quest for the real in our time, even if that means emancipating itself from every apologetic ploy on behalf of the Christian faith."[12] Appealing to his argument that the parables open up an alternative world, Funk claims that "the real *theological* issue is whether human beings can find a concrete context for their existence, a real world to which they can give themselves." Funk sees some hope for such an engagement with reality "where theologians are talking to artists, poets, and those who wish to speak a word for NATURE."[13]

JOHN DOMINIC CROSSAN's *Cliffs of Fall: Paradox and Polyvalence in the Parables of Jesus,* published in 1980, takes seriously Funk's call for religious scholars to engage poets—the title of the book comes from a sonnet by Gerard Manley Hopkins. His thin but complex book engages the post-modern philosophy of Jacques Derrida and a range of literary critics including Paul Ricoeur, Stanley Fish, Roland Barthes and many others. In one passage, he seems to realize that the New Quest, which had frequently relied on the language of existentialism, was no longer sufficient.

> Before proceeding I would like to distinguish this structuralist basis from any existentialist parallel. I consider existentialism to be the end of one era and structuralism to be the start of another. And I consider existentialist nausea to be the ontological disappointment

of one who, having been taught that there is some overarching logical meaning beyond our perception, has come at length to believe there is no such fixed center towards which our searchings strive. Existentialism is, thus, the dull receding roar of classicism and rationalism, while structuralism is a new flood of the tide.[14]

Crossan goes on to use the example of a labyrinth to explore the difference between existentialism and structuralism a bit further. While existentialism laments "that there is no center" to the labyrinth, or "there's nothing in it, or one can't get out," structuralism says:

> that we create the labyrinth ourselves, that it has no center, that it is infinitely expansible, that we create it as play and for play, and that one can no more consider leaving it than one can envisage shedding one's skin.[15]

The structuralist insight—that we human beings exist within the labyrinth of language, and that all of our language, including our language for God, exists as a kind of infinite play within this labyrinth—has consequences for conventional theism. Influenced by ongoing discussions from the early 1960s about the "Death of God," both Funk and Crossan argue that the domesticated "god" of Christian theism no longer represents the heart of Christian theology. In the Epilogue of *Jesus as Precursor*, Funk had written: "the 'god' question . . . is no longer central for theology. Christology survives primarily as a human question—what it means to be human, rather than what it means to be a redeemer figure."[16] For Crossan, thinking in structuralist terms, the paradoxical character of Jesus' parables mirrors the Jewish problem of trying "to imagine an unimaginable God."

> It is, I would maintain, with the Jewish Jesus that the Jewish tradition forced the aniconicity of God onto the surface of language itself and, with inevitable paradox, announced that God could no more be trapped in the forms and genres of linguistic art than in the shapes and figures of plastic art.[17]

Both Crossan and Funk insist that the parables of Jesus open up a world of present and future possibility and, thus, are truly eschatological in the world-transforming sense. But both will also view apocalyptic as an already closed story, the left hand of a domesticated God. Funk writes: "Apocalypticism shirks human responsibility for history: in spite of its lively, reassuring images, an entirely apocalyptic outlook represents a failure in human imagination and resolve."[18] Crossan, writing of Jesus' language of the kingdom of God, also critiques the assumption of apocalypticism:

> Jesus' primary concern is indeed the Kingdom but I would consider it equally clear that his is a very special understanding of this escha-tological Kingdom, one which is, among other things, totally anti-apocalyptic. Not anti-apocalyptic in minor details concerning signs and times but anti-apocalyptic as deriving from a radically non-apocalyptic imagination. Jesus' Kingdom is a permanent possibility and not an imminent certainty.[19]

It is helpful to review the intellectual and theological commit-ments of these two co-chairs of the Jesus Seminar. Both were con-cerned with attempting to locate what Crossan called the "Jesus version" of the parable (in contrast to the readings given by the gos-pel narratives) and to the "voice print" of Jesus. Neither believed one could excavate the *ippissima verba* (the exact words) of Jesus, and neither approached the quest for the teaching of Jesus within anything like the foundationalist assumptions of modernism (i.e., the assumption that once one located a point of certainty one could go on to "build" a body of true knowledge on that "foundation"). Instead, they hoped—in their differing ways—to reawaken a con-temporary audience to the power of Jesus' language that could, in turn, help reorient contemporary understandings of "faith" and "theology."

While both Funk and Crossan had one foot in the New Quest they were also turning in new directions, away from eschatology and toward a new approach to revelation. The same is true for two somewhat younger scholars at the time: Brandon Scott and Marcus Borg. In their voices one hears not only the turn to language but also to the question of how language is heard or received contextually.

BRANDON SCOTT's *Jesus, Symbol Maker for the Kingdom*, published in 1981, opens by differentiating his approach to the parables from Norman Perrin's. Scott acknowledges the significant shift in Perrin's own thought from understanding the phrase "kingdom of God" as a "concept" to seeing it as a "symbol." For Scott, the phrase "kingdom of God" is Jesus' symbolic expression of his ex-perience of God, of God at work in the world in ways hidden to conventional religious wisdom. Scott, thus, disagrees with Perrin's remaining "eschatological" interpretation of the parables.[20] Those apocalyptic interpretations of Jesus' parables, insists Scott, miss the challenge of the parables altogether. At stake is not the end of the world, but Jesus' call to see the world differently.

Scott claims that one can best gain insight into Jesus' symbol of the kingdom of God by interpreting the parables as metaphors.[21] Scott quotes Crossan that a "poetic metaphor attempts 'to articulate a referent so new or so alien to consciousness that this referent can only be grasped within the metaphor itself.'" Scott then draws out the implications of the Crossan quotation for his own understanding of Jesus' parables:

> Parable as metaphor is generated from the experiential world of the teller. Parables, expressing the incomprehensible in terms of the comprehensible, are developed out of Jesus' fundamental vision/ experience of reality. Specifically for Jesus' parables, the experience which comes to expression is the experience of God as symbolized by Kingdom of God.[22]

While this language reminds us of what we have already seen in our discussions of Funk and Crossan, Scott's real contribution is his emphasis on the social world of the parable.

Insofar as the parables open a new world for the hearer, Scott seeks, by "means of historical imagination," to "reconstruct the point of view of the audience to whom the parable was addressed: first-century Palestinian Jews."[23] Influenced here by Wolfgang Iser's notion of "reception theory," or the construction of meaning by analyzing the "implied reader" of a text, Scott captures how Jesus' parables work by showing how the parables challenged the conventional assumptions of Jesus' first-century Palestinian audience.

A classic example of Scott's approach is the parable of the leaven. While Scott works off of previous interpretations of Joachim Jeremias and Funk, he turns the interpretative axis to the reception of the audience. Scott notes the juxtaposition of two images in the parable: the image of leaven, which he demonstrates is an image of moral corruption, and the image of "three measures of flour," a reference to the epiphany story in Gen 8:16.[24] Scott argues that the parable cannot be understood simply as an example story of growth from small beginnings, as Jeremias had suggested. Agreeing with Jeremias that the "three measures of flour" would provide enough bread for about one hundred people, Scott underscores the issue of reception: "A Palestinian audience would have been tipped off that this was no ordinary baking session."[25] But, in addition to this tip, there's also the problem with word "hid" (the woman in this very brief story took the leaven and "hid it" in the meal). Scott points out that the Greek word *kruptō* is not the word one would expect; the word for kneading is *phuraō*. The former has a negative connation, connected to deception. Combining these elements, Scott sees the parable creating real dissonance in his audience:

> To compare Kingdom to leaven means that Kingdom has an inverse relation to what is normally considered religious. . . . If one takes seriously leaven's significance . . . then Kingdom will work its way through everything as a moral perversion, undermining normal religious perceptions. In this sense, it is destructive, subversive and shattering—its own sacramentality is a hidden epiphany.[26]

Scott continues:

> The parable seeks to orient a hearer toward the identification of God with everyday experience. God is at work like leaven, that is, he is undermining the everyday, inverting it. The religious tradition as predictive of God's locus can no longer serve to demarcate where he is at work. . . .

> The hearer's faith is severely challenged because the parable articulates a radical vision of God.[27]

The emphasis of Scott's interpretation falls on the way that Jesus' language reorients his audience's perception and understanding of everyday life. Thus, one sees a new historical focus emerging here, namely, interest in the conventional assumptions of Jesus' audience. While Scott's analysis in this 1981 text retains the New Quest's interest in an implicit Christology,[28] and while one can still see in Scott's interpretation some continuation of the New Quest's existential language of "everydayness," something new is also afoot.

In a somewhat similar vein to Scott's excavation of the social world, MARCUS BORG opens his 1984 book *Conflict, Holiness & Politics in the Teachings of Jesus* by arguing that the dominant model for interpreting Jesus' words and work, namely, the eschatological model descending from Schweitzer and Weiss, has significant problems.

> In the ensuing edifice [eschatological interpretation] no place could be found for the traditions about Jesus which reflect a concern with the institutions of Judaism, which manifest conflict with his contemporaries about the shape and destiny of Israel, and which indicate an awareness of the religio-political threat to Israel by Rome. . . .

The context within which this study places the teaching of Jesus is conflict: the conflict between Rome and Israel as the setting within which conflict occurred between Jesus and his contemporaries concerning the structures and purpose of Israel.[29]

As Scott had begun situating the parables of Jesus in the context of his hearer's expectations, so Borg's analysis explores Jesus' "departure from established patterns of behavior *vis a vis* table fellowship, sabbath and the Temple."[30] He begins with the assumptions that Jesus' words and actions were connected to real questions at issue in first-century Palestine, and that many of those questions were greatly exacerbated by the Roman occupation and Rome's policies of taxation. "The impact of the economic crunch was severe, producing signs of social disintegration, such as widespread emigration, a growing number of landless 'hirelings,' and a social class of robbers and beggars."[31]

One needs to interpret Jesus, claims Borg, within the range of Jewish resistance to Roman rule and occupation. The primary thrust of that resistance to Rome came through Israel's own profound religio-political allegiance to Yahweh.

> During the post-exilic period, the content of the *imitatio dei*, the paradigm of conformity with which national community developed, was *holiness*, understood as separation from everything impure. Intensifying through the Maccabean period and into New Testament times, resting on the two foundational institutions of Torah and Temple, animating the major renewal movements of the period, and drawing part of its vitality from its utility as a program of survival in an increasingly threatening world, the quest for holiness became the dominant cultural dynamic of Israel's corporate life.[32]

By pursuing holiness and purity, Jewish leaders sought to keep Israel apart from the pollution of the Roman occupation, and to remain a holy people dedicated to Yahweh.

In Borg's view, Jesus offers an "alternative" program for Israel's resistance to Rome. By focusing on mercy and compassion rather than holiness, Jesus seeks to hold together a community that is already falling into impurity through poverty.

> But here God's mercy is not limited to those within the covenant; instead, God's mercy is seen in the fact that the sun and the rain come to both the just and the unjust, i.e., to everybody, and not just to those with whom a special relationship exists. Similarly, specific

behavioral applications in the pericope point to the inclusiveness of mercy as a quality of human behavior. The practice of mercy was not to be limited by the expectation of reciprocity: do good even to those who abuse you, lend without expectation of return.[33]

In his inclusion of "tax collectors and sinners" at the table, in his violation of Sabbath regulations for the sake of healing, and in one story after another, Jesus encourages forgiveness, forgiveness of debts, and joyful practice of radical hospitality. While Borg did not suggest that Jesus' formulation of the kingdom of God was in any way a challenge to the Roman empire, he does argue persuasively that the Roman occupation was a major factor in Jesus' disagreement with the Pharisees over how best to preserve Jewish identity under the extraordinary pressures of occupation.

Shifts in Theology: David Tracy and Hans Frei/George Lindbeck

At least some theologians were paying close attention to these developments. Paul Tillich, of course, had underscored the symbolic character of theological language. And Langdon Gilkey, one of Tillich's students, had sought to explore that symbolic character within a more explicitly *empirical* framework as advocated by Funk. In addition, writing in his 1978 classic *Blessed Rage for Order*, DAVID TRACY brings something of a neo-Tillichean perspective into conversation with the work of the New Quest and other recent work on literary theory and the turn to language.

Far from rejecting historical criticism and the work of the New Quest, Tracy actually cites the work of Norman Perrin, Robert Funk, John Dominic Crossan and others to help explore the nature of both religious language and religious experience. Specifically, Tracy turns to many of the very texts that the scholars of the New Quest had identified with the message of Jesus, especially the parables, to support his argument about the specific nature of religious language.[34] In a culture growing increasingly secular, Tracy notes the anxiety surrounding religious language: Does it refer to anything real? Or is religious language illusory? Put another way, are fundamentalism and supernaturalism the only alternatives to a totally secularized and technologized language?

Tracy makes a compelling case for the distinctiveness of religious language by calling attention both to the oddity of religious language and to the human settings or situations in which such odd language is appropriate:

Like poetic metaphors, religious language discloses an odd personal discernment which cannot be described literally but whose reality cannot be denied. In those situations where we find ourselves discerning the meanings of our lives, . . . we find religious language useful and therefore meaningful. Moreover, we notice that the kind of situation to which religious language points has two further distinguishing characteristics. Unlike poetic or ethical language, religious language expresses a *total* commitment (*the* meaning of my life) as well as a meaning which has universal significance (this meaning—e.g., fundamental trust—is applicable to all human life). Such a combination of an odd personal discernment, a total commitment and a universal significance is the *empirical* "place" for religious and theological statements.[35] (Tracy's emphasis)

Tracy invokes the terminology of philosopher Paul Ricoeur to name more accurately these characteristics of religious language. "Limit-language seems a correct way to indicate the logically odd character of religious language and the qualitatively different empirical placing for that language in our common experience."[36] By limit-language, Tracy has in mind language that intensifies, transgresses, exaggerates, and explodes our "ordinary," or "everyday" language, creating a jarring effect that discloses unforeseen possibilities. And Tracy finds these very elements of religious limit-language at work in the parables:

The parables do not merely tell a pleasant (or unpleasant) story to evoke a moral maxim. They are fictions. As with all good fiction, they redescribe ordinary reality in order to disclose a new, an extraordinary possibility for our lives. In the peculiar limit-use of narrative and metaphor in the parables these fictions redescribe the extraordinary in the ordinary in such manner that the ordinary is transgressed and a new and extraordinary, but possible mode-of-being-in-the-world is disclosed. Religious language in general represents that basic confidence and trust in existence which *is* our fundamental faith, our basic authentic mode of being in the world. Further, this parabolic language, as fiction, does not merely re-present such faith. Those fictions redescribe the ordinary existence to show how authentic existence may itself occur: a life lived totally in and by the event, the gift of faith and faith alone.

In reading the parables, we may suddenly find our imaginations conceiving the possibility that, after all, it may yet be possible to live as if in the presence of a God whose love knows no limits.[37]

While one can still hear echoes of Tillichean existentialism in Tracy's argument, what really differentiates it from the generation of Tillich is the turn to the analysis of language. The above passages read like the work of Funk and Crossan we quoted earlier. Tracy is drawing on their innovations in biblical studies—as well as other innovations in philosophy—to craft his theological position.

Noteworthy for our purposes is Tracy's concern to show that fundamentalism and supernaturalism are no longer adequate interpretations of either the religious life or of religious language. In a remarkably strong passage, Tracy, known for both his generosity of interpretation and his irenic spirit, is unusually candid:

> To state the matter with the bluntness needed, for many of us fundamentalism and supernaturalism of whatever religious tradition are dead and cannot return. At their best, Western Christians have learned too well—as Nietzsche reminds us—the truth that Christianity taught. That truth was and remains that one's fundamental Christian and human commitment is to the value of truth wherever it may lead and to that limit-transformation of all values signalized by the Christian demand for agapic love. Fundamentalism of whatever tradition and by whatever criteria of truth one employs seems to me irretrievably false and illusory.[38]

Strong words, and yet, fundamentalism and supernaturalism did, in fact, "return" in virtually all of the major religious traditions, and returned quite emphatically to American political discourse at the very time of Tracy's comments. We will revisit these issues in the next chapter.

The turn to language also reshaped the Barthian tradition. Just as one might speak about a distinct identity for a feminist or African American liberationist theology, "postliberal" theologians HANS FREI and his Yale colleague GEORGE LINDBECK retained Barth's concern about the distinctiveness of a Christian *identity* in the midst of a growing sea of secular discourse. Yet, in his 1975 preface to the book *The Identity of Jesus Christ: The Hermeneutical Bases of Dogmatic Theology*, Frei actually distances himself from the Barthian tradition's emphasis on the otherness of divine revelation. His statement is worth quoting at some length:

> I agree with the recently emerged consensus among a good many theologians that "revelation" is not a wholly unambiguous or satisfying central concept for stating what Christianity is all about. Furthermore, the governing model for construing "revelation"

among modern Protestant theologians, that of a "non-propositional" personal encounter, is even more problematical. When you come right down to it, most of us would hesitate to claim that we encounter God or Christ directly, the way we encounter friends and relations or even the limits of our own potentialities and powers. And if we qualify the description by speaking of an "indirect" encounter, have we anything important or even intelligible left? . . . It is difficult to deny at least a degree of justice to the accusation that "revelation," as construed by neo-orthodox theologians, is a way of intellectualizing the relation between God and man by riveting it to the phenomenon of consciousness or one of its several derivatives. Similarly, there is justice in the cognate criticism that even then "revelation" turns out to be so non-informative as to lack all intellectual content.[39]

Given this critique of neo-orthodoxy's approach to the topic of revelation, how did Frei retain and shape a Barthian perspective? He begins by taking up Barth's sharp distinction between "dogmatic theology" and "apologetics." Insofar as dogmatic theology attempts to interpret the faith for the faithful (Barth's preference), and apologetics attempts to show both Christians and persons living in secular society how Christian faith makes sense of human life (Tillich's preference), Frei argues that the apologetic approach is "largely out of place and self defeating." In keeping with the dogmatic approach, however, Frei is "persuaded that it is possible to state the logic of Christian belief, i.e., the mutual coherence . . . of Christian concepts."[40] Thus, while rejecting the starting point of revelation per se, Frei begins by affirming the self-contained (Christians talking to Christians) character of Barth's dogmatics.

Frei's approach begins, as Barth insisted, with the affirmation of the truths of Christian faith, and thus with faith in Jesus Christ. In addition, this approach, suggests Frei, need not and indeed should not look to historical criticism to understand the biblical text. Thus, on this point as well, Frei (and Lindbeck) rejects the usefulness to theology of historical criticism generally, and of historical Jesus studies even more emphatically. But if theologians should not attend to the historical critical scholarship of their New Testament colleagues, how should they approach the biblical texts?

Frei argues that Christian theology has paid far too much attention to historical criticism in the modern period and not enough to the *narrative* character of the Gospels as the principal story of Christian identity. Here is the basis both of Frei's and Lindbeck's "turn to language," but also to a language of Christian *identity*.

Being a Christian, argues Frei, means being shaped—in one's core identity—by the foundational stories of Christian faith. He suggests that one read the "gospel narrative" (he tends to collapse the four Gospels into a unified story) as a "realistic narrative," as "history-like" in "its language as well as its depiction of a common public world."[41]

Given his preference for dogmatics over apologetics, Frei proceeds to offer a way of interpreting the New Testament "narrative" that virtually ignores historical criticism and that leans toward the formulations of Christian dogma. Over against the New Quest's attempt to locate the message of Jesus in his preaching of the kingdom of God, Frei argues from within this narrative perspective that it is "only in the final sequence in the story [passion and resurrection] that his person as individual figure in a story is most clearly accessible."[42] Frei continues his story-trumps-sayings argument:

> The specific content of a man's preachings, even if we take it that we have direct access to them, does not by itself make the preacher accessible, who might either be quite unknowable or quite different from even full, to say nothing of fragmentary, reports of his sayings. If the depicted Jesus (not even to mention the "historical" Jesus') sayings are to function Christologically, they will have to do so as expressions of the person who comes to be portrayed in the last stage of the story.[43]

But even the "last stage of the story" is not really the last stage of the story for Frei. In his final chapter, which argues for a "pattern" to the gospel narrative, Frei claims that "the climax of the Gospel story is the full unity of the unsubstitutable individuality of Jesus with the presence of God."[44] Frei's "pattern" leans heavily in the direction of the Council of Nicea of 325 CE, and thus in the direction of an orthodox structure. But even here, Frei's insistence that the gospel narrative bends toward an orthodox Christology is not the full picture; the pattern continues. "When Christians speak of the presence of Jesus Christ now . . . they use the term 'Spirit' or 'Holy Spirit.'"[45] And then the pattern, says Frei, speaks of the church, and then of eschatology (or discussion of the consummation of all things within God). In other words, Frei believes that the "realistic narrative" of the gospel story gives rise to the pattern of Christian doctrine—the Trinity, Christology, the church, eschatology. Frei's broadly doctrinal reading of Scripture proved helpful to his Yale colleague, George Lindbeck who crafted the theoretical contours of what he called postliberal theology.

GEORGE LINDBECK's *The Nature of Doctrine*, published in 1984, lays out a postliberal theory of religion and the role of doctrine within it.[46] Working in tandem with Frei's view of faith as a process of being informed and shaped by a narrative, Lindbeck argues that religion itself "can be viewed as a kind of cultural/linguistic framework or medium that shapes the entirety of life and thought."[47] This argument, also informed by anthropologist Clifford Geertz's discussion of "Religion as a Cultural System," emphasizes that aspect of the "turn to language" that claims that far from being a tool which we use, language, in fact, shapes us. Frei and Lindbeck use this aspect of the turn to language to retain Barth's conviction that God's revelation addresses us; we cannot begin to address or even think about God apart from the shaping narrative of the Christian story. The reason Frei and Lindbeck reject historical criticism is similar to Barth's view: because historical Jesus research begins with methodological convictions not informed by Christian faith, its findings are simply irrelevant to Christian faith. Yet even if one argued that the historical Jesus is not an extra- but an intra-theological debate (that is to say a debate within the Christian community), Lindbeck could turn to the following argument to dismiss its significance.

Insofar as religions are analogous to cultural/linguistic systems, argues Lindbeck, the role of doctrine should be understood as analogous to "grammar," that is, to the culture's way of speaking. Lindbeck's choice of grammar as an analogy for doctrine is an interesting one. While grammar is not unchangeable, it changes very slowly. For Lindbeck, who is profoundly interested in Christian ecumenism, the analogy of grammar allowed for some play within and among the various communities of the Christian faith. Thus, one might have different approaches to the topic of the Trinity, but the Trinity is an essential part of a Christian grammar when speaking of God. The problem with historical Jesus research, even if undertaken by Christian scholars, is that it may fail to speak of Jesus Christ in his divinity as well as in his humanity. Such a failure would be a violation of Christian grammar.

With respect to Tracy's revisionist theology as well as Frei/Lindbeck's postliberal approach, it is important to see how both of these significant schools of theology used the "turn to language" to remain intellectually current but also to restate the theological orientations they inherited from their teachers. Now let's turn to how Tracy and Lindbeck responded to Hans Küng's proposal to make the historical Jesus the criterion for Christian theology.

Turning Theology away from
the Historical Jesus

In a 1980 volume edited by Leonard Swidler called *Consensus in Theology?*[48] essays by Hans Küng and Edward Schillebeeckx reflecting on their "Jesus books" formed the basis of a broad-ranging dialogue on theological method. Respondents included not only Roman Catholic and Protestant theologians (including Tracy and Lindbeck) but also Jewish, Muslim, and Hindu scholars. Küng's essay in particular, "Toward a New Consensus in Catholic (and Ecumenical) Theology," placed the search for the historical Jesus at the heart of Christian theology.

> Christianity is not founded on myths, legends or tales, nor solely on a doctrine (or it is not a religion of the book). Rather, it is based primarily on the historical personality of Jesus of Nazareth who was seen as the Christ of God. The New Testament witness—kerygmatic reports—does not enable us to reconstruct Jesus' biography or psychological development. . . . However, they do permit us to accomplish a task that is urgently required today for theological and pastoral reasons. Namely, today we can once again gain an insight into the original outlines of the message of Jesus as well as his personal lifestyle and destiny, which in the course of centuries has been obscured and hidden.[49]

For Küng, historical research is thus vital to establishing the criterion of Christian theology.

> No contradiction can be permitted between the Jesus of history and the Christ of faith. We must be able to identify the Christ of faith as the Jesus of history. Naturally historical-critical research into the life of Jesus neither desires nor has the capacity to prove that the man Jesus of Nazareth is in reality the Christ of God. The recognition of Jesus as the Christ always remains a venture of faith and trust or a *metanoia*.[50]

Influenced by the work of the New Quest, Küng and Schillebeeckx sought to reinvigorate the discourse of theology by appealing to the continuity between the historical Jesus and Christ of faith.[51] They were not alone. Political theologian Johann Baptist Metz had written persuasively about the "dangerous memory" of Jesus.[52] Leonardo Boff had affirmed, "If we identify Jesus with the teaching element of the church, then we lose every critical element and the possibility of legitimate protest."[53] And, Elizabeth Johnson, commenting on the work of the International Theological Commission as well as that of numerous theologians (including Schillebeeckx and Küng) added:

> The reconstructed image of the historical Jesus not only functions today as the equivalent of the memory impression of Jesus in the early Church, but actually is the equivalent of it, i.e., is the means by which significant segments of the present generation of believers remember Jesus who is confessed as the Christ. As such, it is an element of the living tradition of the present Church.[54]

Tracy and Lindbeck both responded directly to Küng's proposal. Both were troubled, in differing ways, by Küng's emphasis on the theological value of historical-critical reconstructions of Jesus.

Tracy's nuanced response, "Particular Questions within General Consensus," agreed that theologians should seek "some correlation" between the fruits of historical research "into the message and person of Jesus correlated with personal Christian faith in Jesus of Nazareth as the Christ." But he expressed reservations about Küng's formulation: "the source, standard and criterion of Christian faith is the living Jesus of history." About that criterion he raised three critical objections. First, Tracy argued that "historical-critical exegesis is a major but not sole method of analysis for these texts." Underscoring the value of hermeneutical-literary approaches in addition to historical-critical analysis, Tracy cited research on the parables by such scholars as Perrin, Dan Via, Funk, Crossan and Jungel as examples of needed, complementary approaches. Second, for Tracy, all methods (e.g., historical-critical, literary, and ideology-critique) "contain corrective but not constitutive truth for Christian theology." He went on to add: "the constitutive truth for Christian faith is to be found elsewhere; in the personal response of faith in the faith-community as that faith is mediated by the community and the tradition." Third, reiterating his second point, Tracy suggested that making historical-critical reflection the constitutive norm of Christian theology leads to "an attempt not merely to correct the tradition but in effect to replace it with historical-critical reconstruction of the message and person of Jesus."[55] Tracy allowed a significant, corrective role for historical-critical reconstructions of the life of Jesus, but sought to limit the influence of such work to a critical phase.

George Lindbeck's response, "The Bible as Realistic Narrative," was a more definite rejection. Obviously influenced by his Yale colleague Frei, Lindbeck proposed an entirely different approach to the Bible.

> It seems to me worth asking whether Scripture does not perhaps supply its own interpretive framework. Everyone recognizes that correct interpretation requires the ascertaining of the literary genre of the work to be interpreted. What then is the literary genre of the Bible as a whole in its canonical unity? What holds together the diverse materials it contains: poetic, prophetic, legal, liturgical, sapiential, mythical, legendary, and historical? These are all embraced, it would seem, in an over-arching story which has the specific literary features of realistic narratives as exemplified in diverse ways. . . . It is as if the Bible were a "vast, loosely-structured, non-fictional novel." . . . Furthermore, we can specify the primary purpose of the canonical narrative. It is to "render a character . . . offer an identity description of an agent," viz., God. . . . Its primary purpose is not to tell the reader what actually happened in the sense of either profane or salvation history, and even less to provide doctrinal propositions, theological concepts, or symbolic expressions or re-presentations of religious experience or authentic *Existenz*—although it may do all these things as well. Given this canonical intent, it is not surprising that the Bible is often "history-like" rather than "likely history."[56]

A narrative approach to Scripture, argued Lindbeck, had two clear advantages over Küng's proposal. First, the canonical approach "gives more theological weight" to the Old Testament with its themes of creation, exodus, the stories of Israel, and so on. Second, the "purpose" of the Gospels is not to provide accurate information about Jesus but "to tell about the risen, ascended, and now-present Christ whose earthly identity as the divine-human agent is irreplaceably enacted in the stories of Jesus of Nazareth."[57] In sharp contrast to Küng's proposal about Jesus, Lindbeck, following Frei, offered an approach to the whole of Scripture that virtually eliminated any *theological* need for historical-critical research of the Scriptures.

The responses of both Tracy and Lindbeck to Küng's essay are telling. While Lindbeck maintains the long-standing Barthian suspicion of historical criticism, albeit from a new linguistic framework, Tracy affirms the work of historical and literary critics—naming Funk and Crossan, among others, to emphasize his support of genuinely critical scholarship—but argues that the work of *theology* is distinct from *biblical criticism*. Thus, for Tracy, while discussions of the historical Jesus can be helpful for correcting the intellectual and moral problems within the Christian tradition's understanding of Jesus as the Christ, historical criticism *alone* cannot provide a criterion for theology that would override the roles of both the Christian community and Christian tradition. That position would be more substantially argued in Tracy's 1981 volume, *The Analogical Imagination.*[58]

In this chapter we have seen how both biblical studies and theology made a turn to language in the 1970s and 1980s. While interest in the historical Jesus was not erased in this period, such interest was carried forward primarily by analysis of the parables. Along the way, one can begin to see scholars—both biblical and theological—wrestling with the tradition of eschatology and moving away from existentialism.

In the variety of moves that we have traced here, one sees the tentative outlines of a new quest for the historical Jesus emerging. Widespread acknowledgment that the concept of revelation must be radically rethought, the critique that existentialism cannot adequately address issues of justice and corporate identity, and suspicions that eschatology really may not capture the heart of Jesus' message, all raise nagging questions about the New Quest's assumptions and proposals. The rejection of Küng's 1979 proposal suggests a type of closure to the New Quest, but the confidence in "tradition," or "narrative," as expressed by both Tracy and Lindbeck, in varying ways, would prove problematic as reactionary Christians moved to the forefront of American politics in the 1980s. What we might call not simply the "Renewed Quest" but the "American Quest" was still several years away.

CHAPTER

11

The Jesus Seminar and the
Renewed Quest for a Public Jesus

When one looks at the scholarly work of the founding members of the Jesus Seminar, as we did in the previous chapter, one sees a range of professional scholars whose writings are immersed in the technical language of their disciplines. Yet, it is impossible to pick up the works of Funk, Crossan, Borg, Scott, Patterson and others written during, but especially after, the initial work of the Jesus Seminar (post 1993) and not notice a seismic shift in their writing. The commitment to engage a wider public audience on the topic of Jesus—with what Jesus most likely said and did, what he cared about, stood for, and died for—was a startlingly bold project in public education. What prompted such an effort, such a shift in focus and style?

At the very time that scholarly discussions of the Bible and Christian theology were becoming ever more sophisticated in the university, religion in American public life was moving dramatically toward what Canadian theologian Douglas John Hall calls "religious simplism."[1] In a 1967 essay entitled, "Is There a Third Force in Christendom?" sociologist William McGloughlin noted a positional symmetry between an emergent group that he called the "new evangelicals" and the politics of the Republican nominee for the Presidency in 1964:

> The new evangelicals . . . are lock, stock, and barrel with Senator Barry Goldwater. For them, applied Christianity is still basically evangelistic soul-winning; they equate Christianity with "the American way of life"; . . . they are hysterically anti-Communist in foreign policy and totally opposed to any extension of the Welfare State in domestic policy. And while they profess sympathy with the civil rights movement and oppose die-hard segregation, they still believe that the principle function of the Christian churches in

social reform is "proclamation of the gospel" and not social action to "legislate" reform. . . . For the evangelicals, as for Billy Graham, the greatest problems facing America today are the Supreme Court's rulings on Bible reading and school prayer in the public schools, the "spiraling divorce rate," . . . the upsurge of juvenile delinquency, the increase of illegitimate births, and the spread of addiction to alcohol and dope.[2]

In actuality, however, the political reemergence of white, evangelical-to-fundamentalist Christians had been taking shape for decades. While many sociologists, looking at headcount numbers only, saw the 1960s as a watershed period of mainline Protestant decline, Rodney Stark and Roger Finke, in their 1992 book *The Churching of America* took a different look at the data. Studying the rise and fall of "each denomination's share of the total sum of religious adherents in the United States,"[3] they spotted significant shifts in denominational strength much earlier. Conservative commentator Kevin Phillips, using their data in his book *American Theocracy: The Peril and Politics of Radical Religion, Oil, and Borrowed Money in the 21st Century*, called attention to the longer trend.

> By the calculations of Stark and Finke, between 1940 and 1985 mainline Protestantism's share of all U.S. religious adherents was steadily plummeting. The largest group, the United Methodists, dropped from 124.7 adherents per thousand total church members in 1940 to 93.0 in 1960 and to just 64.3 in 1985. For the Presbyterians (USA), the simultaneous decline was from 41.7 to 36.4 to 21.3, while the Episcopalian fall was from 30.9 to 28.6 to 19.2. Meanwhile the United Church of Christ (Congregationalists) slid from 26.5 to 19.6 to 11.8. . . .
>
> The ascendant Southern Baptists, during the same period, climbed from 76.7 adherents per thousand total church members in 1940 to 85.0 in 1960 and to 101.3 in 1985. The Pentecostal Assemblies of God vaulted from 3.1 in 1940 to 4.4 in 1960 and to 14.6 in 1985. These, in the 1940s and 1950s, were national outsider denominations, found more often in unfashionable locales than in wealthy ones.[4]

What one sees in Starke and Finke's numbers, according to Phillips, is not just the decline in absolute numbers among the mainline denominations but, more importantly, the relative loss of religious vitality to the rising tide of Pentecostal, evangelical, and fundamentalist churches. Reflecting on that trend, Phillips adds that "changes in theological dominance . . . proved to be harbingers of broader political and societal changes."[5]

By the 1980 presidential campaign, Christian fundamentalism was a resurgent force in the election of Ronald Reagan. The partnership was no mere coincidence. In a 1977 speech at the 4th Annual CPAC (Conservative Political Action Council) Convention, entitled, "The New Republican Party," Ronald Reagan argued that the longstanding split between social conservatives and fiscal conservatives was no longer necessary. Bridging this divide between conservatives, he argued, could forge a new conservative majority in the nation.

> Yes, conservatism can and does mean different things to those who call themselves conservatives.
>
> You know, as I do, that most commentators make a distinction between what they call "social" conservatism and "economic" conservatism. The so-called social issues—law and order, abortion, busing, quota systems—are usually associated with blue-collar, ethnic and religious groups themselves traditionally associated with the Democratic Party. The economic issues—inflation, deficit spending and big government—are usually associated with Republican Party members and independents who concentrate their attention on economic matters.
>
> Now I am willing to accept this view of two major kinds of conservatism—or, better still, two different conservative constituencies. But at the same time let me say that the old lines that once clearly divided these two kinds of conservatism are disappearing.
>
> In fact, the time has come to see if it is possible to present a program of action based on political principle that can attract those interested in the so-called "social" issues and those interested in "economic" issues. In short, isn't it possible to combine the two major segments of contemporary American conservatism into one politically effective whole?
>
> I believe the answer is: Yes, it is possible to create a political entity that will reflect the views of the great, hitherto, conservative majority.[6]

Reagan's vision of entwining the interests of fiscal and religious conservatives proved a powerful strategy. Reagan courted not only Jerry Falwell and his Moral Majority (founded in 1979), but conservative Roman Catholics, who were especially angry over the 1973 Supreme Court decision of *Roe v. Wade*. Prior to the election of 1980

Reagan had been in contact with the Vatican and, once elected, he named William Wilson as his personal envoy to the Vatican, with Wilson becoming ambassador in 1984 once diplomatic ties with the Vatican were reestablished.[7] Later, Pentecostal minister and talk-show personality Pat Robertson and the Christian Coalition (founded by Robertson in 1988 with Ralph Reed as head of the organization) emphasized a method of grass-roots community organizing that brought Christian conservatives into the center of local, regional, and national Republican politics.

As documented by Phillips, the influence of this religious viewpoint profoundly narrowed the vision and commitments of the Republican Party, not only in the Reagan years but even more throughout the 1990s and especially through the first decade of the twenty-first century.[8] Grounded in religious and cultural resentments dating back to Supreme Court decisions of the early 1960s over school prayer and Bible reading in public schools, and to resentments over the anti-war movement, the civil rights movement, the feminist movement, and gay rights movement, as well as to resentments toward the increasingly secular orientation of colleges and universities, which seemed to tolerate and foster those other, "liberal" movements, Jerry Falwell's "I Love America" rallies of 1976–78 and his Moral Majority argued that liberal society's permissiveness and lack of individual responsibility (recall Reagan's famous epithet, "L-word—Liberals") had led to the moral decline of America. Reagan took up this theme with the enthusiasm of a self-proclaimed "crusader," famously concluding his 1979 Convention Address: "I'll confess that I've been a little afraid to suggest what I'm going to suggest—I'm more afraid not to—that we begin our crusade joined together in a moment of silent prayer."[9]

The alliance between fiscal and Christian "conservatives," using an inerrant Bible on the one hand and *laissez faire* economic simplism on the other, sought to secure not just a *de facto* religious establishment along Christian fundamentalist and conservative Catholic lines, but also an economic establishment, committed religiously to the oaths of no-new taxes, no government regulation of the marketplace, no limits on contributions to political candidates, and at the very least strict limitation on social programs. It is a testimony to the power of that movement that in 2011/2012, Congressman Paul Ryan, head of the powerful Congressional Budget Committee, and Republican Vice Presidential candidate couldn't really distinguish whether his political philosophy had come from Ayn Rand or Thomas Aquinas.

But it was not just the public face of American Protestantism that was changing. Within Roman Catholicism, as well, a traditionalist backlash to the liberalizing mood of the Second Vatican Council was taking shape. Suspicious of growing secularism, including the sexual revolution of the 1960s, the feminist movement, and the Supreme Court's willingness to allow women access to birth control (*Griswold v. Connecticut*, 1965), the Vatican had condemned the use of "artificial means" of birth control in Pope Paul VI's encyclical *Humane Vitae* ("On Human Life,"1967). Still, it would be the Supreme Court's *Roe v. Wade* decision of 1973 that would become a defining moment for a Vatican convinced that secularism posed a profound danger to the dignity of the human person. While the American bishops would write two major Pastoral Letters on social issues in the 1980s (the "Pastoral Letter on War and Peace" in 1983 and "Justice for All: Pastoral Letter on Catholic Social Teaching and the Economy" in 1986), by the mid-1980s the Vatican had made abortion its clear number one social-justice issue, demoting all other social-justice commitments by comparison.

The year 1978 witnessed the election of a Polish Pope, Karol Cardinal Wojtyla of Kraków (Pope John Paul II). By the mid-1980s the new, charismatic pope had moved to reclaim the primacy of the papacy in Roman Catholic life and had moved against the theological movements related to the New Quest. During the Pope's 1979 visit to the United States, Sister Teresa Kane, then president of the Leadership Conference of Women Religious, appealed publicly to the Pope to reconsider the Roman Catholic ban on ordaining women priests. The Vatican rebuffed all such entreaties and, in 1994 John Paul II officially closed the subject of women's ordination. In December of 1979, the Vatican stripped Hans Küng of his license to teach as a professor of Roman Catholic theology. In 1984, the Vatican issued an "Instruction on Certain Aspects of Liberation Theology," condemning "Marxist" elements and liberation theology's eschatological focus on history to the exclusion of eternal life. In 1985 the Congregation for the Doctrine of the Faith headed by Josef Cardinal Ratzinger (now Pope Benedict XVI) silenced Brazilian and Franciscan liberationist theologian Leonardo Boff for a year for his book, *The Church: Charism and Power*. Under the threat of being silenced a second time, Boff left the priesthood in 1992. In the Vatican, proponents of feminist and liberation and political theology became suspect (even challenging an academic appointment of Johann Baptist Metz in Germany), as the Vatican increasingly interpreted the documents of the Second Vatican Council through a more traditionalist lens. Thus, on both Protestant and Roman Catholic fronts, powerful currents were moving American religious discourse in far more conservative directions.

A Public Project

What Robert Funk would call the Renewed Quest—the work of the Jesus Seminar—must be understood to be as much informed by the public character of the First Quest of the historical Jesus as by the ecclesial character of the New Quest. The signature publication of the Jesus Seminar, *The Five Gospels: The Search for the Authentic Words of Jesus* (1993) underscores the concern about the character of American public and political discourse. In their Introduction, Robert Funk and Roy Hoover lament that "the level of public knowledge about the Bible borders on the illiterate," and they go on to say that the "church and synagogue have failed in their historic mission to educate the public in the fourth 'R,' religion."[10] While many theologians and church officials can rightly claim that their primary obligation is not to the public generally but to the faithful of their religious communities, such a response raises the question: but what is the church's obligation to respond publicly to the overtly political discourse of Christian fundamentalism? Do churches, synagogues, pastors, rabbis, and theologians not have some obligation to educate the public?[11]

In the wake of mainline churches' and theological schools' failure to mount a significant response to the politicized fundamentalism of the late 1970s and early 1980s, Funk and Hoover called on scholars to engage in the work of public education.

> Academic folk are a retiring lot. We prefer books to lectures, and solitude to public display. Nevertheless, we have too long buried our considered views of Jesus and the gospels in technical jargon and in obscure journals. We have hesitated to contradict TV evangelists and pulp religious authors for fear of political reprisal and public controversy. And we have been intimidated by promotion and tenure committees to whom the charge of popularizing or sensationalizing biblical issues is anathema. It is time for us to quit the library and speak up.[12]

By 1997 Funk could report that eventually "more than two hundred professionally trained specialists, called Fellows, joined the group."[13] The idea of gathering a group of scholars—a seminar—to study and report to the public on its research was an innovative one. To the extent that a scholar's research would be published typically only in an academic journal or book and never really see the light of public discourse, the idea of a group of scholars working together, discussing papers, voting on the consequent issues under discussion, and reporting those results to news organizations, generated a different kind of public work. In addition to the Fellows who gathered for a particular meeting, there were also Associate Members of the Seminar who attended the working sessions as well as special conversational meetings with several of the Fellows. These Associates gave the Seminar meetings both a public and an educational feel. The Westar Institute, the parent non-profit organization that sponsored The Jesus Seminar and subsequent projects including the Acts Seminar, the Paul Seminar, and, most recently, the Bible Seminar, also sponsored weekend "Jesus Seminar on the Road" programs for interested congregations and other groups interested in Westar's work, and several publications, *The Fourth R*, a quarterly publication, and an academic journal, *Forum*.

The initial work of the Jesus Seminar was to determine those sayings and parables that had the best probability of belonging to the earliest strand of the Jesus tradition, and thus of going back to Jesus himself. Robert Miller, in his book *The Jesus Seminar and Its Critics*, put it this way: "The agenda of the Seminar was to evaluate the historicity of every utterance and deed attributed to Jesus in Christian sources from the first three centuries."[14] Trying to ensure their own critical distance on the material, the Seminar—from the outset—focused on the sayings and not on the theological interpretation of those sayings. Here again are Funk and Hoover:

> The goal of the Seminar was to review each of the fifteen hundred items [attributed to Jesus] and determine which of them could be ascribed with a high degree of probability to Jesus. The items passing the test would be included in a database for determining who Jesus was. But the interpretation of the data was to be excluded from the agenda of the Seminar and left to individual scholars working from their own perspectives.[15]

Lane McGaughy reflects on the scholarly origins of what Funk would call "The Renewed Quest" in a *Fourth R* article from 1996 entitled, "The Search for the Historical Jesus: Why Start with the Sayings?"

> The quick answer to why the Jesus Seminar started with the sayings is "Because Bultmann did." The outline of his *History of the Synoptic Tradition* provided the ten-year agenda of the Jesus Seminar:

1. The Tradition of the Sayings of Jesus
2. The Tradition of the Narrative Material[16]

McGaughy goes on to chart the focus on sayings material between Bultmann and the work of the Jesus Seminar:

> The scholarly route from Rudolf Bultmann's *History of the Synoptic Tradition* to *The Five Gospels* of the Jesus Seminar can be traced through studies like Gunther Bornkamm's *Jesus of Nazareth* (1956), which contains about twenty-five pages on Jesus' biography and about one hundred sixty-five on his message; Norman Perrin's *Rediscovering the Teaching of Jesus* (1967); such monographs on the parables of Jesus as Robert Funk's *Language, Hermeneutic, and Word of God* (1966) and *Jesus as Precursor* (1975); John Dominic Crossan's *In Parables* (1973); and Bernard Brandon Scott's *Jesus, Symbol-Maker for the Kingdom* (1981) and *Hear Then the Parable* (1989).
>
> Before the Jesus Seminar, the forum for this renewed quest was the Parables Seminar of the 1970s and the journal *Semeia*, which Robert Funk launched in 1974. Both were projects of the Society of Biblical Literature, the professional association for biblical scholars.[17]

Underscoring the scholarly continuity between the quests, McGaughy argues that the Jesus Seminar was following a fairly traditional script. In their critical reflection upon the sayings, however, the Fellows developed a more rigorous and complex set of historical criteria than the New Quest, with specific rules under three headings: "rules of attestation," "rules of oral evidence," and rules of "distinctive discourse."[18] By "rules of attestation" Fellows meant the analysis of the written sources and settings in which a particular saying occurs; the point of these rules, says Funk, is to identify sayings that can be "assigned to the oral period [of the tradition] with a high degree of probability."[19] By "rules of oral evidence" Fellows meant the analysis of oral tradition that attempts to locate the "earliest layer" of the sayings tradition.[20] And by "rules of distinctive discourse" Fellows meant the analysis of those markers that distinguish Jesus' voice from other "sages of his day and time," also called the criterion of dissimilarity.[21] As McGaughy notes, the Seminar debated the relative priority of these criteria in the early years of its work:

> This attention to method started with a paper that was presented by Jesus Seminar Fellow Eugene Boring at the second meeting of the Seminar (Fall 1985) and was subsequently published in the journal

Forum. Boring extended Perrin's criteria from three to ten and arranged them in order of priority beginning with multiple attestation.

Also writing in *Forum,* John Dominic Crossan proposed a chronological sequence for dating the various sources that he has elaborated in his later works on the historical Jesus. As a result of this methodological debate, a gradual shift from stressing the criterion of dissimilarity to emphasizing the priority of multiple attestation occurred during the first phases of the Seminar's work.[22]

With respect to process, the Seminar used scholarly papers such as Boring, as mentioned above, to focus its deliberations on key sayings, with scholars voting their particular judgments on the authenticity of the texts by dropping colored beads "into voting boxes to permit all members to vote in secret."[23] Critics of the Jesus Seminar love to mock its process of voting with colored beads, emblematic for them of the whole enterprise as a kind of circus, with Funk in the role of P. T. Barnum. The idea of using votes to assess truth, they charge, is ludicrous, a cheap appeal to democracy. Yet, the idea of voting came not from democracy, but from the disciplined work of Bible translation committees, a very traditional scholarly practice.[24]

About the practice of voting itself, Funk and Hoover point out that Fellows "were permitted to cast ballots under two different options for understanding the four colors."

Option 1

Red: I would include this item unequivocally in the database for determining who Jesus was.

Pink: I would include this item with reservations (or modifications) in the database.

Gray: I would not include this item in the database, but I might make use of some of the content in determining who Jesus was.

Black: I would not use this item in the primary database.

Option 2

Red: Jesus undoubtedly said this or something very like it.

Pink: Jesus probably said something like this.

Gray: Jesus did not say this, but the ideas contained in it are close to his own

Black: Jesus did not say this; it represents the perspective or content of a later or different tradition.[25]

In calculating the votes about a particular saying or issue, the Fellows rejected the possibility of recording either a simple majority or general average of the individual votes. They opted instead for reporting the "weighted average" of the Fellows' votes.

> The weighted average is the numerical value assigned to each saying and parable by vote of the Fellows of the Jesus Seminar. Votes are weighted as follows: red . . . is given a value of 3; pink . . . is given the value of 2; gray . . . has a value of 1; and black . . . has a value of zero. Each value is multiplied by the number of votes in each category and the sum of values divided by the total number of votes. . . . Had the Fellows adopted majority rule, some Fellows would have lost their votes on each ballot; the weighted average means that every vote counts in the final determination of the color designation.[26]

Utilizing the weighted average, the Seminar sought to integrate individual scholarly attention within a communal practice and discipline of reaching a judgment. About the process, Miller writes:

> Scholars love discussions but are notorious for postponing judgment because they want to think over every possible aspect of an issue, weigh every piece of evidence, ponder every argument, and make precise distinctions and clarifications before making up their minds. These are good intellectual habits in themselves, but they can tempt some to avoid the accountability that comes with taking a stand. . . . Votes were therefore held at the end of each session, forcing members to focus their attention and make up their minds quickly.[27]

If one asks Miller, "what do you mean by 'taking a stand,'" he means more, I believe, than "reaching a judgment." He means the willingness to acknowledge one's position publicly. Insofar as the votes of the Seminar would be published in newspapers, and immediately available to a broad audience, Miller's language of "taking a stand" also has a stronger sense to it, one that he conveys in speaking about the public orientation of the Seminar itself. "The surprising success of *The Five Gospels* has raised the Seminar's hopes that it just might influence public perceptions about Jesus by providing an alternative to the unchallenged fundamentalist assumptions that pervade American discourse about the Bible."[28]

My point in rehearsing these basic elements of the structure of the Jesus Seminar is to demonstrate that the procedures and disciplines that governed the work of the Seminar stemmed from its core preoccupation: bringing the practice and judgments of biblical scholarship into public life. Here again is Miller:

> Scholars using the historical-critical approach have known for over a century that the gospels are a blend of historical remembrance and Christian interpretation, which means that not every deed and word attributed to Jesus in the gospels can actually be traced to him. Biblical scholars presuppose this in writings addressed to their peers. Yet almost no one, professors and clergy alike, tries to communicate this way of understanding Jesus to the public. The vast majority of Christians, including those in Catholic and mainline Protestant churches, are surprised, even stunned, when they hear a scholar or clergyperson assert that the gospels are part fact and part fiction. The Jesus Seminar aims to bridge the gap between scholars and the public by communicating the results of its historical study clearly, honestly, and in terms understandable to a lay audience.[29]

By framing its work in opposition to the unexpected reemergence of biblical fundamentalism in American politics and public life, the Jesus Seminar established its own distinctive voice from that of the New Quest.

Theological Shifts

By moving its conversation among biblical scholars to a public, non-theological setting in Santa Rosa, California, the Seminar sought on the one hand to address an issue of American public life, namely, the growing prominence of a politicized Christian fundamentalism. On the other hand, it also sought—in pursuing its distinctly *historical* work—to differentiate itself from the kind of theological claims that had anchored the New Quest. For example, at the basic level of how and where to situate the study of Jesus of Nazareth, while the New Quest followed Bultmann's suggestion that Jesus needed to be interpreted within the first-century Jewish context, many scholars of the Renewed Quest would come, over time, to realize that Jesus needed to be understood not only in the religious context of first-century Judaism but also within the context of the Mediterranean world ruled by Rome. We saw this shift already in Borg's 1984 book, but further work on the pervasive influence of Roman power and policies in Palestine would continue to shape the scholars' sensitivity to the political and not just religious nuances in Jesus' words and acts.

On another issue, with respect to the focus of Jesus' teaching: while the biblical scholars of the New Quest had assumed the eschatological character of Jesus' teaching of the kingdom of God, scholars of the Renewed Quest would find not only eschatological but wisdom themes in the earliest strata. This wisdom theme was supported, in part, by Seminar votes that located most of the parables within the very early strata of Jesus material. But such a determination also followed from recognition that elements of the Gospel of Thomas and Q contain very early material. Miller notes that this judgment, "that Jesus did not proclaim that God's kingdom was coming soon, that he did not predict that the world would end during the lifetime of his early followers, and that he did not speak of his own second coming on judgment day" met with real opposition from many New Testament scholars convinced by the earlier paradigm.[30]

Lest one jump to the conclusion that the Fellows of the Seminar had simply found a Jesus they were looking for — a caution recited continually in the sessions of the Seminar itself and noted in *The Five Gospels*[31] — the scholars affirmed that Jesus was an exorcist and healer, hardly the assumptions of modern liberal scholarship. Crossan, for example, puts Jesus as exorcist on the first page of his 1991 book, *The Historical Jesus: The Life of a Mediterranean Jewish Peasant*:

> He [Jesus] speaks about the rule of God, and they listen as much from curiosity as anything else. They know all about rule and power, about kingdom and empire, but they know it in terms of tax and debt, malnutrition and sickness, agrarian oppression and demonic possession. What, they really want to know, can this kingdom of God do for a lame child, a blind parent, a demented soul screaming its tortured isolation among the graves that mark the edges of the village? Jesus walks with them to the tombs, and, in the silence after the exorcism, the villagers listen once more.[32]

As a result of discerning a Jesus more fully situated in the religious, cultural, and political tensions of first-century Palestine, the Jesus Seminar began to open up new interpretive angles on Jesus that could provide alternative models to orthodoxy for reimagining the life of discipleship and faith. And it is just here that the most significant *theological* difference between the New Quest and the Renewed Quest comes into clear view. While the scholars of the New Quest had sought to demonstrate the "continuity" between the Jesus of history and the Christ of faith, the scholars of the Renewed Quest sought to develop a "data base" of sayings with strongest likelihood of going back to the historical Jesus. As one of the rules for evidence of the Jesus Seminar put it, "Canonical boundaries are irrelevant in critical assessments of the various sources of information about Jesus."[33]

By distancing itself from the New Quest's concern for "continuity" with the tradition, the public stance of the Jesus Seminar inevitably renewed questions in the theological community about the necessity and/or adequacy of traditional doctrine and belief as a norm for following Jesus. While, again, this *theological* concern was not an issue for the Fellows in their *historical* work, it became an issue, as we'll see for a range of Christian theologians. And, of course, the concern itself was no surprise to the Seminar's leadership. Funk had been arguing for the inadequacy of Christian doctrine as a norm of authentic faith at least since *Jesus as Precursor*. What the political rise of fundamentalism gave to Funk and to the Seminar was an obvious public concern over the misuse of the Bible that opened up the theological question in a new way. Thus, the theological issue was not simply: What if the sayings and deeds of Jesus' message, as discerned by historical methodology, did not support the assertions and practices of later Christian orthodoxy? Instead, by pointing to the prevalence of Christian fundamentalism as a destructive force in both US politics and US churches, the Seminar implicitly raised a broader and deeper theological suspicion: Was the structural norm of Christian identity, namely, religious orthodoxy, or right belief, in part responsible for the emerging anti-intellectualism of American life—suspicious of science, suspicious of women, suspicious of foreigners, and suspicious of educational institutions? Put another way: Was the affirmation of Christian orthodoxy—which is not simply a theological norm but a political norm required of all participants of the church—a vital and morally viable axis around which to organize Christian faith? Or was that approach to Christian identity no longer intellectually or morally persuasive?

While we will be exploring this question further in the final chapter, it is important to acknowledge the force of the suspicion about orthodoxy as an appropriate norm of faith—a suspicion in no way limited to the critical scholarship of the Jesus Seminar. In the context of an increasingly globalized, postmodern and postcolonial world, the interpretation of Jesus outside the pre-fit categories of traditionalism enabled a sense of fresh encounter across these multiple contemporary contexts. For many, this new sense of encounter did not ruin their faith, but reawakened it. In a variety of publications and in Jesus Seminar on the Road programs, the

Seminar helped raise the question in both churches and in public alike: "Why haven't we been told this before?"

Critiques

Not all scholars applauded the work of the Jesus Seminar. Examining the range of that criticism may help illuminate the most significant areas of disagreement with, and anxiety over, the experiment of the Seminar. A range of clerics and scholars rightly perceived that the Seminar was not simply a continuation of the New Quest's search for a more humanistic *continuity* with church teaching but an appeal to understanding the message of Jesus apart from explicit Christian faith. Some of these same critics were scandalized by the public character of the Seminar. Just as clerics in the eighteenth and nineteenth and centuries thought that debates over the Scriptures should be conducted in Latin, without placing the faith of ordinary persons at risk, so contemporary critics were scandalized by the Seminar's working in the public eye. Many of these critics—as well as others—criticized the process of voting, described above. To them the idea that solid scholarship could emerge from such a gathering—what some derisively called a "circus"—was nonsense, as was the publication of such poorly gathered "findings" in newspapers.

The most bitter and outspoken critic of the Seminar, Luke Timothy Johnson, published *The Real Jesus: The Misguided Quest for the Historical Jesus and the Truth of the Traditional Gospels* in 1996. In the book, Johnson engages in a broad-ranging *ad hominem* attack against Funk and the Fellows of the Seminar, while essentially repeating Martin Kähler's late nineteenth-century position, updated to some extent with the neo-Barthian logic of Frei and Lindbeck.

Johnson portrays himself as a theological moderate operating sensibly between two extremes. On the one hand, he critiques the theological problem of fundamentalism:

> The fundamentalists' claim to take the literal meaning of the New Testament seriously is controverted by their neglect of any careful or sustained reading. . . . When texts are used at all, they are lifted atomistically from their context as adornment for a sermon or lesson that has not in any fashion actually derived from the text. Such a method (if it can be called such) of using the New Testament enables fundamentalists to make claims about inerrancy and noncontradiction in the Gospels, because they have never actually engaged

the texts in a way that would enable some basic critical issues to emerge.[34]

Johnson dismisses the kind of scholarship practiced in "conservative theological seminaries" that "support conclusions already determined by doctrine."[35] Such approaches to theology are clearly not modern, or self-critical enough. But Johnson is not really concerned at all with these ultraconservative theologies; in fact, he mocks the Jesus Seminar's "war on fundamentalism." The real enemy, according to Johnson—and here he conjures up the vitriolic language of Barth—is the influence of historical criticism on biblical and theological studies. At one point, Johnson asks the reader to identify with naïve, conservatively-minded students in their introductory course-work in seminary, who are, for all intents and purposes attacked by professors armed with the tools of historical criticism.

> For generations, the clergy of these [mainline] denominations have been prepared for ministry in seminaries or schools of theology where the categories of modernity have shaped scholarship, and above all biblical scholarship. First-year students, who often come to seminary with deeply conservative convictions concerning the inspiration and inerrancy of the Scripture, are exposed at once to the "shock therapy" of the historical critical method. They are told by eminent professors, often in tones of scarcely contained glee, that everything they ever believed is wrong, and that to be part of this new academic environment they must accept the "historical critical view" of the Bible.[36]

Johnson gets very exercised over this image of "gleeful," abusive professors. It is a strange comment. Can one also imagine, I wonder, the gall of professors in other graduate departments, in physics, for example, or psychology, or cultural anthropology "forcing" their students to learn a methodology: How outrageous! Just as there is something unseemly in Johnson's implied accusation that New Testament and Hebrew Bible professors are not concerned about their students, there is also something unprofessional in Johnson's special pleading for students unprepared for graduate work while avoiding any discussion of students who welcome such critical studies. But Johnson is just getting started. He continues to vent his Barthian-like fury on the "popularity of liberation theology in many liberal Protestant and Catholic seminaries." Lamenting the widening "gap between the critically educated clergy and the people they were called to serve,"[37] Johnson takes umbrage on behalf of the poor, unsuspecting, white, middle-class, male parishioner fending off the poor and destitute of the world.

> Such liberation has tended to base itself squarely on a "historical Jesus" that has been critically reconstructed from the Gospels after they have been subjected to the appropriate ideological criticism. The distinction between "Jesus" and "Christianity" is ideologically exploited. In the feminist reading, the "woman-defined Jesus" who preaches a version of female wisdom and displays all the appropriate gender-inclusive attitudes is supplanted by patriarchal Paul, who, despite his nod to egalitarianism, suppresses women in his churches, and through his letters also suppresses women through the entire history of the church. In the Latin American reading, the Jesus who proclaimed a Jubilee year for the poor and followed an itinerant lifestyle is supplanted by the bourgeois tendencies of Pauline Christianity, which softens the countercultural edge of the Jesus movement. In the radical gay liberationist reading, the anti-establishment Jesus is declared "as queer as you or me" and the heroic enemy of heterosexist hegemony. Once more, Paul's statements against homosexuality represent the enemy. In each version, Jesus is pitted against the church, and the Gospels are pitted against the rest of the New Testament, but only when read against their plain sense to yield a portrait of Jesus that fits the ideological commitments of the readers.[38]

Johnson's simplistic reading of feminist and liberation theologies points to the real source of his anger; he cannot abide the influence that critical biblical scholarship has had upon the field of theology.

Johnson comes close to arguing explicitly that the decline of "mainline Protestant denominations" is due to ministers formed by a historical-critical approach to the Bible on the one hand and a liberationist approach to theology on the other. Johnson's intellectual and professional resentments, therefore, are by no means limited to the Jesus Seminar, but are considerably broader in scope. Rather than encouraging congregations to promote intellectual curiosity, Johnson blames professors of graduate-school education for engaging in "shock therapy." Instead of encouraging churches to engage in thoughtful consideration of how faith wedded to social power can create and justify social and religious patterns of injustice, Johnson dismisses the work of theological colleagues as mere "ideological commitments." Instead of calling for denominations to improve their own theological curricula for lay persons, Johnson blames graduate theological schools for encouraging students to ask about the real-world, socio-political effects of Christian tradition on global culture as part of their ministerial education.

When Johnson turns to the "Real Jesus" his arguments remind one of Kähler's as discussed in Part Two, or even Pastor Göze's as discussed in Part One: "Christians direct their faith not to the historical Jesus but to the living Lord Jesus."[39]

> The "real Jesus" for Christian faith is the resurrected Jesus. . . . It is Jesus as risen Lord who is experienced in the assembly of believers, declared by the word of proclamation, encountered in the sacramental meal, addressed by prayers of praise and petition. It is "in the name" of *this* Jesus that powerful deeds of healing are performed. . . . So it was at the birth of the Christian faith, and so is it today wherever Christianity is spiritually alive and identifiably Christian in character.[40]

While Johnson had early-on criticized conservative theological schools that use the "paraphernalia of the academy . . . to support conclusions already determined by doctrine,"[41] he now introduces Frei's narrative structure of Christian faith to close off any historical questioning of Jesus' or Christian "identity."

> Christianity has credibility, both with its adherents and with its despisers, to the degree that it claims and lives by its own distinctive identity. This means, at a minimum, recognizing that Christianity is not measured by cultural expectations but by the experiences and convictions by which it lives. A church that has lost a sense of its boundaries—that is, a grasp of its self-definition—can only recover it by reasserting its character as a community of faith with a canon of Scripture and a creed.[42]

Anxious to preserve a "distinctive identity" in the face of modern and postmodern secular culture, postliberal scholars like Frei and Lindbeck and Johnson have sought continually to insulate traditional Christian faith from historical critical studies. Yet the historic question that historical Jesus studies continue to raise against the specter of creedal infidelity is whether there are historic moments when both creed and canon have been tools of ecclesiastical abuse or ecclesiastical failure of nerve, both in the public sphere and in the church at large. Are there moments when the defense of authentic faith must challenge the use of creed and canon to close off debates of both moral justice and intellectual credibility?

What really irks Johnson is that historical Jesus studies have been consistently effective in raising critical questions about the proper role of ecclesiastical authority in public life and about the importance of human experience in coming to grasp the message of Jesus at the heart of Christian faith. Opening a space of inquiry at the heart of the Christian tradition, the quests for the historical Jesus have raised real and persuasive concerns about the adequacy of contemporary Christian authorities (whether in the eighteenth, nineteenth, twentieth, or twenty-first centuries) to confront humbly and honestly the complexities of modern life. While Johnson urges those who would seek change within the church to argue from the guidance of the Holy Spirit, the prophetic character of historical Jesus studies may be far more aligned with the guidance of the Spirit than Johnson will ever be willing to admit.

In an essay, "Jesus and the Politics of Interpretation," ELIZABETH SCHÜSSLER FIORENZA takes aim at both Johnson for his "canonical" "theological positivism," and the Jesus Seminar for offering only "historical positivism," a continuation of "liberal bourgeois Jesus research."[43] In contrast to Johnson, who argued that the Jesus Seminar was too modern in its rejection of the canon and creed as a norm for scholarship, Schüssler Fiorenza claims that the Seminar has not been postmodern enough. "The politics of meaning requires that any presentation of Jesus, scientific or otherwise, must own that it is a 're-construction,' . . . and must open up its historical models or patterns to public reflection and critical scrutiny."[44] While Schüssler Fiorenza herself insists that she "would not advocate abandoning historical criticism as constitutive for Christian self-understanding,"[45] she believes that the Seminar's and Crossan's "portrayal of the historical Jesus, still remains caught up in the liberal framework of the old quests, envisioning Jesus as an extraordinary and heroic individual."[46]

Arguing, in particular, that the Jesus Seminar and scholars including John Dominic Crossan have not been sufficiently attentive to feminist scholarship, Schüssler Fiorenza suggests that her own category of "memory" provides a "reconstructive frame" that "does not require one to construe a sharp contrast and dualistic opposition between history and theology."[47]

> If one shifts from the frame of reference that centers on Jesus as exceptional human being or as "God striding over the earth" to that of memory in the discipleship of equals, one can no longer hold

that wo/men did not influence the Jesus traditions and movements. Rather than taking rhetorical texts and sources at face value, one must unravel their politics of meaning.[48]

While Schüssler Fiorenza's critique is helpful in underscoring the "politics of interpretation," I believe she too easily collapses the Jesus Seminar into the assumptions of previous quests (even as she skips over the liberative dimensions of those quests). In the process, she overlooks the very straightforward "politics of interpretation" at work in the Seminar's structures and publications.

As we have seen in previous chapters, Funk, Crossan, and other Fellows of the Seminar were at the forefront of biblical and theological scholars embracing postmodernity's "turn to language" and moving away from naïve claims to objectivity. Any discussion that side-steps their contributions to the development of a postmodern discourse in biblical and theological studies misses an important aspect of their work. In addition, the Introduction to *The Five Gospels* clearly indicates the broader "agenda" of the Seminar. Funk and Hoover are clear in the Seminar's attempt to confront the biblical illiteracy of the country among both secular and religious persons, an illiteracy which has eased the Christian Right's access to political influence. Insofar as the Seminar was attempting, quite explicitly, to challenge the Christian Right's appeals to an inerrant Bible as a legitimate basis for US public policy, the development of the Seminar's database was significantly deconstructive in character. Moreover, while locating what Jesus may have actually said and taught, on the basis of historical argument, the Seminar's procedure of voting clearly underscores the partial, provisional, and far from certain character of their public conclusions. Far more than any other quest, the work of the Jesus Seminar was conducted in public and its voting procedures set forth in extraordinarily publicly accessible and accountable ways. Finally, while Schüssler-Fiorenza is certainly correct to encourage greater engagement with feminist scholarship in attending to the politics of interpretation, the range of constructive projects engaged by Fellows of the Jesus Seminar over the last fifteen years argues against any easy accusation that the Jesus Seminar can be reduced to mere liberal bourgeois scholarship.

Two other critiques that affirm historical critical studies deserve specific mention. BART EHRMAN, a prolific scholar of religion—not a New Testament scholar—has no problem with the idea of a quest for the historical Jesus. In his book *Jesus: Apocalyptic Prophet of the*

New Millennium, Ehrman argues that the apocalyptic school (but not the specific conclusions) of Schweitzer and Weiss was correct, and that Jesus "predicted that the God of Israel was about to perform a mighty act of destruction and salvation for his people. And he thought that some of those listening to him would be alive when it happened."[49] Erhman, who is not a Christian, argues that academic debates are natural and important realities in intellectual life. "Radical shifts in scholarly opinion occur throughout all the disciplines of all the humanities all the time; they are as natural as vine-ripened tomatoes." He cites work by "Marcus Borg, John Dominic Crossan, . . . Robert Funk" as among "the most interesting . . . recent studies that take a nonapocalyptic view of Jesus."[50]

Still, Ehrman believes that the case for the apocalyptic Jesus is the easiest, and therefore, best historical argument to make. By apocalyptic, however, Ehrman does not believe Jesus was predicting the end of time as such, but rather the beginning of God's reign:

> Throughout the earliest accounts of Jesus' words are found predictions of a Kingdom of God that is soon to appear, in which God will rule. This will be an actual kingdom here on earth. When it comes, the forces of evil will be overthrown, along with everyone who has sided with them, and only those who repent and follow Jesus' teachings will be allowed to enter.[51]

Insofar as virtually all of the early sources include data that "portray Jesus apocalyptically," Ehrman believes such evidence should tilt toward an interpretation of Jesus as apocalyptic and not toward an interpretation of the early church as apocalyptic. For Ehrman, however, the major argument has to do with context.

> Jesus' ministry began with his association with John the Baptist, an apocalyptic prophet, and ended with the establishment of the Christian Church, a community of apocalyptic Jews who believed in him. The only connection between the apocalyptic John and the apocalyptic Christian church was Jesus himself. How could both the beginning and the end be apocalyptic, if the middle was not as well? My own conclusion is that Jesus himself must have been a Jewish apocalypticist.[52]

Ehrman, of course, is aware of alternative views, and tries to set them aside quickly, but not always with obvious success. He makes much of the fact, for example, that Q is a hypothetical document, and thus a still-suspect historical source. In addition, the complex theories of Q, while suggestive, according to Ehrman, also muddy the waters of a clear, historical judgment. Ehrman acknowledges the argument of non-apocalyptic wisdom materials in Q, but finds the presence of apocalyptic elements more persuasive. In addition, while Ehrman acknowledges the possibility of Crossan's argument that the apocalyptic stratum is not, in fact, the earliest stratrum of the tradition, he suggests that Crossan's evidence for that claim is strained.[53]

While I appreciate the tenor of Ehrman's arguments, I suspect, first, that John Kloppenborg's body of work, including *Q the Earliest Gospel: An Introduction to the Original Stories and Sayings of Jesus*, along with the work of other Q scholars will become more convincing, not less, over time. Secondly, with respect to Ehrman's major argument about the popularity of apocalyptic discourse in Jewish thought of the time, I think Crossan's argument is more compelling. While Jesus was drawn initially to John, there is evidence that he rethought John's apocalyptic message in light of John's death, after which no great revelatory event occurred. Jesus did not stay in the desert. Instead, Jesus was accused of consorting with sinners, tax collectors, and prostitutes. It is quite possible that Jesus turned away from an apocalyptic perspective in order to encourage his largely peasant community to *be* a people of God by forgiving one another, forgiving debts, and resisting Roman occupation — not through purity but through social solidarity. Seen in this way, Crossan's emphasis on Jesus' pointing to the kingdom of God as already present shifts significantly how one views the ethical teaching of Jesus. Such teaching may not fit as neatly within the apocalyptic worldview as Ehrman suggests.

There is another problem with Ehrman's argument about apocalyptic as the governing genre of Jesus' discourse. One need not be an apocalyptic thinker in order to use an apocalyptic image. Ehrman points to Matt 25:31–46, the parable of the last judgment as evidence of Jesus' apocalyptic point of view.[54] But must that be so? Is not this "final judgment" scene also a wisdom text, in which the "final judgment" is used as a backdrop to ask a question analogous to "what is the greatest commandment?" Ehrman believes that in this apocalyptic story of ultimate judgment the fact that "belief" does not matter at all to the question of salvation suggests that this "apocalyptic" story would not have been invented by the early church. While I enjoy that part of his argument, I think Ehrman misses the point that the real question of this "last judgment" is a wisdom question about how to live here and now. To be sure, if one starts out with the assumption that Jesus was an apocalypticist, then this text looks like an apocalyptic story. But if one starts with the story itself, there is no intrinsic reason to believe that the image of a final judgment is an apocalyptic setting, much less that Jesus was using the story in an apocalyptic way. Instead, it appears as a story about what "finally," ultimately matters.

BURTON L. MACK in his 2001 book *The Christian Myth* offered a broader critique of the quest for the historical Jesus. In contrast to Ehrman's skepticism about the existence of Q, Mack places Q1 (the earliest stratum of Q material) and its Cynic-like sayings material at the heart of his project. But Mack's argument that the early stratum of Jesus materials reflects a Cynic-like voice is *not* a claim about either the personality or viewpoint of a historical figure named Jesus. Instead, Mack believes that the proper focus of any historical analysis of Christian origins cannot be the person of Jesus but analysis of the earliest traditions about him. What one can and should try to capture, according to Mack, is the process of Christian mythmaking about Jesus, demonstrating the multiplicity and complexity of early interpretations of Jesus and his message.

> But the earliest layers of the teachings are not at first documentation *for* the historical Jesus. They are documentation for the teachings of the Jesus schools, groups that thought of their Cynic-like discourse as the "teachings of Jesus."[55]

Even though Mack acknowledges the inevitability that some question about the identity of Jesus of Nazareth remains, given the various *Christos* groups that traced their origins to him, he argues that the proper analytical focus is on the groups and not on Jesus. "Thus the more important observation is that the many views of Jesus are mythic and that each mythic view corresponds to a particular group's way of thinking about itself."[56]

Mack presents his argument about Christian origins not simply as the result of his own personal scholarship but in the context of the "Christian Origins Seminar," organized within the scholarly guild of the Society of Biblical Literature, and staffed with scholars such as Arthur Dewey, Hal Tausig, and Dennis Smith, who have made significant contributions to Westar's Jesus Seminar, the Acts Seminar, and the Paul Seminar. Mack's final chapter points to the fruits of the Origins Seminar's work, noting that "the Seminar is poised to make a significant contribution both to early Christian studies and to studies in the theory of myth and social formation."[57]

The critiques of Ehrman and Mack are interesting in a way that Johnson's is not. One sees real continuity with the Jesus Seminar in the intellectual assumptions that Ehrman and Mack bring to their work even as they disagree strongly with its focus and its conclusions. Ehrman disagrees with the conclusions of several Seminar scholars; Mack disagrees over the object of research. Yet both of these popular books explore the territory of biblical scholarship in ways that demonstrate that the Jesus Seminar is not at all "out of touch" with the practice of New Testament scholarship. Ehrman's and Mack's work, in addition to Schüssler-Firoenza's, contribute to a wider, public discussion about Jesus and the origins of Christian communities as do several debate-format books including: *The Meaning of Jesus: Two Visions* by Marcus Borg and N.T. Wright, and *The Apocalyptic Jesus: A Debate* by Dale C. Allison, Marcus Borg, John Dominic Crossan, and Stephen Patterson.[58] Such conversations have once again opened spaces in which new interpretations of faith—Christian and post-Christian—have begun to emerge.

CHAPTER

12

Beyond Belief
Re-Imagining Faith

As we saw in the opening chapter of Part III, the historic turn to language began to move theology—including the neo-Barthian theology of postliberalism—away from the claims of supernatural revelation and toward the realization that claims of Christian tradition should not be understood propositionally, or literally, but figuratively. We saw there, as well, how the pre-Seminar work of Funk, Crossan, Scott, and Borg, contributed to this re-imagination of revelation and faith within a literary, social, and political framework.

In the previous chapter we explored how the Seminar utilized its public stance to critique both the politicization of Christian fundamentalism in American politics and, more implicitly, the rule of Christian orthodoxy as the appropriate, exclusive norm for a faith that follows Jesus. In this final chapter I take up the work of these and other Seminar fellows in order to trace out four rather distinct trajectories of inquiry that align with other, similar projects in contemporary theological scholarship: (1) a revisionist, or new-paradigm, model, (2) a political, post-colonialist model, (3) a constructionist, postmodern model, and (4) a poetic, re-imagination model. While these models or approaches to scholarship certainly overlap at points, they express differing priorities within a range of commitments to re-imagine the dynamics of Christian and post-Christian faith in the contemporary world.

From the Collaborative Seminar
to Particular Interpretations

Recalling Funk's caution that the work of the Seminar itself was to provide a "data base" of the sayings of Jesus and *not* to interpret that data base, it did not take long before Seminar participants began to publish their own interpretations of Jesus in light of the Seminar's recently completed research. John Dominic Crossan's study, *The Historical Jesus*, was published in 1991 prior to the publication of *The Five Gospels*. That book was the basis for Crossan's more accessible 1994 work, *Jesus: A Revolutionary Biography*, dedicated to Funk and to fellow members of the Westar Institute's Jesus Seminar "for their courage, collegiality, and consistency." Marcus Borg's *Meeting Jesus Again for the First Time* premiered in 1995, and was followed rather quickly by two texts with a stronger theological bent, *The God We Never Knew* (1997) and *The Heart of Christianity* (2003). Robert Funk published *Honest to Jesus* in 1996, and Stephen Patterson published *The God of Jesus: The Historical Jesus and the Search for Meaning* in 1998. In these studies, one finds varying interpretations of the historical Jesus, as well as a variety of theological positions.[1]

Marcus Borg, Hal Taussig, and Stephen Patterson —A Revisionist, Integrationist Model

Among those scholars who have had a close relationship to the work of the Jesus Seminar, Marcus Borg has been most forceful in arguing that historical Jesus scholarship can help renew mainline denominations to enable them to speak both faithfully and convincingly to contemporary Christians and seekers. His writing and presentation style, at once scholarly and pastoral, have made him the most accessible and most comfortable conversation partner for those in mainline and progressive communities of faith seeking to grow beyond the catechisms that shaped them.

In *Meeting Jesus Again for the First Time*, Borg seeks to hold together the importance of both Christian tradition and historical Jesus scholarship for the life of faith. He draws on his own "spiritual journey" to show how the questioning of his own childhood faith intersected with the questions and viewpoints of his seminary studies that led him to a new place of spiritual integration.

> I sometimes joke that if I were ever to write my spiritual autobiography, I would call it "Beyond Belief." The fuller title would be "Beyond Belief to Relationship." That has been my experience. My own journey has led beyond belief (and beyond doubt and disbelief) to an understanding of the Christian life as a relationship to the Spirit of God—a relationship that involves one in a journey of transformation.

Borg, who interprets the historical Jesus using the history-of-religions category of "spirit person,"[2] also prefers the language of "Spirit" for God in a way that allows him to re-imagine the language of the Trinity in more relational, and contemporary language. By working the interconnections between contemporary biblical scholarship and the traditions of Christian faith, Borg's work in *Meeting Jesus* was already moving in the direction of reframing theological tradition. In his follow-up book, *The God We Never Knew*, Borg extended his theological meditation on Jesus as spirit person, developing an explicitly panentheistic model of God as Spirit.[3] In *The Heart of Christianity*, Borg argued that contemporary Christians live in a time of "two quite different" visions, or worldviews, of what it means to be Christian: "The first is an earlier vision of Christianity; the second, an emerging vision," which incorporates insights from his two earlier books.[4]

Seeing his work as part of an ongoing process of conversation, conflict, and renewal within the Christian community, Borg argues in *The Heart of Christianity* that the changes currently being debated within Christian communities are not simply conflicts about one particular issue or another, but about two competing "comprehensive ways of seeing Christianity as a whole."[5] While fully acknowledging that people living within both the "earlier paradigm" and the "emerging paradigm" are fully Christian, and while trying to be fair to both, Borg clearly wants his readers not only to understand both paradigms but to see the growing persuasiveness of the newer paradigm. Thus, while underscoring the point that affirming historical Jesus research is in no way "essential to being a Christian," Borg does show how historical Jesus research can make a contribution to faith. "My claim is more modest: that the historical study of Jesus is relevant for our time in particular. It can help to flesh out the incarnation."[6]

It is just here that one can see Borg's interest in continuing to draw out the insights of the New Quest, discussed in Part II. The above words could have been written by Norman Perrin, James Robinson, or Ernst Käsemann. And Robinson did! It is helpful, therefore, to understand Borg as consolidating the insights of the New Quest and the Renewed Quest in language that can help people of faith make new connections and move to a paradigm which, while new, will also be continuous with the past. Borg uses the traditional phrase "born again," for example, to describe the need for the shift from the earlier paradigm to the emergent one, and he emphasizes the role of the Spirit in moving the person of faith from the one paradigm to the other.

Part of the importance of Borg's work is that it popularizes in broad strokes much of the revisionist Christian theology over the past four decades. Borg would be at ease—if not always in agreement with—the company of David Tracy and other revisionists, such as Peter Hodgson, Sallie McFague, Elizabeth Johnson, Rita Nakashima Brock, Leonardo Boff, Roger Haight and others. Commitments to women's issues, to liberation and justice, to the environment and poverty are all part of the intellectual paradigm shift to which Borg calls our attention. And in the work of Emergent Church theologians such as Brian McLaren, working within the Protestant, evangelical community, one can see others paying attention to both Borg's content and style of presentation.

Hal Taussig

Hal Taussig's *A New Spiritual Home: Progressive Christianity at the Grass Roots*, published in 2006, provides empirical documentation of the paradigm shift described by Borg. In his Introduction, Taussig writes:

> New voices celebrating a lively, open-minded, and openhearted Christianity are emerging at the grass roots across America. Comfortable with their own faith, they also know that they are not better than Jews or Muslims. In contrast to the old liberals of the 1960s and 1970s, these new voices are just as interested in spirituality as they are in justice. With much more confidence than Christians of the mid-twentieth century, this new momentum strongly affirms both intellectual analysis and emotional expression of one's own faith. With constituencies of both inspired youth and seasoned leaders, new groups advocate strongly for the causes of women, gays and lesbians, and the environment. Weary of materialistic decadence, these voices proclaim a Christian practice that helps individuals resist the dominant American paradigms.[7]

Taussig acknowledges that his name for this movement, "progressive Christianity," is not a "perfect term." He justifies it as a preliminary designation, however, because others, pursuing similar objectives, have used it, including: the Center for Progressive Christianity, theologian John Cobb and Borg himself. Taussig, pointing to the diversity of the communities he has studied, notes that some are "somewhat uncomfortable with the self-designation 'Christian.'" Yet, he argues "there does not seem to be a better term for people who talk about Jesus, read the Bible regularly, and practice the rites of breaking bread and baptizing those new to the community as this new movement does."[8]

In his book, Taussig documents the presence of a thousand or more congregations which have already made something akin to Borg's paradigm shift. Taussig is not so much defending or justifying such a shift, as he is documenting its occurrence. Pointing to more than a thousand such progressive communities across the country and providing an appendix listing the names of these denominationally diverse communities/congregations, Taussig underscores—among other things—the search by many of the persons in these communities for a faith with greater intellectual integrity.

Taussig, himself a member of Westar's Jesus Seminar and the Society of Biblical Literature's Christian Origins Seminar, locates the interest in historical studies as only one among a broad array of approaches to integrate knowledge from the sciences and social sciences within a postmodern spiritual orientation. Taussig sees these emergent, progressive faith communities as committed to a kind of organic sensibility in which faith and reason connect. In these communities, Taussig hears descriptions of God and Jesus that align with the kind of panentheistic model of God proposed by Borg and others, including Sallie McFague, and models of Jesus that are resonant with Jesus' full humanity but that also often affirm Jesus' divinity in the sense that "God is in every human being."[9] While Luke Timothy Johnson might view such testimonies with suspicion, Taussig would encourage seminaries and divinity schools to respect and reach out to this newly emerging audience within progressive Christianity and not only to those constituencies rooted in what Borg calls the "earlier paradigm."

Stephen Patterson

Another member of the Jesus Seminar who seeks to bridge the widening gulf between critical scholarship and the life of the church is Stephen Patterson. In his book, *The God of Jesus: The Historical Jesus and the Search for Meaning*, Patterson opens by acknowledging the very real tension that exists between the scholarly and the faith community.

> New Testament scholarship in North America is currently involved in a great struggle and a fundamental realignment. This struggle, which has been developing behind the scenes and in polite conversation, has now been forced out into the open, as groups like the Jesus Seminar . . . have produced materials for public

consumption, exposing a wide audience to some of the most challenging critical work being done in New Testament scholarship today. To this has come an equally public and strident response from persons . . . who, more than challenging the work of . . . the Jesus Seminar, really have expressed basic misgivings about the value and validity of critical scholarship as it has emerged in the late twentieth century. This is where we are today. . . . And so the gulf widens. Critical scholarship eschews any interest in the church, and conservatives tell the church that it ought to have no interest in critical scholarship.[10]

Finding this situation "intolerable," Patterson argues that critical scholarship needs the church and the church needs critical scholarship.

Biblical scholarship that ignores the church risks losing the one genuine constituency that could take what it has to say to heart. Apart from the church, does anyone really care about the Bible or biblical scholars and their work? And a church that adores the Bible but ignores biblical scholarship is a house built on sand, and its foundations are already beginning to fall away.[11]

While the church should attend seriously to the insights of scholars, Patterson also argues that scholars "must also be willing to say what they think their work means."[12] One can hear echoes of Martin Kähler's argument in the lines above—namely, Kähler's assertion that the only reason one cares about Jesus is because of the historic impact of "faith" that Jesus' life, death, and resurrection generated. Patterson, however, turns that argument to a reciprocal need, reminiscent of Ernst Käsemann's position that faith needs to be rooted in the message of Jesus, and not simply in whatever story was told about him.

Patterson is clearly aware of the reality of conflict here, noting that if the church would take contemporary scholarship seriously "it would have to begin to rethink some of its basic theological commitments."[13] Yet, he remains committed both to the scholarly work and to sharing his own scholarly judgments about what that scholarship means for the church.

Patterson's commitment to the language of "meaning" connects him to the existentialist heritage of the New Quest. In fact, he is quite explicit in crediting both Willi Marxsen and Shubert Ogden for helping him think through the contours of what he (Patterson) calls his "existentialist Christology." Such a Christology, says Patterson,

> is based on the idea that the early followers of Jesus did not make claims about him because they had somehow sensed in him a different essence, a palpable divinity. When they said of him, "Behold, the Son of God," it was not because they had seen a halo circling his head. It was because they had heard him say and seen him do certain things. They experienced him acting in their lives. And what they experienced in the company of this person, Jesus, moved them deeply. They heard in his words profound truth about the world, about human nature, and about God. They experienced in his actions what authentic human being can and should be. In his life they experienced a depth of meaning that tapped into what they knew to be true, ultimately true.[14]

Thus, at least in part, one can see Patterson agreeing with the general tendency in Borg's work to attempt to speak to the church in the existential language of the New Quest. What differentiates Patterson's position from Borg's is its relatively stronger emphasis on Jesus' alternative vision to the power of the Roman Empire. While Borg, who himself had been among the first to call attention to the Roman Empire as a significant element of Jesus' context, understands Jesus through the image of a "spirit person," Patterson, following theologian Shubert Ogden on the theological side, and Crossan on the exegetical side, links Jesus' opposition to the Empire more explicitly to aspects of liberation theology. At the conclusion of his chapter, "The Death of Jesus the Jew," Patterson quotes the liberationist Virgilio Elizondo's *Galilean Journey*:

> In our times, and in all times, Christ has to go his way to Jerusalem. Again he has to face the structures of oppression in today's world. As his Galilean followers were called to go with him, so today his followers are likewise called to go with him and in him to the Jerusalem of today's world. . . . It is a call to be prophetic in both deeds and words. It is a call to live a new alternative in the world and to invite others to this new way.[15]

For Patterson, the deepened historical and cultural analysis of Jesus within the world of the first century, and especially within the stifling dynamics of the Roman Empire, opens onto an existentialist and liberationist understanding of the Christian faith. Patterson's own scholarship deepens the connections between these approaches in hopes of helping churches embrace a new understanding, a new meaning of Jesus.

John Dominic Crossan—Political, Post-Colonial Model

If Stephen Patterson's *The God of Jesus* incorporates political and liberationist themes into its largely existential engagement with the church, John Dominic Crossan's 1994 book *Jesus: A Revolutionary Biography* transposes those priorities. Crossan's work is less concerned with the church per se than with interpreting the words, acts, and death of Jesus in the first-century religio-political context of Roman imperialism. While Taussig is correct, in my view, in noting that "Borg and Crossan are not quite as divisive within mainstream Christianity as is the Jesus Seminar,"[16] and while Crossan and Borg have worked together on several best-selling publications, Crossan's commitment is relatively more weighted than Borg's to understanding the public, political dimensions of Jesus' discourse.

Crossan's method involves locating the historical Jesus at the intersection of three analytical "vectors": cross-cultural anthropology, Greco-Roman and Jewish history, and literary or textual analysis. Using these vectors to establish a context in which an audience might hear and understand Jesus' words and actions, Crossan then places those sayings and actions of Jesus that are "most plausibly" from the "earliest stratum of the tradition" within that context so that contemporary readers can "hear" those sayings and actions with a fuller sense of their original resonance. The effect of Crossan's book is that it offers not so much a revolutionary *biography* as a revolutionary rhetoric, a compelling, historical re-imagination of Jesus' words and actions in the political-religious context of the Roman Empire in first-century Palestine.

At the end of *Jesus*, Crossan frames the relevance of his book for the ongoing work of Christian theology with the following: "Is Christian faith," he asks, "always (1) an act of faith (2) in the historical Jesus (3) as the manifestation of God?"[17] By framing the question of faith as a linkage of these three moments, Crossan asserts a *theological* role for historical Jesus scholarship.

> I presume that there will always be divergent historical Jesuses, that there will always be divergent Christs built upon them, but I argue, above all, that the structure of Christianity will always be: *this is how we see Jesus-then as Christ-now*. Christianity must repeatedly, generation after generation, make its best historical judgment about who

Jesus was *then* and, on that basis, decide what that reconstruction means as *Christ now*.[18]

In his 2007 book, *God and Empire*, Crossan plays out the above three moments of Christian faith, using the historical Jesus' critique of Roman imperial power to challenge the easy accommodation that many American Christians have made with the politics of the American Empire. He connects his understanding of *Jesus-then* to pose the question: how do we in America interpret *Christ-now*? Crossan asks in effect: what does 1) Christian faith in this American political context mean, if it truly attends to 2) the historical Jesus, 3) as a manifestation of God? In his prologue, Crossan notices that his work on the historical Jesus may have a previously unforeseen relevance to contemporary culture.

> But now there is a new reason for studying the textual and archeo-logical history of the Roman Empire. I have been hearing recently two rather insistent claims from across the spectrum of our religio-political life. The first one claims that America is now—and may always have been—an empire and that, in fact, the virus of imperial-ism came—like so many others—on those first ships from Europe. The second and subsidiary claim is that America is Nova Roma, the New Roman Empire, Rome on the Potomac.[19]

In *God and Empire*, Crossan also follows up in a much more ex-plicit way on the Jesus Seminar's commitment to address the prob-lem of American biblical illiteracy. Pointing out how contemporary fundamentalists have interpreted the Bible in the language of apocalyptic violence, Crossan draws upon his cumulative work on the historical Jesus, Paul, and early Christianity to demonstrate the ideological use of those apocalyptic readings in recent American culture and politics. His work is a more theologically informed companion to Kevin Phillips' 2007 book *American Theocracy*, dis-cussed in chapter eleven. By the time Crossan reaches the Epilogue, he has three questions that have emerged from his study for "any-one who is both Christian and American today":

> How is it possible to be a faithful Christian in the American
> Empire? . . .
> How is it possible to be a non-violent Christian within a violent
> Christianity based on a violent Christian Bible? . . .
> How is it possible to be a faithful Christian in an American Empire
> facilitated by a violent Christian Bible?

In *God and Empire* and in numerous public conversations with post-colonial theologian Joerg Rieger discussing variations on the theme of "God and Empire: Jesus and Economic Justice,"[20] Crossan shares his conviction about the importance of a distinctive Christian *identity* that seeks to heal the earth while acknowledging the importance of other views and voices.

> I make no presumption that my own Christianity is the first, best, last, or only vision for global peace on our distracted earth. But I have talked primarily about Christianity, the Bible, and America in this book because I have spent all of my life as a Christian, half of my life as a biblical scholar, and the end of my life as an American. This book is therefore less an exercise in historical reconstruction than a witness in religious responsibility. . . .
>
> The good news . . . is that the violent normalcy of human civilization is not the inevitable destiny of human nature. Christian faith and human evolution agree on that point. Since we *invented* civilization some six thousand years ago along the floodplains of great rivers, we can also *un-invent* it—we can create its alternative. In the challenge of Christian faith, we are called to cooperate in establishing the Kingdom of God in a transformed earth. In the challenge of human evolution, we are called to Post-Civilization, to imagine it, to create it, and to enjoy it on a transfigured earth.

Along with post-colonial Christian theologians such as Rieger and Catherine Keller, Crossan's work on Jesus' teaching of the Kingdom of God leads him to a profound critique of the presumptive purity of American and Christian power. Even in the last lines quoted above, one hears from Crossan a much humbler assessment of Christian faith's capacity to share in the project of peace making.[21]

Bob Funk—Strong Constructivist, Postmodern Model

In *Honest to Jesus*, Funk sounds the most clearly post-Christian note of the group. Stating that his odyssey "began in the church," Funk recalls his 1975 work *Jesus as Precursor*, "a book I wrote while teaching in the Divinity School" (of Vanderbilt University). In that book, says Funk, "I concluded that theologians should abandon the cloistered precincts of the church and seminary where nothing real was on the agenda. I soon followed my own advice."[22] If that sounds as if Funk has left the church, it is because he has. In a portion of his introduction, Funk includes a brief discussion of alienated Christians:

I am running into increasing numbers of both clergy and laypersons who are quitting or have quit the church. For them *Honest to Jesus* may have come too late. Yet they have not lost their interest in the Jesus question. They have channeled their energies into other venues, such as social work or carpentry or counseling. I have a special affinity for them because I belong to their number.[23]

How did Funk come to the point of quitting the church?

I am a spiritual descendant of Rudolf Bultmann and Karl Barth, Reinhold Niebuhr and Paul Tillich, and the neo-orthodox movement they sponsored. I am deeply indebted to my mentors, and I have nothing but respect for that legacy. Nevertheless, I now believe that neo-orthodoxy (and its Catholic counterparts) was the dying gasp of creedal Christianity—a last effort to salvage it for the modern world. In the half century that follows the end of the Second World War, it has become clear that neo-orthodoxy has failed, that we have moved beyond the reach of that noble effort. In plain language, neo-orthodoxy is dead. As that fact dawned on me, slowly and painfully, I found myself forced to reevaluate all those doctrines that constitute the orthodox creed. I have done so at the behest of Jesus as the subverter of theological litmus tests.[24]

If Funk has quit the church, he still cares passionately about it; he still seeks to reform it. "Christianity," he says, "is a tradition worth reforming and saving."[25] If he has placed himself outside the church, it is, in part at least, to identify with those who have left because they can no longer affirm with integrity the traditional dogmas of the church. Funk returns to this theme at the end of the book, saying "If what we have to say about Jesus does not matter to those outside the precincts of traditional Christianity, it probably will not matter at all, at least not for the long term."[26] Instead of giving up on Christianity, he argues for a "new age" of faith in which "[w]e should either revise or eliminate the creeds," and in which we should "substitute right behavior—orthopraxis—for right doctrine—orthodoxy."[27]

While some might see only hubris in Funk's recommendation to revise or eliminate the creeds, Funk's strong constructivist position is not that far from the work of Harvard theologian Gordon Kaufman's focus on "constructing" the concept of God in his 1995 book *In Face of Mystery*, or of Vanderbilt theologian Sallie McFague, who called in 1993 for an ecological theology based in a panentheistic model of the cosmos as God's body in her book *The Body of God*, or from Australian theologian Lloyd Geering's call for a *Christianity without God* (2002) or English theologian Don Cupitt's even more radical suggestions since writing *Taking Leave of God* in 1980. In his 2001 book *Emptiness and Brightness*, for example, Cupitt opens by discussing Christian orthodoxy, within which there was "little or no space . . . for personal intellectual exploration and development."[28]

> This theologically dominated approach to religion is still not dead, even though today the authority of the Church and of orthodox creedal belief has declined to almost nothing. There yet remain numerous vestiges of the old assumptions, and this puts us in some difficulty. For we are now all of us aware that new religious thinking is urgently needed, but we don't know how to set about it. How do you *do* religious thinking without the Church and its belief system, without God, and without the old supernatural world? What *is* religion, in a time when everything that we were brought up to think of as defining religion has disappeared? Theology has been dominant for so long that we no longer know what pure and free religious thinking is. [29]

Despite the very significant differences among the above theologians, they are all committed to constructing a vision of faith within the contours of the best understandings of reality available to us and beyond the contours of Christian orthodoxy. While Funk does not address the contemporary theological problem of God, for example, in *Honest to Jesus*, he does discuss at some length the "collapse of the old symbolic universe," namely, the end of Christian supernaturalism,[30] and the collapse of the "orthodox creed" discussed above. For Funk, the creative work of the Jesus Seminar was to pull the study of Jesus away from both fundamentalism and the preoccupation with orthodoxy. Closer to Cupitt, I suspect, than to Borg, Funk longed for a more robust rethinking of faith and theology within a humanistic and naturalistic paradigm.

Bernard Brandon Scott— Poetic Re-Imagination Model

I discuss Brandon Scott's work last in this discussion because it is a bit more difficult to locate along the continuum that extends from Borg to Funk. Scott has never written a "Jesus book," because he does not believe such a substantive reconstruction of the historical Jesus to be possible. But the parables are another matter. In his 2001 book *Re-Imagine the World: An Introduction to the Parables of*

Jesus, Scott claims that "in terms of writing a biography of Jesus, they [the parables] furnish us almost nothing." Yet to this he adds, "But as a way of making sense of who Jesus was, they furnish the foundation."[31]

In Scott's view, working with the parables as primary data, Jesus was a rebel, but not one with a fully developed social blueprint. Instead, says Scott, Jesus "revolts in parable."

> I see no evidence that Jesus was leading a political revolution or that he had a social program in mind. He clearly affected the lives of people, but he was not a social organizer or activist. Although the idea is now out of fashion, Jesus the oral storyteller seems to me closer to a poet. The activist will always be dissatisfied with the poetic vision, but change comes about because a creative individual has that vision.[32]

The parables' line of vision is an important image, for Scott, because they open up a "counter reality" to what he calls, using computer imagery, the "default world,"[33] namely, the world of wealth and power and influence that governs every age. Scott picks up the language of "counter reality" from the 1995 Nobel Address of Irish poet Seamus Heaney, in which Heaney writes:

> And in the activity of poetry, too, there is a tendency to place a counter-reality in the scales—a reality which may be only imagined but which nevertheless has weight because it is imagined within the gravitational pull of the actual and can therefore hold its own and balance out against the historical situation. This redressing of poetry comes from its being a glimpsed alternative, a revelation of potential that is denied or constantly threatened by circumstances. And sometimes, of course, it happens that such a revelation, once enshrined in the poem, remains as a standard for the poet, so that he or she must then submit to the strain of bearing witness in his or her own life to the place of consciousness established in the poem.[34]

Heaney's image of the "standard" in the above lines also helps Scott express his understanding of Jesus' relation to the parables— namely, that they functioned as a "standard" for Jesus, as that consciousness for which and toward which he submitted to "the strain of bearing witness in his . . . own life." Because the parable is a "glimpsed alternative" and not a fully "worked out program," "it is," says Scott, "always temporary, glimpsed. It is a possibility not a reality."[35] But again, with Heaney, Scott affirms the power of the parable because it is imagined "within the gravitational pull of the actual." The parable's critical leverage on the default world, says Scott, means that Jesus—and those standing with Jesus—say to their communities and societies: "things do not have to be this way."[36] And while Scott believes it is possible for us to base our lives on the "re-imagined world of the parables," he is convinced that doing so involves our faithfulness to a Jesus who dwells at the margins of the default world.

In the epilogue of the book, Scott speaks of his own experience at the Community of Hope in Tulsa, Oklahoma, modeled on the base communities of Central and South America. For the Community of Hope and its pastor, Leslie Penrose, the "principal outreach," says Scott, "was to those suffering with HIV/AIDS." When he was asked to give several talks at the Community of Hope on the parables, Scott writes that he began with the parable of the leaven. As we saw in Chapter 10, Scott's interpretation of the parable centers on the ancient world's understanding of leaven as a metaphor for moral corruption. Here Scott describes his rationale for opening with that particular parable, and the surprise he encountered with the Community of Hope audience.

> I frequently draw on the parable of the Leaven with church groups because it gives such a powerful insight into Jesus' vision. But usually the parable scares congregations. . . . Most middle class Americans, those who inhabit the world of mainline Christian churches, belong to the default world against which the parable is re-imagining the empire of God. They intuitively sense that they are the target of the parable.
>
> The Community of Hope immediately sensed what was at stake because the parable related their life story. As gays and lesbians they were the leaven of this society. Many had been asked to leave a church, or at least had felt unwelcome and judged. Many, through a long journey from self-hatred to self-acceptance, had at last come to see that they were not cursed or an abomination, but loved and cherished by God—even when their churches told them otherwise. For them, the Leaven was their story. As one said, "the kingdom of God is like a queer . . ."[37]

Scott's story of the Community of Hope is indicative of his own stance toward contemporary Christianity. The problem, as Scott sees it, is the church's tradition of understanding faith as right be-lief. "The question we should be asking is not who Christ is, but the nature of God Jesus hides in his parables."[38] The point of faith, for Scott, is not the logic of belief, nor the set of beliefs that constitute the orthodox tradition, but the practice of living in the parables. "Ultimately we have faith not *in* Jesus, but faith *with* Jesus. In the re-imagined world of the parables we stand beside Jesus and trust that his world will work."[39]

In Scott's balance of glimpsed insight with existential commitment, I hear the work of philosopher/theologian John Caputo, who in his 1993 book *Against Ethics* sought to write a "poetics of obligation."[40] In one passage, commenting on the parable of the widow who deposits two copper coins in the temple treasury, Caputo critiques the operating assumptions of what Scott might call the default world.

> In general, I would say that the problem that besets this [present] time of greed, this epoch of protecting the rich against the poor, this age of defending the strong against the weak, is not the secret, serpentine motives of giving to the poor or helping the needy. The problem lies in the indifference with which obligation is treated, the silence, invisibility, and lack of idiom with which the neediest and most destitute people are cloaked.[41]

Caputo, whose work is deeply influenced by the writing of Jacques Derrida, claims in a later work that religious truth is not definable or circumscribable with a name, be that name God, or Democracy, or Justice, or Liberty. Instead, says Caputo, religious truth is what he calls an "event," that unsayable, unstable something which is "astir" within the name. It is that "event" within the name that moves us and turns the world, and our established systems upside down.

> The name is a kind of provisional formulation of an event, a relatively stable, if evolving structure, while the event is ever restless, on the move, seeking new forms to assume, seeking to get expressed in still unexpected ways.[42]

Caputo's "event" and Scott's parable do not project new systems, but resist the closure of the name, or the closure of Jesus into the name of Christ. They seek, as poets, to stir, to provoke, to prompt a re-imagining of language and experience, and so to hold open a space for thought and action.

Conclusion: Change for the Better?

Of course, Scott and Caputo are not thinking the *same* thing, any more than Crossan is saying the same thing as Rieger or Keller, or Funk is saying the same thing as Gordon Kaufman or Sallie

McFague or Don Cupitt. My point in discussing these distinctive interpretations flowing from the collaborative work of the Jesus Seminar is to demonstrate—once again—the participation of the quest for the historical Jesus within broader currents that, taken together, pose a historic question. By entitling this final chapter, "Beyond Belief: Re-Imagining Faith," I mean to name what I believe is the wider, historic question to which the Renewed Quest has contributed.

In varying ways, I identify with each of the above perspectives insofar as I feel pulled by the audiences to which they are addressed. I long for the now "old" mainline churches—both Protestant and Catholic—to re-imagine faith in a way that embraces more enthusiastically the complexity of knowing and the range of knowledge—including studies of the historical Jesus—that shape our world. Such longing connects the creativity of those like Borg, Taussig, and Patterson, who seek to demonstrate that at least some audiences of the church are, in fact, adopting new models of thought, faith, and ritual; with the courage of those like Cupitt and Funk, who feel compelled to say that the institutional structures of Christian faith—too attached as they are to an ancient cosmology—are incapable of adequate change; and with the insight of those like Scott who glimpse the "counter reality" of the gospel among the very ones the church has dismissed and cast out as leaven. And such longing seeks a wider flexibility of spirit to underwrite a more open model of coherence than the grammar of orthodoxy in theological studies.

While I agree with David Tracy that historical criticism cannot provide by itself a criterion of faith, what I see occurring in the movements described in Part III is not the establishment of a criterion of faith but the clearing of a space in which the message of Jesus reverberates in the shifting structures of literary, political, social, and theological language. In other words, as I have tried to argue throughout, the question of the "historical Jesus" is never simply about the historical Jesus, narrowly understood. It is always caught up in the multi-dimensional play of discourse that moves— and that moves us—beyond belief to both insight and obligation. It is in this way that historical Jesus research has provided not so much a criterion of faith as a space in which new models of faith are glimpsed . . . and lived both within and beyond the boundaries of tradition.

Have these three historic quests really changed theology for the better? I can easily imagine readers for whom such a claim would be both ridiculous and scandalous. If one believes, for example, that all true theological questions have already been answered by the tradition, that each apparently "new" question, is merely the repetition of a previously resolved heresy; or if one believes that on the basis of authority the question of the historical Jesus is simply disallowed because it pursues Jesus beyond the boundaries of canon and creed; then the attempt to raise the question of the historical Jesus appears always already as a kind of insolence, disobedience, and treason against the tradition and the faith—hence the scandal.

When Paul uses the Greek word *skandalon* in 1 Cor 1:20–25, he does so in connection with the theme of wisdom. He argues that the Cross, which appears to be foolishness and a scandal to some, is at its depths the wisdom and power of God. He argues, in effect, that one must look beyond the appearances of shame and humiliation that accompany the Cross in order to see that the Cross and resurrection of Jesus constitute a historic breakthrough, requiring the breaking open of traditional assumptions in order to see a new reality that is taking shape and moving toward completion.

My argument about these three historic quests is indebted to Paul's argument. For these quests have in each time and place challenged the dominant conventions of Christian faith in order to: open up a space for civil discourse; allow a new worldview to inform the traditions of faith; assert the rootedness of faith in human experience and across the breadth of gender, racial, and cultural diversity; and advance proposals for interpretations of Jesus and faith that occur in the context of reorienting Christian faith, even to models that move beyond belief. In each time and place, what has appeared initially as a threat and as a scandal, has brought both greater openness and vitality to discussions of faith even as it has brought Jesus' teaching of the kingdom into clearer view.

So, if one can imagine times and places where church authority itself seems to have lost its own compass of humility; if one senses that it was morally and theologically important to free civil society from ecclesiastical control; if one believes that it was morally and theologically important to affirm the creative role of human experience and cultural diversity in the work of theological interpretation; and if one can see the importance for models of faith that go beyond official claims of right belief and supernaturalism to speak in publicly accessible ways, then what appears to others as scandal assumes the weight of a risk worth taking.

Chapter One

1. B. Moyers, "Salman Rushdie." Quotations below are from the program; transcripts available.

2. For an interesting approach to the life of Jesus through the lens of class consciousness, see D. Georgi, "The Interest in Life of Jesus Theology as a Paradigm for the Social History of Biblical Criticism."

3. R. Williams, "Bloudy Tenent of Persecution."

4. R. Williams, "Bloudy Tenent of Persecution."

5. R. Williams, "Bloudy Tenent of Persecution."

6. H. Grotius, *Freedom of the Seas*, 10.

7. H. Grotius, *Freedom of the Seas*, 12.

Chapter Two

1. Lord Herbert of Cherbury, *De religione*.

2. J. Locke, *A Letter on Toleration*, 59.

3. J. Locke, *A Letter on Toleration*, 65.

4. J. Locke, *A Letter on Toleration*, 65.

5. J. Locke, *A Letter on Toleration*, 67.

6. J. Locke, *A Letter on Toleration*, 69.

7. J. Locke, *A Letter on Toleration*, 71.

8. J. Locke, *A Letter on Toleration*, 73.

9. J. Locke, *A Letter on Toleration*, 77.

10. J. Locke, *A Letter on Toleration*, 81, 83.

11. J. Locke, *The Reasonableness of Christianity*, 92.

12. J. Locke, *The Reasonableness of Christianity*, 98.

13. E. G. Waring, *Deism and Natural Religion*, 12.

14. E. G. Waring, *Deism and Natural Religion*, 35–36.

15. C. H. Talbert, *Reimarus: Fragments*, 14–18.

16. Hume referred to attempts to provide a rational grounding for revelation pejoratively as providing a "shelter" for religious "superstition." While "superstition" was Protestant code at the time for the Catholic Church and its hierarchical priesthood, and thus rhetorically helpful to Hume, he clearly intended his critique for those Protestant formulations of dogmatic truth that grounded their claim to public authority.

17. D. Hume, *Political Essays*, 33–39.

18. D. Hume, *Political Essays*, 38–39.

19. Quoted in S. Buckle, *Hume's Enlightenment Tract*, 160.

20. N. K. Smith, "Hume's Argument against Miracles," 45.

21. F. Schüssler Fiorenza, *Foundational Theology: Jesus and the Church*, 7.

22. D. Hume, "Of Miracles," 84.

23. D. Hume, "Of Miracles," 85.

24. D. Hume, "Of Miracles," 86.

25. D. Hume, "Of Miracles," 86.

26. D. Hume, "Of Miracles," 87.

27. D. Hume, "Of Miracles," 88.

28. D. Hume, "Of Miracles," 88.

29. D. Hume, "Of Miracles," 88.

30. D. Hume, "Of Miracles," 88.

31. D. Hume, "Of Miracles," 89.

32. D. Hume, "Of Miracles," 89.

33. D. Hume, "Of Miracles," 90.

34. D. Hume, "Of Miracles," 90: The religionist, says Hume, may "know his narrative to be false," but continues in it for the "best intentions," "for the sake of promoting so holy a cause." In addition, "vanity . . . operates on him [the religionist] more powerfully than on the rest of mankind," as well as "self interest."

35. D. Hume, "Of Miracles," 92.

36. D. Hume, "Of Miracles," 92.

37. D. Hume, "Of Miracles," 92.

38. D. Hume, "Of Miracles," 101.

39. D. Hume, "Of Miracles," 100.

Interlude

1. The adjective "amateurish" is used by J. Pelikan in his "Afterword: Jefferson and his Contemporaries," 160. In this brief excursus, I am indebted to Pelikan and F. Forester Church's introduction to *The Jefferson Bible*.

2. F. Forrester Church, "The Gospel According to Thomas Jefferson," 31.

3. In J. Pelikan's "Afterword," 160–62, Pelikan rightfully argues that Hume's suspicion of "natural religion," as expressed in his *Dialogues concerning Natural Religion*, which he delayed publishing until after his death for fear of reprisal, would cast doubts on all Deist attempts (including Jefferson's and Reimarus') to develop an understanding of God as a "necessarily existent being." That being said, I am not sure Jefferson would mind.

4. L. Brenner, *Jefferson and Madison*, 9.

5. L. Brenner, *Jefferson and Madison*, 87.

6. L. Brenner, *Jefferson and Madison*, 88.

7. The deeper problem with miracles—for Hume, for Reimarus, and for Jefferson—was the way in which they were used as public arguments to defend the power of the established church over society and public discourse. It wasn't simply that miracles contradicted nature; more importantly, they contradicted public reasoning and discourse. The real focus wasn't nature per se but theological constructions of natural law, which

were, in turn, used to structure both government and civil society under the authority of the church.

8. L. Brenner, *Jefferson and Madison*, 88.

9. While Jefferson had generally sought to keep his religious views to himself, he had written in his 1782 pamphlet, *Notes on the State of Virginia,* that the powers of government should be limited with respect to religion. "The legitimate powers of government extend to such acts only as are injurious to others. But it does me no injury for my neighbor to say there are twenty gods, or no God. It neither picks my pocket nor breaks my leg."

10. L. Brenner, *Jefferson and Madison*, 49.

11. E. J. Larson, *A Magnificent Catastrophe*, 165.

12. E. J. Larson, *A Magnificent Catastrophe*, 171.

13. Influenced and encouraged over the years by correspondence and conversation with Benjamin Rush, John Adams, and Joseph Priestly, Jefferson developed three distinct pieces on Jesus, written between his initial discussions with Rush in 1798 and the completion of *The Life and Morals of Jesus of Nazareth* in 1820.

14. F. Forrester Church, "The Gospel According to Thomas Jefferson," 12.

15. F. Forrester Church, "The Gospel According to Thomas Jefferson," 11.

16. F. Forrester Church, "The Gospel According to Thomas Jefferson," 11.

17. F. Forrester Church, "The Gospel According to Thomas Jefferson," 11.

18. F. Forrester Church, "The Gospel According to Thomas Jefferson," 11.

19. F. Forrester Church, "The Gospel According to Thomas Jefferson," 12.

20. F. Forrester Church, "The Gospel According to Thomas Jefferson," 29.

21. F. Forrester Church, "The Gospel According to Thomas Jefferson," 31.

22. Notice, that if someone approached Jefferson with the kind of Schweitzerian charge that he had "reduced" Jesus to fit his own time and interests, Jefferson might respond that the state-churches in particular had reduced the nobility of Jesus' teaching to that "groundwork of vulgar ignorance, of things impossible, of superstitions, fanaticisms and fabrications," that are the miracles, resurrections and second-comings of New Testament lore, and that the prelates had used *that* Jesus in support of their own temporal power.

23. Schweitzer, *Quest of the Historical Jesus*, 28.

Chapter Three

1. A. Schweizer, *Quest of the Historical Jesus*, 400.

2. M. Kähler, *The So-Called Historical Jesus*, 141.

3. C. H. Talbert, *Reimarus: Fragments*, 7.

4. C. H. Talbert, *Reimarus: Fragments*, 8. In addition to Schmidt's

translation of the Penteteuch, Reimarus would also have known Schmidt's 1741 translation of Tindal's *Christianity as Old as the Creation*.

5. C. H. Talbert, *Reimarus: Fragments*, 8.

6. See C. H. Talbert, *Reimarus: Fragments*, 5.

7. I am influenced here by C. H. Talbert, *Reimarus: Fragments*, 10.

8. Wolff had himself suffered for a time for these views. Writes Talbert: "Whereas in 1723 the pietistic theologians had been able to secure Frederick William I's banishment of Wolff from Prussia within forty-eight hours under pain of death, in 1743, after Frederick the Great had succeeded to the throne of Prussia, Wolff was invited to return to Halle as chancellor" (10). By the time of Reimarus' writing, however, Frederick the Great had died and his religiously reactionary nephew had assumed the Prussian throne.

9. See Talbert's discussion of the various copies and versions of the manuscript, including the "fragments" published by Lessing, in C. H. Talbert, *Reimarus: Fragments*, 18–25.

10. D. F. Strauss, "Hermann Samuel Reimarus and His Apology," 54.

11. C. H. Talbert, "Concerning the Intention of Jesus and His Disciples, Part One," §10, 76.

12. C. H. Talbert, *Reimarus: Fragments*, 86.

13. C. H. Talbert, *Reimarus: Fragments*, 67–68, 69–70.

14. C. H. Talbert, *Reimarus: Fragments*, 150.

15. C. H. Talbert, *Reimarus: Fragments*, 134.

16. C. H. Talbert, *Reimarus: Fragments*, 164.

17. C. H. Talbert, *Reimarus: Fragments*, 151–52.

18. C. H. Talbert, *Reimarus: Fragments*, 152.

19. C. H. Talbert, *Reimarus: Fragments*, 159.

20. C. H. Talbert, *Reimarus: Fragments*, 176.

21. C. H. Talbert, *Reimarus: Fragments*, 163.

22. C. H. Talbert, *Reimarus: Fragments*, 164.

23. C. H. Talbert, *Reimarus: Fragments*, 164.

24. C. H. Talbert, *Reimarus: Fragments*, 197.

25. C. H. Talbert, *Reimarus: Fragments*, 200.

26. C. H. Talbert, *Reimarus: Fragments*, 249–50.

27. C. H. Talbert, *Reimarus: Fragments*, 240.

28. C. H. Talbert, *Reimarus: Fragments*, 240–41.

29. C. H. Talbert, *Reimarus: Fragments*, 242–43.

30. C. H. Talbert, *Reimarus: Fragments*, 245.

31. C. H. Talbert, *Reimarus: Fragments*, 246.

32. C. H. Talbert, *Reimarus: Fragments*, 246.

33. C. H. Talbert, *Reimarus: Fragments*, 234–35.

34. C. H. Talbert, *Reimarus: Fragments*, 86

35. C. H. Talbert, *Reimarus: Fragments*, 85.

36. C. H. Talbert, *Reimarus: Fragments*, 259.

37. C. H. Talbert, *Reimarus: Fragments*, 268–69.

Chapter Four

1. H. Chadwick, *Lessing's Theological Writings*, 14.

2. In fact, Reimarus was not known officially as the author of the

Fragments, until 1815 when his son acknowledged this in donating a copy of his father's *Apology* to the library of the University of Göttingen. See C. H. Talbert, *Reimarus: Fragments*, 7.

3. H. Chadwick, *Lessing's Theological Writings*, 15.

4. See discussion of Schmidt in Chapter 3.

5. H. Chadwick, *Lessing's Theological Writings*, 15.

6. Chadwick notes, for example, that Lessing had met the Jewish philosopher Moses Mendelsohn in Berlin in 1749 and that the two had become friends, and that as early as 1754 in a work entitled *Vindication of Hieronymous Cardanus*, Lessing had expressed concern that claims for the superiority of Christianity over Judaism and Islam were based on historical arguments that English Deists had already undermined.

7. H. Chadwick, *Lessing's Theological Writings*, 16.

8. H. Chadwick, *Lessing's Theological Writings*, 17.

9. H. Chadwick, *Lessing's Theological Writings*, 17–18.

10. H. Chadwick, *Lessing's Theological Writings*, 20.

11. E. Schillebeeckx, *Jesus: An Experiment in Christology*, 583.

12. See Chadwick's introduction to *Lessing's Theological Fragments*, 30.

13. H. Chadwick, *Lessing's Theological Fragments*, 30.

14. E. Schillebeeckx, *Jesus: An Experiment in Christology*, 583.

15. H. B. Nisbet, *Lessing, Philosophical and Theological Writings*, 85.

16. H. B. Nisbet, *Lessing, Philosophical and Theological Writings*, 86.

17. H. B. Nisbet, *Lessing, Philosophical and Theological Writings*, 87.

18. H. Chadwick, *Lessing's Theological Fragments*, 53.

19. H. B. Nisbet, *Lessing, Philosophical and Theological Writings*, 87.

20. H. Chadwick, *Lessing's Theological Fragments*, 23.

21. M. C. Massey, *Christ Unmasked*, 47.

22. Quoted in M. C. Massey, *Christ Unmasked*, 46.

23. See Chadwick's introduction to *Lessing's Theological Writings*, 22–23.

24. See the discussion of this fragment in Chapter 3.

25. H. Chadwick, *Lessing's Theological Writings*, 26.

26. H. Chadwick, *Lessing's Theological Writings*, 26–27.

27. I am using William Taylor's translation of Lessing's *Nathan the Wise*, published in 1830. ISBN # 1-60424-503-4.

28. G. E. Lessing, *Nathan the Wise*, 89.

29. G. E. Lessing, *Nathan the Wise*, 91–92.

30. G. E. Lessing, *Nathan the Wise*, 93.

31. For H. Richard Niebuhr's discussion of "internal" versus "external" history, see his book, *The Meaning of Revelation*, 44–66.

32. G. E. Lessing, *Nathan the Wise*, 94.

33. G. E. Lessing, *Nathan the Wise*, 95.

Chapter Five

1. I am aided throughout this chapter by M. C. Massey's *Christ Unmasked*.

2. M. C. Massey, *Christ Unmasked*, 37–38.

3. M. C. Massey, *Christ Unmasked*, 43.

4. M. C. Massey, *Christ Unmasked*, 36.

5. M. C. Massey, *Christ Unmasked*, 39–40.

6. R. Bigler, *The Politics of German Protestantism,* quoted in M. C. Massey, *Christ Unmasked*, 45.

7. D. F. Strauss, Life of Jesus, li. By "supernaturalism," I mean a philosophical/theological stance which argues on behalf of supernatural causes for natural phenomena. "Rationalism" and "Naturalism" are related. Rationalism often sought to defend the "truth" of Scripture, for example, by offering rational explanations for miraculous events. "Naturalism," even more directly opposed to supernaturalism than rationalism, argued that all phenomena could be accounted for by natural causes.

8. D. F. Strauss, *Life of Jesus*, §14, 78.

9. D. F. Strauss, *Life of Jesus*, §14, 80.

10. D. F. Strauss, *Life of Jesus*, §13, 69.

11. D. F. Strauss, *Life of Jesus*, §13, 69.

12. D. F. Strauss, *Life of Jesus*, §13, 69.

13. D. F. Strauss, *Life of Jesus*, §14, 81.

14. It would be a mistake, however, to conclude that Strauss was not sympathetic to rationalism. As Peter Hodgson observes in his Introduction to *The Life of Jesus Critically Examined,* Strauss dismissed supernaturalistic interpretations of the biblical text virtually out of hand, and, far more quickly than rationalistic ones.

15. The return of religious supernaturalism as a political force in Germany caused Strauss to lament that rationalism was now more "antiquated" than supernaturalism.

16. M. C. Massey, *Christ Unmasked*, 92.

17. M. C. Massey, *Christ Unmasked*, 93.

18. M. C. Massey, *Christ Unmasked*, 93.

19. M. C. Massey, *Christ Unmasked*, 100.

20. M. C. Massey, *Christ Unmasked*, 100.

21. M. C. Massey, *Christ Unmasked*, 101.

22. D. F. Strauss, *Life of Jesus*, §151, 780–81.

23. D. F. Strauss, *Life of Jesus*, xxiv.

24. D. F. Strauss, *Life of Jesus*, xxiv.

25. A. Schweitzer, *Quest of the Historical Jesus*, 99.

26. A. Schweitzer, *Quest of the Historical Jesus*, 99–100.

27. The term "evangelical" here is not synonymous with American evangelicalism; instead it is a term for the Lutheran Church.

28. M. C. Massey, *Christ Unmasked*, 49.

29. M. C. Massey, *Christ Unmasked*, 50.

30. M. C. Massey, *Christ Unmasked*, 49.

31. Quoted in A. Schweitzer, *The Quest of the Historical Jesus*, 106.

32. M. C. Massey, *Christ Unmasked*, 144.

33. M. C. Massey, *Christ Unmasked*, 144.

34. D. F. Strauss, *Life of Jesus*, liv.

Chapter Six

1. A. Schweitzer, *Quest of the Historical Jesus*, 181.

2. A. Schweitzer, *Quest of the Historical Jesus*, 182.

3. A. Schweitzer, *Quest of the Historical Jesus*, 4.

4. Schweitzer discusses a third phase, in which he includes himself, that corrects the abuses of the 1860s and moves toward solving the quest.

5. To take only two obvious examples: first, Vatican I (1868–70) promulgated the doctrine of papal infallibility in matters of faith and morals, and second, by the turn of the century one saw in the United States the development of biblical fundamentalism, which rejected the findings of historical criticism and argued for the factual inerrancy of God's word.

6. A. Schweitzer, *Quest of the Historical Jesus*, 188.

7. A. Schweitzer, *Quest of the Historical Jesus*, 200.

8. M. Arnold, *Complete Prose Works*, 143.

9. A. Schweitzer, *Quest of the Historical Jesus*, 311.

10. Quoted in *Encyclopedia Britannica*, vol. 15, 468.

11. A. Schweitzer, *Quest of the Historical Jesus*, 238.

12. A. Schweitzer, *Quest of the Historical Jesus*, 221.

13. A. Schweitzer, *Quest of the Historical Jesus*, 84.

14. A. Schweitzer, *Quest of the Historical Jesus*, 351.

15. A. Schweitzer, *Quest of the Historical Jesus*, 351–52.

16. A. Schweitzer, *Quest of the Historical Jesus*, 251.

17. A. Schweitzer, *Quest of the Historical Jesus*, 252.

18. A. Schweitzer, *Quest of the Historical Jesus*, 363.

19. A. Schweitzer, *Quest of the Historical Jesus*, 402.

20. A. Schweitzer, *Quest of the Historical Jesus*, 402.

Chapter Seven

1. M. Kähler, *The So-Called Historical Jesus*.

2. C. E. Braaten, "Martin Kähler on the Historic Biblical Christ," 99.

3. C. E. Braaten, "Martin Kähler on the Historic Biblical Christ," 100.

4. C. E. Braaten, "Martin Kähler on the Historic Biblical Christ," 88.

5. M. Kähler, *The So-Called Historical Jesus*, 56.

6. M. Kähler, *The So-Called Historical Jesus*, 56–57.

7. Quoted in J. M. Robinson, *A New Quest of the Historical Jesus*, 74–75.

8. J. M. Robinson, *A New Quest of the Historical Jesus*, 74–75.

9. As noted in J. Macquarrie, *In Search of Humanity*, 165.

10. In this respect—underscoring the impact or influence of a heroic figure on others, Kähler follows E. Rénan's *Life of Jesus*. Unlike Rénan, however, who sought to interpret the life of Jesus with a history-of-religions model of interpretation, Kähler shaped that sense of historical influence to argue first for Jesus' divinity and second that the shape of Jesus' influence was "faith."

11. M. Kähler, *The So-Called Historical Jesus*, 63–64.

12. M. Kähler, *The So-Called Historical Jesus*, 90.

13. M. Kähler, *The So-Called Historical Jesus*, 64.

14. M. Kähler, *The So-Called Historical Jesus*, 58.

15. M. Kähler, *The So-Called Historical Jesus*, 77.

16. M. Kähler, *The So-Called Historical Jesus*, 141.

17. Twentieth-century German Catholic theologian Karl Adam is known for his comment that Barth's early work *The Epistle to the Romans* "fell like a bomb on the playground of the theologians."

18. K. Barth, *The Epistle to the Romans*, 45.

19. K. Barth, *The Epistle to the Romans*, 341.

20. K. Barth, *The Epistle to the Romans*, 341–42.

21. K. Barth, *The Epistle to the Romans*, 225.

22. P. Tillich, *On the Boundary*, 52.

23. P. Tillich, *On the Boundary*, 50.

24. P. Tillich, *On the Boundary*, 50.

25. P. Tillich, *On the Boundary*, 62.

26. P. Tillich, *Systematic Theology*, vol. 1, 61–62.

27. P. Tillich, *On the Boundary*, 60.

28. P. Tillich, *On the Boundary*, 57.

29. P. Tillich, *Systematic Theology*, vol. 2, 79.

30. P. Tillich, *Systematic Theology*, vol. 2, 79.

31. P. Tillich, *Systematic Theology*, vol. 2, 80.

32. K. Rahner, "Philosophy and Theology," 76.

33. K. Rahner, "Philosophy and Theology," 73.

34. K. Rahner, "Philosophy and Theology," 81.

Chapter Eight

1. R. Bultmann, *Jesus Christ and Mythology*, 13.

2. R. Bultmann, *Jesus Christ and Mythology*, 15.

3. R. Bultmann, *Jesus Christ and Mythology*, 18.

4. Quoted in J. M. Robinson, *A New Quest of the Historical Jesus*, 45.

5. While Bultmann's *Jesus and the Word* was published in 1926, and thus before Martin Heidegger's *Being and Time*, Bultmann had begun correspondence with Heidegger at least since 1925.

6. R. Bultmann, *Jesus and the Word*, 4. The book was first published in German in 1926.

7. R. Bultmann, *Jesus and the Word*, 5.

8. R. Bultmann, *Jesus and the Word*, 6.

9. R. Bultmann, *Jesus and the Word*, 5.

10. R. Bultmann, *Jesus Christ and Mythology*, 51–52.

11. R. Bultmann, *Jesus and the Word*, 10–11.

12. R. Bultmann, *Jesus and the Word*, 31.

13. R. Bultmann, *Jesus and the Word*, 35.

14. R. Bultmann, *Jesus and the Word*, 37.

15. R. Bultmann, *Jesus and the Word*, 38.

16. R. Bultmann, *Jesus and the Word*, 217.

17. R. Bultmann, *Jesus and the Word*, 218.

18. R. Bultmann, *Jesus and the Word*, 218.

19. See R. Bultmann, *New Testament Theology*, vol. 1, pt. 1, 42–43. See also Bultmann's discussion of Paul's theology on this point in pt. 2, 293–94.

20. To underscore the extent to which the community of faith is not indebted to the teaching of Jesus, Bultmann takes issue with Kähler's understanding of the "historic" person. "Nothing preceding the faith which acknowledges the risen Christ can give insight into the reality of *Christ's resurrection*. . . . For in the proclamation Christ is not in the same way present as a great historical person is present in his work and its

historical after-effects. For what is here involved is not an influence that takes the effect in the history of the human mind; what does take place is that a historical person and his fate are raised to the rank of the eschatological event. The word which makes this proclamation is itself a part of this event; and this word, in contrast to all other historical tradition, accosts the hearer as personal challenge." R. Bultmann, *Theology of the New Testament*, pt. 2, 305–6.

21. E. Käsemann, "The Problem of the Historical Jesus."

22. E. Käsemann, "The Problem of the Historical Jesus," 24.

23. E. Käsemann, "The Problem of the Historical Jesus," 31.

24. E. Käsemann, "The Problem of the Historical Jesus," 31.

25. E. Käsemann, "The Problem of the Historical Jesus," 31.

26. E. Käsemann, "The Problem of the Historical Jesus," 34.

27. E. Käsemann, "The Problem of the Historical Jesus," 20.

28. E. Käsemann, "The Problem of the Historical Jesus," 46. After acknowledging that one cannot reconstruct a life of Jesus based on the Gospels, Käsemann adds: "But conversely neither am I prepared to concede that, in face of these facts, defeatism and skepticism must have the last word and lead us on to a complete disengagement of interest from the earthly Jesus. If this were to happen, we should either be failing to grasp the nature of the primitive Christian concern with the identity between the exalted and the humiliated Lord; or else we should be emptying that concern of any real content, as did the docetists."

29. E. Käsemann, "The Problem of the Historical Jesus," 20.

30. See N. Perrin, *Rediscovering the Teaching of Jesus*, 226.

31. E. Käsemann, "The Problem of the Historical Jesus," 37.

32. E. Käsemann, "The Problem of the Historical Jesus," 37.

33. E. Käsemann, "The Problem of the Historical Jesus," 43.

34. E. Käsemann, "The Problem of the Historical Jesus," 37–38.

35. E. Käsemann, "The Problem of the Historical Jesus," 39.

36. E. Käsemann, "The Problem of the Historical Jesus," 46.

37. Quoted in E. Käsemann, "Blind Alleys in the 'History of Jesus' Controversy," 57.

38. E. Käsemann, "Blind Alleys in the 'History of Jesus' Controversy," 57–58.

39. E. Käsemann, "Blind Alleys in the 'History of Jesus' Controversy," 63.

40. E. Käsemann, "Blind Alleys in the 'History of Jesus' Controversy," 64.

41. J. M. Robinson, *A New Quest of the Historical Jesus*, 68.

42. J. M. Robinson, *A New Quest of the Historical Jesus*, 76–77.

43. J. M. Robinson, *A New Quest of the Historical Jesus*, 86.

44. N. Perrin, *The Kingdom of God in the Preaching of Jesus*.

45. N. Perrin, *The Kingdom of God in the Preaching of Jesus*, 126.

46. N. Perrin, *The Kingdom of God in the Teaching of Jesus*, 186.

Chapter Nine

1. L. Gilkey, *Naming the Whirlwind*, 102.

2. L. Gilkey, "Dissolution and Reconstruction in Theology," quoted in *Naming the Whirlwind*, 8–9.

3. N. Perrin, *Rediscovering the Teaching of Jesus*, 47.

4. E. Käsemann, "On the Subject of Primitive Christian Apocalyptic," 110.

5. J. B. Metz, *Theology of the World*, 13–14.

6. J. B. Metz, *Theology of the World*, 82–83.

7. J. B. Metz, *Theology of the World*, 128.

8. J. B. Metz, *Theology of the World*, 128–29.

9. J. B. Metz, *Theology of the World*, 93.

10. J. B. Metz, *Theology of the World*, 94.

11. J. B. Metz, *Theology of the World*, 114–15.

12. J. H. Cone, *A Black Theology of Liberation*, 112–13.

13. J. H. Cone, *A Black Theology of Liberation*, 113.

14. J. H. Cone, *A Black Theology of Liberation*, 117.

15. J. H. Cone, *A Black Theology of Liberation*, 116–17.

16. G. Gutierrez, *A Theology of Liberation*, 224.

17. G. Gutierrez, *A Theology of Liberation*, 224–25.

18. G. Gutierrez, *A Theology of Liberation*, 225.

19. G. Gutierrez, *A Theology of Liberation*, 231–32.

20. H. Küng, *On Being a Christian*, 27–28.

21. H. Küng, *On Being a Christian*, 35.

22. H. Küng, *On Being a Christian*, 157.

23. H. Küng, *On Being a Christian*, 157.

24. H. Küng, *On Being a Christian*, 237.

25. H. Küng, *On Being a Christian*, 240.

26. H. Küng, *On Being a Christian*, 242–43.

27. H. Küng, *On Being a Christian*, 266.

28. H. Küng, *On Being a Christian*, 266–67.

29. H. Küng, *On Being a Christian*, 601.

30. H. Küng, *On Being a Christian*, 602.

31. H. Küng, *On Being a Christian*, 224.

32. H. Küng, *On Being a Christian*, 225.

33. M. Daly, *Beyond God the Father*, 71.

34. M. Daly, *Beyond God the Father*, 79.

35. R. Radford Ruether, *Sexism and God-Talk*, 134–35.

36. R. Radford Ruether, *Sexism and God-Talk*, 135.

37. R. Radford Ruether, *Sexism and God-Talk*, 135.

38. R. Radford Ruether, *Sexism and God-Talk*, 135–36.

39. R. Radford Ruether, *Sexism and God-Talk*, 138.

40. E. Schüssler Fiorenza, *In Memory of Her*, 7.

41. E. Schüssler Fiorenza, *In Memory of Her*, xxi.

42. E. Schüssler Fiorenza, *In Memory of Her*, xxii.

43. E. Schüssler Fiorenza, *In Memory of Her*, xxii–xxiii.

44. E. Schüssler Fiorenza, *In Memory of Her*, 121.

45. E. Schüssler Fiorenza, *In Memory of Her*, 105ff.

46. E. Schüssler Fiorenza, *In Memory of Her*, 119.

47. E. Schüssler Fiorenza, *In Memory of Her*, 119–20.

48. E. Schüssler Fiorenza, *In Memory of Her*, 121.

49. E. Schüssler Fiorenza, *In Memory of Her*, 122.

50. E. Schüssler Fiorenza, *In Memory of Her*, 132.

51. E. Schüssler Fiorenza, *In Memory of Her*, 134.

52. E. Schüssler Fiorenza, *In Memory of Her*, 135.

Chapter Ten

1. R. W. Funk, *Language, Hermeneutic, and Word of God*, 158–59.

2. R. W. Funk, *Language, Hermeneutic, and Word of God*, 162.

3. R. W. Funk, *Language, Hermeneutic, and Word of God*, 222.

4. R. W. Funk, *Language, Hermeneutic, and Word of God*, 220.

5. R. W. Funk, *Language, Hermeneutic, and Word of God*, 220.

6. R. W. Funk, *Jesus as Precursor*, 79.

7. R. W. Funk, *Jesus as Precursor*, 39.

8. R. W. Funk, *Jesus as Precursor*, 63.

9. R. W. Funk, *Jesus as Precursor*, 63–64.

10. R. W. Funk, *Jesus as Precursor*, 63.

11. R. W. Funk, *Jesus as Precursor*, 141.

12. R. W. Funk, *Jesus as Precursor*, 142.

13. R. W. Funk, *Jesus as Precursor*, 142.

14. J. D. Crossan, *Cliffs of Fall*, 71–72.

15. J. D. Crossan, *Cliffs of Fall*, 72.

16. R. W. Funk, *Jesus as Precursor*, 142.

17. J. D. Crossan, *Cliffs of Fall*, 20.

18. R. W. Funk, *Jesus as Precursor*, 142.

19. J. D. Crossan, *Cliffs of Fall*, 49.

20. B. B. Scott, *Jesus, Symbol Maker for the Kingdom of God*, 10

21. B. B. Scott, *Jesus, Symbol Maker for the Kingdom of God*, 17.

22. B. B. Scott, *Jesus, Symbol Maker for the Kingdom of God*, 14, 15.

23. B. B. Scott, *Jesus, Symbol Maker for the Kingdom of God*, 26.

24. B. B. Scott, *Jesus, Symbol Maker for the Kingdom of God*, 74: "The story deals with Abraham's reception of the three visitors, one of them the Lord, at the Oaks of Mamre. He instructs Sarah, 'Make ready quickly three measures of fine meal, knead it, and make cakes.'"

25. B. B. Scott, *Jesus, Symbol Maker for the Kingdom of God*, 74.

26. B. B. Scott, *Jesus, Symbol Maker for the Kingdom of God*, 76.

27. B. B. Scott, *Jesus, Symbol Maker for the Kingdom of God*, 76.

28. B. B. Scott, *Jesus, Symbol Maker for the Kingdom of God*, 176: "His [Jesus'] language implies claims about his own relation to Yahweh. The teller of parables and the exorcist makes direct claims about his ability to focus the real."

29. M. J. Borg, *Conflict, Holiness & Politics*, 2.

30. M. J. Borg, *Conflict, Holiness & Politics*, 75.

31. M. J. Borg, *Conflict, Holiness & Politics*, 33.

32. M. J. Borg, *Conflict, Holiness & Politics*, 51.

33. M. J. Borg, *Conflict, Holiness & Politics*, 129.

34. D. Tracy, *Blessed Rage for Order*, 119–45.

35. D. Tracy, *Blessed Rage for Order*, 122.

36. D. Tracy, *Blessed Rage for Order*, 123–24.

37. D. Tracy, *Blessed Rage for Order*, 134.

38. D. Tracy, *Blessed Rage for Order*, 135.

39. H. Frei, *The Identity of Jesus Christ*, vii–viii. First published in 1967 under the title "The Mystery of the Presence of Jesus Christ."

40. H. Frei, *The Identity of Jesus Christ*, xxi–xxiii.

41. H. Frei, *The Identity of Jesus Christ*, xiii–xiv.

42. H. Frei, *The Identity of Jesus Christ*, 142.

43. H. Frei, *The Identity of Jesus Christ*, 142.

44. H. Frei, *The Identity of Jesus Christ*, 154.

45. H. Frei, *The Identity of Jesus Christ*, 155.

46. G. Lindbeck, *The Nature of Doctrine*.

47. G. Lindbeck, *The Nature of Doctrine*, 33.

48. L. Swidler, *Consensus in Theology?* Originally published as *Journal of Ecumenical Studies*, 17,1 (Winter 1980).

49. L. Swidler, *Consensus in Theology?* 6–7.

50. L. Swidler, *Consensus in Theology?* 7.

51. See B. B. Scott, "From Reimarus to Crossan," 256.

52. J. B. Metz, *Faith in History and Society*, esp. 90.

53. L. Boff, *Jesus Christ Liberator*, 11.

54. E. A. Johnson, "The Theological Relevance of the Historical Jesus," 25. Johnson's essay is an important response to David Tracy's hermeneutical approach to the question. For a helpful discussion of their debate, see W. P. Loewe, "From the Humanity of Christ to the Historical Jesus," 314. While noting the importance of the Jesus Seminar, Loewe dismisses the Seminar as "scholarship with an agenda."

55. L. Swidler, *Consensus in Theology?* 37–39.

56. L. Swidler, *Consensus in Theology?* 84–85.

57. L. Swidler, *Consensus in Theology?* 85.

58. D. Tracy, *The Analogical Imagination*, 233–47.

Chapter Eleven

1. See D. J. Hall's discussion of this element of the North American context in *Thinking the Faith*, 228–35.

2. W. McGloughlin, "Is There a Third Force in Christendom?" 43.

3. Quoted in K. Phillips, *American Theocracy*, 113.

4. K. Phillips, *American Theocracy*, 218.

5. K. Phillips, *American Theocracy*, 218.

6. R. Reagan, "The New Republican Party."

7. There was no diplomatic relations between the United States and the Vatican between 1867 and 1984.

8. K. Phillips, *American Theocracy*, 99–265. To be clear, not all members of the Republican Party stood for such positions, but the party, as such, countenanced such positions implicitly if not explicitly in its pursuit of electoral gains. Phrases like "teach the controversy" with respect to evolution, when there was no scientific controversy, became Republican mantras even among Republicans who knew better. A similar situation exists in the current "debate" over climate change.

9. R. Reagan, 1980 Acceptance Speech at the Republican National Convention.

10. R. W. Funk et al., *The Five Gospels*, 34.

11. Indeed, in The Pastoral Letters on "War and Peace" (1983) and

"Economic Justice for All" (1986) the bishops sought to engage a range of experts and policy makers as part of a conversation that contributed to the drafting of the letters. In other words, these documents, inspired by the call of Vatican II, were not simply drafted behind closed doors in a theological library. By the early 1990s, however, the Vatican had made opposition to abortion its official priority.

12. R. W. Funk et al., *The Five Gospels*, 34.

13. R. W. Funk et al., *The Five Gospels*, 34. Seventy-six scholars are listed in a roster of the Jesus Seminar in *The Five Gospels*. Of course, that two-hundred number does not indicate a constant working group or account for those who stopped attending the Seminar, or who became members but never attended, and so on.

14. R. J. Miller, *The Jesus Seminar and Its Critics*, 15.

15. R. W. Funk et al., *The Five Gospels*, 35.

16. L. McGaughy, "The Search for the Historical Jesus," 72.

17. L. McGaughy, "The Search for the Historical Jesus," 73–74.

18. R. W. Funk et al., *The Five Gospels*, 25–32.

19. R. W. Funk et al., *The Five Gospels*, 26.

20. R. W. Funk et al., *The Five Gospels*, 26.

21. R. W. Funk et al., *The Five Gospels*, 26.

22. L. McGaughy, "The Search for the Historical Jesus," 75.

23. R. W. Funk et al., *The Five Gospels*, 36.

24. R. J. Miller, *The Jesus Seminar and Its Critics*, 65.

25. R. W. Funk et al., *The Five Gospels*, 36.

26. R. W. Funk et al., *The Five Gospels*, 548.

27. R. J. Miller, *The Jesus Seminar and Its Critics*, 13. Miller adds, "Decisions reached by deadlines may be efficient, but they can also be hasty. To guard against this danger, the Seminar provided for reconsiderations" (13).

28. R. J. Miller, *The Jesus Seminar and Its Critics*, 9.

29. R. J. Miller, *The Jesus Seminar and Its Critics*, 11.

30. R. J. Miller, *The Jesus Seminar and Its Critics*, 24.

31. R. W. Funk et al., *The Five Gospels*, 5: "Beware of finding a Jesus entirely congenial to you."

32. J. D. Crossan, *The Historical Jesus*, xi.

33. R. W. Funk et al., *The Five Gospels*, 35.

34. L. T. Johnson, *The Real Jesus*, 63.

35. L. T. Johnson, *The Real Jesus*, 63.

36. L. T. Johnson, *The Real Jesus*, 64.

37. L. T. Johnson, *The Real Jesus*, 65.

38. L. T. Johnson, *The Real Jesus*, 65.

39. L. T. Johnson, *The Real Jesus*, 142.

40. L. T. Johnson, *The Real Jesus*, 142.

41. L. T. Johnson, *The Real Jesus*, 63.

42. L. T. Johnson, *The Real Jesus*, 168–69.

43. E. Schüssler Fiorenza, "Jesus and the Politics of Interpretation," 345, 351.

44. E. Schüssler Fiorenza, "Jesus and the Politics of Interpretation," 345.

45. E. Schüssler Fiorenza, "Jesus and the Politics of Interpretation," 350.

46. E. Schüssler Fiorenza, "Jesus and the Politics of Interpretation," 347.

47. E. Schüssler Fiorenza, "Jesus and the Politics of Interpretation," 353.

48. E. Schüssler Fiorenza, "Jesus and the Politics of Interpretation," 354.

49. B. Ehrman, *Jesus*, 18–19.

50. B. Ehrman, *Jesus*, 250.

51. B. Ehrman, *Jesus*, 128.

52. B. Ehrman, *Jesus*, 139.

53. See arguments in B. Ehrman, *Jesus*, 133–34.

54. B. Ehrman, *Jesus*, 136.

55. B. L. Mack, *The Christian Myth*, 58.

56. B. L. Mack, *The Christian Myth*, 205.

57. B. L. Mack, *The Christian Myth*, 215.

58. See *The Meaning of Jesus: Two Visions* by Marcus Borg and N. T. Wright, and *The Apocalyptic Jesus: A Debate* by Dale C. Allison, Marcus Borg, John Dominic Crossan, and Stephen Patterson.

Chapter Twelve

1. For a broader sampling of how Seminar Fellows interpreted the work of the Seminar in shaping particular portraits of Jesus, see R. Hoover, *Profiles of Jesus*.

2. M. Borg, *Meeting Jesus Again*, 17.

3. Panentheism differs from pantheism. In the latter "all things are God," thus giving rise to the worship of nature itself. By contrast, panentheism is the view that "God is in all things," or that "all things are in God."

4. M. Borg, *Heart of Christianity*, xi.

5. M. Borg, *Heart of Christianity*, 5.

6. M. Borg, *Heart of Christianity*, 89.

7. H. Taussig, *A New Spiritual Home*, 2.

8. H. Taussig, *A New Spiritual Home*, 3, 4.

9. H. Taussig, *A New Spiritual Home*, 27.

10. S. J. Patterson, *The God of Jesus*, xii.

11. S. J. Patterson, *The God of Jesus*, xii–xiii.

12. S. J. Patterson, *The God of Jesus*, xiii.

13. S. J. Patterson, *The God of Jesus*, xii.

14. S. J. Patterson, *The God of Jesus*, 53.

15. S. J. Patterson, *The God of Jesus*, 210. Quoted in V. Elizondo, *Galilean Journey*, 104.

16. H. Taussig, *A New Spiritual Home*, 31.

17. J. D. Crossan, *Jesus*, 199.

18. J. D. Crossan, *Jesus*, 200.

19. J. D. Crossan, *God and Empire*, 2.

20. See, e.g., the video of their 2011 Chatauqua presentations.

21. See esp. C. Keller, *Face of the Deep* (2003), *Apocalypse Then and Now* (2004), and *God and Power* (2005). For Keller's critique of Crossan, see the discussion of Schüssler Fiorenza in Chapter 11. J. Rieger, along with Don H. Compier and Kowk Pui-Lan, has also edited the 2007 book, *Empire and the Christian Tradition: New Readings of Classical Theologians.*

22. R. W. Funk, *Honest to Jesus*, 5.

23. R. W. Funk, *Honest to Jesus*, 13.

24. R. W. Funk, *Honest to Jesus*, 304.

25. R. W. Funk, *Honest to Jesus*, 306.

26. R. W. Funk, *Honest to Jesus*, 298.

27. R. W. Funk, *Honest to Jesus*, 312.

28. D. Cupitt, *Emptiness and Brightness*, 1.

29. D. Cupitt, *Emptiness and Brightness*, 2.

30. R. W. Funk, *Honest to Jesus*, 74–76.

31. B. B. Scott, *Re-Imagine the World*, 119.

32. B. B. Scott, *Re-Imagine the World*, 138.

33. B. B. Scott, *Re-Imagine the World*, 138.

34. B. B. Scott, *Re-Imagine the World*, 138.

35. B. B. Scott, *Re-Imagine the World*, 139.

36. B. B. Scott, *Re-Imagine the World*, 139.

37. B. B. Scott, *Re-Imagine the World*, 142–43.

38. B. B. Scott, *Re-Imagine the World*, 147. Scott immediately adds the caution: "I use 'hide' deliberately because God is no more the explicit topic of the parables than Jesus."

39. B. B. Scott, *Re-Imagine the World*, 149.

40. See, e.g., J. D. Caputo, *Against Ethics.*

41. J. D. Caputo, *Against Ethics*, 67.

42. Quoted in K. Armstrong, *The Case for God*, 315–16. See J. D. Caputo, "Spectral Hermeneutics."

Works Cited

Allison, Dale C., Marcus Borg, John Dominic Crossan, and Stephen
Patterson. *The Apocalyptic Jesus: A Debate*. Santa Rosa, CA:
Polebridge, 2001.

Armstrong, Karen. *The Case for God*. New York: Anchor Books, 2009.

Arnold, Matthew. *The Complete Prose Works of Matthew Arnold*. Vol. 6. Ed.
R. H. Super. Ann Arbor, MI: University of Michigan, 1964.

Barth, Karl. *The Epistle to the Romans*. Trans. Edwyn C. Hoskyns. London:
Oxford University, 1977.

Boff, Leonardo. *Jesus Christ Liberator*. New York: Orbis Books, 1984.

Borg, Marcus J. *Conflict, Holiness & Politics in the Teaching of Jesus*. New
York: Edwin Mellen, 1984.

———. *The Heart of Christianity: Rediscovering a Life of Faith*. New York:
HarperCollins, 2003.

———. *Meeting Jesus Again for the First Time*. New York: HarperCollins,
1994.

Borg, Marcus J., and N. T. Wright. *The Meaning of Jesus: Two Visions*. New
York: HarperOne, 2007.

Braaten, Carl E. "Martin Kähler on the Historic Biblical Christ." *The
Historical Jesus and the Kergymatic Christ: Essays on the New Quest
for the Historical Jesus*. Eds. Carl E. Braaten and Roy A. Harrisville.
Nashville, TN: Abingdon, 1964.

Brenner, Lenni, ed. *Jefferson and Madison on Separation of Church and State:
Writings on Religion and Secularism*. Fort Lee, NJ: Barricade, 2004.

Buckle, Stephen. *Hume's Enlightenment Tract: The Unity and Purpose of An
Enquiry concerning Human Understanding*. Oxford: Clarendon, 2001.

Bultmann, Rudolf. *Jesus Christ and Mythology*. New York: Charles
Scribner's Sons, 1958.

———. *Jesus and the Word*. Trans. Louise Pettibone Smith and Ermine
Huntress. New York: Charles Scribner's Sons, [1926] 1934.

———. *New Testament Theology*. Vol. 1. Trans. Kendrick Grobel. New York:
Charles Scribner's Sons, 1957.

Caputo, John D. *Against Ethics*. Bloomington: Indiana University, 1993.

———. "Spectral Hermeneutics: On the Weakness of God and the Theology of the Event," in John D. Caputo and Gianni Vattimo, *After the Death of God*. Ed. Jeffrey W. Robbins. New York: Columbia University, 2007.

Chadwick, Henry. Introduction. *Lessing's Theological Writings*. London: Adam & Charles Black, 1956.

Church, F. Forester. Introduction. *The Jefferson Bible*. Boston: Beacon, 1989.

———. "The Gospel According to Thomas Jefferson." *The Jefferson Bible*. Boston: Beacon, 1989.

Cone, James H. *A Black Theology of Liberation*. Maryknoll, NY: Orbis, 1990.

Crossan, John Dominic. *Cliffs of Fall: Paradox and Polyvalence in the Parables of Jesus*. New York: Crossroad, 1980.

———. *God and Empire*. New York: HarperOne, 2007.

———. *The Historical Jesus: The Life of a Mediterranean Jewish Peasant*. New York: HarperCollins, 1991.

———. *Jesus: A Revolutionary Biography*. New York: HarperCollins, 1994.

Crossan, John Dominic, and Joerg Rieger. "God and Empire: Jesus and Economic Justice." 2011 Chatauqua Presentations. http://fora. tv/2011/08/08/Crossan_and_Rieger_Prophecy_Economics_as_ Religion. Accessed May 21, 2012.

Cupitt, Don. *Emptiness and Brightness*. Santa Rosa, CA: Polebridge, 2001.

Daly, Mary. *Beyond God the Father: Toward a Philosophy of Women's Liberation*. Boston: Beacon, 1973.

Ehrman, Bart. *Jesus: Apocalyptic Prophet of the New Millennium*. Oxford: Oxford University, 1999.

Elizondo, Virgilio. *Galilean Journey: The Mexican American Promise*. Maryknoll, NY: Orbis, 1983.

Encyclopedia Britannica. Vol. 15. Ed. Mortimer Adler and Charles Van Doren. William Benton Publishers, 1968.

Frei, Hans. *The Identity of Jesus Christ: The Hermeneutical Bases of Dogmatic Theology*. Philadelphia: Fortress, 1975.

Funk, Robert W. *Honest to Jesus*. New York: HarperSanFrancisco, 1996.

———. *Jesus as Precursor*. Santa Rosa: Polebridge, [1975] 1994.

———. *Language, Hermeneutic, and Word of God: The Problem of Language in the New Testament and Contemporary Theology*. New York: Harper & Row, 1966.

Funk, Robert W., Roy W. Hoover, and The Jesus Seminar. *The Five Gospels: The Search for the Authentic Words of Jesus*. New York: HarperCollins, [1993] 1997.

Georgi, Dieter. "The Interest in Life of Jesus Theology as a Paradigm for the Social History of Biblical Criticism." *Harvard Theological Review*, Vol. 85,1 (Jan 1992): 51–83.

Gilkey, Langdon. *Naming the Whirlwind: The Renewal of God Language*. Indianapolis: Bobbs-Merrill, 1969.

Grotius, Hugo. *The Freedom of the Seas* [*Mare Liberum, 1609*]. Kitchener, Ontario, CA: Batoche, 2000.

Gutierrez, Gustavo. *A Theology of Liberation*. Maryknoll, NY: Orbis, 1973.

Hall, Douglas John. *Thinking the Faith*. Minneapolis: Fortress, 1993.

Herbert of Cherbury, Lord. *De religione Gentilium errorumque apud eos causes*. London, 1645. http://www.iep.utm.edu/deismeng/. Accessed December 23, 2011.

Hoover, Roy, ed. *Profiles of Jesus*. Santa Rosa, CA: Polebridge, 2002.

Hume, David. "Of Miracles." *An Enquiry concerning Human Understanding*. New York: Barnes and Noble, [1772] 2004.

———. *Political Essays*. Ed. Knud Haakonssen. Cambridge Texts in the History of Political Thought. Eds. Raymond Geuss and Quentin Skinner. Cambridge University Press, 1994.

John of Salisbury. *Policraticus: The Statesman's Book*, Abridged and ed. Murray F. Markland. Milestones of Thought in the History of Ideas. New York: Frederick Ungar Publishing, 1979..

Johnson, Elizabeth A. "The Theological Relevance of the Historical Jesus: A Debate and a Thesis." *The Thomist* 48 (1984): 1–43.

Johnson, Luke Timothy. *The Real Jesus: The Misguided Quest for the Historical Jesus and the Truth of the Traditional Gospels*. New York: HarperSanFrancisco, 1996.

Kähler, Martin. *The So-Called Historical Jesus and the Historic Biblical Christ* [*Der sogenannte historische Jesus under der geschictliche biblische Christus*]. Trans. Carl Braaten. Seminar Editions. Ed. Theodore G. Tappert. Philadelphia: Fortress, [1892] 1964.

Käsemann, Ernst. "Blind Alleys in the 'History of Jesus' Controversy." *New Testament Questions of Today*. Trans. W. J. Montague. London: SCM, 1969.

———. "On the Subject of Primitive Christian Apocalyptic." *New Testament Questions of Today*. Trans. W. J. Montague. London: SCM, 1969.

———. "The Problem of the Historical Jesus." *Essays on New Testament Themes*. Philadelphia: Fortress, 1954.

Keller, Catherine. *Apocalypse Then and Now*. Minneapolis: Augsburg Fortress, 2004.

———. *The Face of the Deep: A Theology of Becoming*. New York: Routledge, 2003.

———. *God and Power: Counter-Apocalyptic Journeys*. Minneapolis: Fortress, 2005.

Küng, Hans. *On Being a Christian*. Trans Edward Quinn. Garden City, NY: Doubleday, 1976.

Larson, Edward J. *A Magnificent Catastrophe: The Tumultuous Election of 1800, America's First Presidential Campaign*. New York: The Free Press, 2007.

Lessing, Gotthold Ephraim. *Nathan the Wise*. Trans. William Taylor. 1830. ISBN # 1-60424-503-4.

Lindbeck, George. *The Nature of Doctrine: Religion and Theology in a Postliberal Age*. Philadelphia: Westminster, 1984.

Locke, John. *A Letter on Toleration*. Latin text ed. Raymond Klibansky. Trans. J. W. Gough. Oxford: Clarendon, 1968.

———. *The Reasonableness of Christianity*. Ed. I. T. Ramsey. A Library of Modern Religious Thought. Ed. Henry Chadwick. Stanford, CA: Stanford University, 1958.

Loewe, William P. "From the Humanity of Christ to the Historical Jesus." *Theological Studies* 61,2 (June 2000): 314–31.

Macquarrie, John. *In Search of Humanity: A Theological and Philosophical Approach*. New York: Crossroad, 1983.

Mack, Burton L. *The Christian Myth: Origins, Logic, and Legacy*. New York: Continuum, 2001.

Massey, Marilyn Chapin. *Christ Unmasked: The Meaning of the Life of Jesus in German Politics*. Chapel Hill, NC: University of North Carolina, 1983.

McGaughy, Lane. "The Search for the Historical Jesus: Why Start with the Sayings?" *Finding the Historical Jesus*. Ed. Brandon Scott. Santa Rosa, CA: Polebridge, 2008.

McGloughlin, William. "Is There a Third Force in Christendom?" in Martin H. Belsky and Joseph Bessler-Northcutt, *Law and Theology: Cases and Readings*. Durham, NC; Carolina Academic, 2005.

Metz, Johann Baptist. *Faith in History and Society*. New York: Seabury, 1980.

———. *Theology of the World*. Trans. William Glen-Doepel. New York: Herder and Herder, 1969.

Miller, Robert J. *The Jesus Seminar and its Critics*. Santa Rosa, CA: Polebridge, 1999.

Moyers, Bill. "Salman Rushdie." *Faith and Reason*. PBS. Aired Friday, June 23, 2006. http://www.pbs.org/moyers/faithandreason/watch.html. Accessed July 19, 2012.

Niebuhr, H. Richard. *The Meaning of Revelation*. New York: Macmillan, 1941.

Nisbet, H. B., ed. *Lessing, Philosophical and Theological Writings*. Cambridge: Cambridge University, 2005.

Patterson, Stephen J. *The God of Jesus: The Historical Jesus & the Search for Meaning*. Harrisburg, PA: Trinity, 1998.

Pelikan, Jaroslav. "Afterword: Jefferson and his Contemporaries." *The Jefferson Bible*. Boston: Beacon, 1989.

Perrin, Norman. *The Kingdom of God in the Preaching of Jesus*. The New Testament Library. London: SCM, 1963.

———. *Rediscovering the Teaching of Jesus*. New York: Harper & Row, 1967.

Phillips, Kevin. *American Theocracy: The Peril and Politics of Radical Religion, Oil, and Borrowed Money in the 21st Century*. New York: Penguin, 2006.

Radford Ruether, Rosemary. *Sexism and God-Talk: Toward a Feminist Theology*. Boston: Beacon, 1983.

Rahner, Karl. "Philosophy and Theology." *Theological Investigations*. Vol. 6. Trans. Karl-H. Kruger and Boniface Kruger. New York: Crossroad, 1982.

Reagan, Ronald. "The New Republican Party." Speech at the 4th Annual Conservative Political Action Council Convention. Delivered February 6, 1977. http://reagan2020.us/speeches/The_New_Republican_Party.asp. Accessed July 15, 2012.

———. 1980 Convention Address. Delivered July 17, 1980. http://www.presidency.ucsb.edu/ws/index.php?pid=25970#axzz1siOrSZNj. Accessed April 21, 2012.

Rénan, Ernest. *Life of Jesus*. New York: A. L. Burt, 1863.

Robinson, James M. *A New Quest of the Historical Jesus*. Chatham: SCM, 1959.

Schillebeeckx, Edward. *Jesus: An Experiment in Christology*. Trans. Hubert Hoskins. New York: Crossroad, 1985.

Schüssler Fiorenza, Elisabeth. *In Memory of Her: A Feminist Theological Reconstruction of Christian Origins*. New York: Crossroad, 1983.

———. "Jesus and the Politics of Interpretation." *Harvard Theological Review* 90,4 (1997): 343–58.

———. *Jesus and the Politics of Interpretation*. New York: Continuum, 2001.

Schüssler Fiorenza, Francis. *Foundational Theology: Jesus and the Church*. New York: Crossroad, 1984.

Schweitzer, Albert. *The Quest of the Historical Jesus* [*Von Reimarus zur Wrede*]. Trans. William Montgomery. Originally published 1906.

Scott, Bernard Brandon. "From Reimarus to Crossan: Stages in a Quest." *Currents in Research* 2 (1994): 253–280.

———. *Jesus, Symbol Maker for the Kingdom of God*. Philadelphia: Fortress, 1981.

———. *Re-Imagine the World: An Introduction to the Parables of Jesus*. Santa Rosa, CA: Polebridge, 2001.

Smith, Norman Kemp. "Hume's Argument against Miracles, and His Criticism of the Argument from Design, in the *Enquiry*," in David Hume, *Dialogues concerning Natural Religion*. Ed. Norman Kemp Smith. The Library of Liberal Arts. Indianapolis, IN: Bobbs-Merrill, 1981.

Strauss, David Friedrich. "Hermann Samuel Reimarus and His Apology." Trans. Ralph S. Fraser. *Reimarus: Fragments*. Ed. Charles H. Talbert. Philadelphia: Fortress, 1970.

———. *The Life of Jesus Critically Examined*. Ed. Peter Hodgson. Trans. George Eliot. Lives of Jesus Series. Ed. Leander E. Keck. Philadelphia: Fortress, 1972.

Swidler, Leonard. *Consensus in Theology? A Dialogue with Hans Küng and Edward Schillebeeckx*. Philadelphia, PA: Westminster, 1980.

Originally published as *Journal of Ecumentical Studies* 17,1 (Winter 1980).

Talbert, Charles H., ed. *Reimarus: Fragments*. Lives of Jesus Series. Ed. Leander Keck. Philadelphia: Fortress, 1970.

Taussig, Hal. *A New Spiritual Home: Progressive Christianity at the Grass Roots*. Santa Rose, CA: Polebridge, 2006.

Tillich, Paul. *On the Boundary: An Autobiographical Sketch*. New York: Charles Scribner's Sons, 1966.

———. *Systematic Theology*. 2 vols. Chicago: University of Chicago, 1963.

Tracy, David. *The Analogical Imagination*. New York: Crossroad, 1981.

———. *Blessed Rage for Order*. New York: Crossroad, 1978.

United States Conference of Catholic Bishops. Pastoral Letter on "War and Peace." 1983.

———. Pastoral Letter on "Economic Justice for All." 1986.

Waring, E. Graham, ed. *Deism and Natural Religion: A Source Book*. Milestones of Thought. New York: Frederick Ungar, 1967.

Williams, Roger. "The Bloudy Tenent of Persecution." http://press-pubs. uchicago.edu/founders/documents/amendI_religions4.html. Accessed December 21, 2011.

Index

German Restorationists 83, 110
German Romanticism 94
German Revolution 92, 97
Geschichte (see also *Historie*) 1, 2, 112, 113, 146
Gesenius, Wilhelm 88
Gilkey, Langdon ix, 143, 144, 151, 158, 168, 176, 237, 246
God-consciousness 102
Goldwater, Barry 187
Göschel, Karl Friedrich 85
Gospel of John 53, 96, 97
Gospel of Mark (see Synoptic Gospels)
Gospel of Matthew (see Synoptic Gospels)
Gospel of Luke (see Synoptic Gospels)
Gospel of Thomas 198
Göze, Johann Melchior 52, 70, 71, 87, 88, 203
grace 5, 21, 117–19, 122–24, 127, 132, 166
Graham, Billy 188
grammer (see Postliberal)
Grotius, Hugo 18–20, 23, 24, 26, 28, 229, 247
Gutierrez, Gustavo 148, 149, 158, 238, 247

Haight, Roger 214
Hall, Douglas John 187, 240, 247
Heaney, Seamus 223
Hebrew Bible 51, 65, 201
Hegel, G. W. F. 79, 80, 81, 83–87, 89
Heidegger, Martin 121–23, 125, 127–30, 139, 141, 142, 164, 167, 168, 236
Heine, Heinrich 77
Hengstenberg, Ernest Wilhelm 88, 89
Herbert of Cherbury, Lord 23, 229, 247
hermeneutics 57, 155, 164
Historie (see also *Geschichte*) 1, 2, 112, 113
historical criticism 62, 64, 70, 115, 117, 135, 176, 179–81, 184, 185, 201, 204, 226
Hobbes, Thomas 28
Hodgson, Peter 87, 214, 234, 249
Holtzmann, Heinrich Julius 99
Hopkins, Gerard Manley 170
Home, Henry 34
Hoover, Roy 192, 193, 195, 205, 242, 246, 247
hubris 221
humanism 78, 121, 150, 151, 153
Hume, David 23–42, 44, 46, 50–52, 55–57, 229, 230, 245, 247, 249

Imago Dei 117
immortality of the soul 65
imperialism, Roman 218, 219
indulgences 20
International Theological Commission 183
invulnerable space (see *sturmfreis Gebiet*)
Ionesco, Eugene 170
Iser, Wolfgang 173
Islam 9–11, 20, 82, 182, 214
Israel 53–55, 57, 65, 156–58, 174, 175, 184, 206

Jefferson, Thomas 5, 32, 40–47, 52, 115, 230, 231, 245, 246, 248
James II 25, 26, 110
Jeremias, Joachim 173
Jesus (historical) ix, 1, 5, 9, 11, 12, 18, 21, 23, 41, 42, 46, 49, 50, 53, 84, 86, 91–93, 95, 96, 98, 102, 103, 107–12, 114–16, 120, 124, 126, 128, 133–36, 141, 145, 148, 149, 154, 158, 159, 163, 165, 166, 179, 180–85, 192–95, 198, 200, 202–5, 208, 212, 213, 215, 218, 219, 222, 226, 227
  atonement 21, 52, 150
  biblical Christ 2, 49, 107, 109, 111, 114
  divinity 25, 35, 43, 84, 94, 136, 154, 181, 215, 217
  exorcist 198
  healer 198
  messiah 31, 53, 55, 57, 134, 137, 155, 168
  miracles 21, 25, 29–32, 34, 35, 37–40, 44, 45, 50, 51, 53, 55–58, 61, 67–70, 84, 94, 95, 97
  of Nazareth 1, 3, 11, 13, 109, 125, 134, 135, 182–84, 194, 197, 208
  poet 173, 211, 222–25
  pre–Easter 135
  rebel 223
  resurrection 31, 37, 39, 55–58, 65–67, 69, 83, 84, 94, 113, 132, 134, 150, 151, 180, 216, 227
  salvation 27, 52, 54, 56, 65, 86, 116, 122, 156, 184, 206, 207
  self–consciousness of 139, 141
  son of God 52, 53, 59, 69, 137, 141, 217
  son of Man 101, 141
  voice print of 166, 172
Jesus movement 109, 110, 156–58, 202

the Jesus Seminar 4, 163–67, 172, 187–209, 212, 215, 216, 218, 219, 222, 226
critique of 200–209
John the Baptist 156, 206
John of Salisbury 12, 247
Johnson, Elizabeth 182, 214, 240, 247
Johnson, Luke Timothy 200–204, 208, 215, 241
Judaism 156, 174, 197, 233

Kafka, Franz 168, 170
Kaftan, Julius 128
Kähler, Martin 1–3, 11, 12, 49, 107–15, 119, 120, 126, 127, 130, 133, 140, 158, 200, 203, 216, 231, 235, 236, 245, 247
Kane, Sister Theresa 101
Kant, Immanual 34, 94
Käsemann, Ernst 135–41, 145, 146, 148, 151, 152, 168, 213, 216, 237, 247
Kaufman, Gordon 221, 225
Keim, Theodor 96
Keller, Catherine 220, 225, 243, 247
Kennedy, President John F. 144
kerygma 134, 136–38, 140, 141, 148, 151, 182
Khomeini, Ayattollah Ruhollah 9
Kierkegaard, Søren 111, 112, 114, 118, 122, 125, 133
King George III 41
kingdom of God (see also basileia) 53–55, 58, 71, 99, 100, 109, 121, 128, 131, 132, 134, 141, 142, 144, 145, 147–53, 159, 166–68, 172, 173, 176, 180, 198, 206, 207, 220, 224
Kloppenborg, John 207
Küng, Hans 150–53, 157–59, 165, 181–85, 191, 236, 249, 247

Lamartine, Alphonse de 98
language (turn to) 163–85, 205, 211, 213, 216, 225
Larson, Edward J. 44, 231, 247
Leadership Conference of Women Religious 191
leap of faith 112
Leibnitz, Gottfried 33, 51, 68
Lessing, Gotthold Ephraim 50, 62–76, 82, 83, 88–90, 93, 232, 233, 246–48
liberal theology 51, 55, 91–103, 108, 109, 115, 117, 119
liberation theology 159, 191, 201, 217
Lindbeck, George 165, 176, 178–85, 200, 203, 240, 248
Livy 42

Locke, John 23–442, 51, 52, 74, 110, 229, 248
Loewe, William 240, 248
logos 13, 154, 155
the Lord's Prayer 144, 152
Loti, Pierre 98
Lutheranism 15, 20, 21, 51, 59, 64, 70, 75, 107, 111
Luther, Martin 59, 70, 122

Macaulay, Thomas Babington 110
Macquarrie, John 235, 248
Mack, Burton 208, 209, 242, 248
Mani 122
Manichaeanism 122, 123, 138
Markland, Murray F. 247
Marxism 89, 191
Marx, Karl 97
Marxsen, Willi 216
Massey, Marilyn Chapin 71, 77, 78, 85, 89, 233, 234, 248
McFague, Sallie 214, 215, 221, 226
McGaughy, Lane 193, 194, 241, 248
McGloughlin, William 187, 240, 248
McLaren, Brian 214
messiah (see Jesus)
messianic secret 100
Metz, Johann Baptist 145–49, 151, 158, 182, 191, 238, 240, 248
Michelet, Jules 98
Middle Ages 13, 14, 32
Miller, Robert 193, 196–98, 241, 248
Millet, Jean-François 98
miracles (see Jesus)
modernity 15, 102, 103, 108, 117, 119, 201
Mohammed 10, 11
Montgomery, William 49, 249
moralism 138
the Moral Majority 164, 189, 190
Mosaic Law 31
Moses (biblical) 18, 59, 80, 137, 152
Moyers, Bill 9, 10, 229, 248
Muslims (see Islam)
Mysticism 45, 138
myth (see also demythologizing) 79, 81–84, 129, 136, 141, 146, 147, 154, 155, 182, 184, 208

Nakashima Brock, Rita 214
Napoleon 77
National Socialism 89
naturalism 79, 86, 89